# Editor's Note

**Jonathan Wilson, Editor**

**And so *The Blizzard* approaches its fourth Christmas, which is far more than ever seemed likely when we started out. That wouldn't have been possible without a huge number of people making sacrifices, from those who man the office to the writers to you, the readers. Our pay-what-you-want policy was open to abuse, but the vast majority of people have respected the principle that if we all give what we can, then the magazine will have far greater reach than would otherwise be possible. So a huge thank you for that.**

(Relative) longevity, though, doesn't mean that we're any more flush with cash than we were back in March 2011 when we launched; just because we're still here doesn't mean we're not still largely dependent on word of mouth and social media for our marketing. So if there's anybody you know who you think may like the magazine, particularly if they're somebody who might not be on Twitter, do tell them. Getting this far the only way we're going to keep going, the only way we're going to thrive. The effort has to be ongoing.

It's not just about driving on, though. When we launched, our plan was always to try to promote the sort of football writing we feel is important that doesn't necessarily get an airing elsewhere, and that's why we've started publishing books: two to start with, but there will be more to come next year and beyond.

*Johnny Cook: The Impossible Job* is a novel by Iain Macintosh. Football fiction as a genre has a pretty awful reputation, something that in most cases is probably deserved. One of the real problems of any sports fiction is that the dramatic finishes that are so gripping in real life can feel contrived on the page. Liverpool coming from 3-0 down in Istanbul, Manchester United scoring twice in injury-time in Barcelona, Sunderland beating Leeds in 1973... they're the greatest things about football, the occasions that are transcendent, but any novel that finished with one of those three finals would seem absurd. It's become a cliché to say of a sudden transformation in a game that you couldn't make it up; actually the problem is usually that you could make it up very easily, but it would sound rubbish. Even the climactic baseball scene in Chad Harbach's well-regarded novel *The Art of Fielding* feels absurd, banal in its implausibility.

The key to a successful football novel, I suspect, is to make the sport itself almost incidental, the device that drives the novel forward but on which it doesn't depend for its drama or emotional punch. I'm not going to give away what happens in *The Impossible Job*, but it left me moved in a way I hadn't been expecting, largely because the characters of Johnny and his girlfriend, Debbie, are so acutely drawn. The novel's as amusing as you'd expect from Iain, and there are well-aimed jabs at megalomaniac chairmen, self-absorbed players and the endlessly shifting impulses of the news cycle, but it's rather more than that. It's a satire with a very human heart.

Dominic Bliss's biography of Egri Erbstein is very different. Erbstein's story is an astonishing one and it's baffling that it's not already better known. He deserves to be recognised for his pioneering work as a coach, and for his role putting together the great Torino side that had won four successive *scudetti* and was well on the way to a fifth before he and his players were killed in the air crash at Superga. But for me the most fascinating section of the novel is the part dealing with the end of the Second World War in Budapest, as Erbstein and his family dodged the SS and right-wing Hungarian thugs as the Soviet Army closed in. Their survival was down to a combination of remarkable resourcefulness in extraordinary circumstances and good fortune. Dominic has done an incredible job in tracking down witnesses and documentary evidence and piecing together just what did happen in 1945: the moment when Erbstein and Béla Guttmann, two of the greats of the rich Jewish coaching culture of 1930s Budapest, escape the prison camp where they've been digging graves is barely credible.

I'm very proud that *Blizzard* has been able to put out two books of such quality, and particularly that they have so little in common. From the start we've tried to be eclectic and we've run fiction in every issue. There seems to be a perception (from people who don't read the magazine, I assume) that *The Blizzard* is very worthy and all we care about are the serious issues, whether that's football's relationship with politics or war or poverty, corruption or tactics, but I hope we've also looked at lighter topics. Certainly the Q&As always seem a pleasing mix of the important and the comic. There'll be another event in London in February and others later in the year (and we'll do everything we can to come to Scotland this time). Full details of the books and how you can order them, and forthcoming events and how you can buy tickets for them, are on the website.

The books are a leap into the unknown for us, but the impetus is the same as it was for the magazine: to offer a platform for a particular type of writing or for stories the mainstream deems too obscure. Of necessity we're outsiders, but together, if you keep spreading the word, we can make this work.

*December 2014*

# FOOTBALL IS NOT A GAME. IT IS A LIFESTYLE.

CANNONIERE.EU

# Contents

***The Blizzard*, Issue Fifteen**

## Introduction



## The North-East



## Strikers



## Davids and Goliaths

## Theory



## The Sense of an Ending



## Fiction



## Greatest Games



## Eight Bells



## Information

# 8

## The North-East

"For the most part, the club has been owned by idiots."

# A Sentimental Journey

*In a world of superclubs, what's the point of the ordinary teams?*

**By Jonathan Wilson**

**There was a book we used to have at home that contained a photograph of Wearmouth Bridge taken on a Saturday afternoon sometime in the 1930s. It looks north, the camera peering into a faint hint of sun, and shows the backs of thousands of men, all in dark coats, most wearing flat caps, traipsing to the match. On either side of the bridge, smoke billowed from chimneys. Slightly out of focus on the banks, there were cranes and lattices and funnels: there was industry, an extraordinary amount of it, the backdrop to everyday life. These days, there is nothing: just walls and bushes. But the most striking thing is the sheer number of people – and they were going, of course, to Roker Park, another mile or so on, not simply turning left under the railway to the Stadium of Light. I don't know the details of when the photograph was taken and I don't know where the book is now, but if anybody asks what football means to Sunderland that image is what comes to mind, a whole community engaged in one collective act.**

Football is changing. Last year, at an event in West Hampstead to publicise the release of Patrick Barclay's biography of Herbert Chapman, the issue of franchising came up. I was dismissive: the glory of European football, I argued, of our clubs that had grown up organically, was that they had a rich history, roots in the local community, that they so transparently meant something – which is why it's not an irregular occurrence on Twitter to find, say, a Barcelona fan from Bangalore arguing with a Real Madrid fan from Montreal about arcane details of the Spanish Civil War. Increasingly, though, I wonder if I was wrong.

It's the messing about with kits that's really done it. It's a trivial thing and yet it's hugely revealing of football's values. When West Ham played Manchester City at Upton Park this year, City wore dark blue shirts that were actually harder to differentiate from West Ham's than their home kit would have been. Swansea wore purple at Everton last season, which made the sides almost impossible to tell apart on television. Tottenham wore black at City this season, denying us the classic sky blue versus lilywhite clash that's gone on for over a century. Hearts wore pale blue and white stripes at Hibernian. Every weekend there's some egregious insult to tradition. Does it matter? Perhaps not: Tottenham are Tottenham in white or black. But given the extraordinary throughput of players at some clubs, it does feel at times that football has become a series of games between random collections of players wearing random kits – a bit, in other words, like the IPL.

More seriously, the financial structures of modern football dictate that the same handful of teams dominate perpetually. Occasionally the likes of Atlético Madrid rise from the second rank to challenge the superclubs, but it would be something miraculous if they could sustain their success for more than a couple of seasons. In that regard Borussia Dortmund provide the paradigm: however good the coach and the underlying structure, it only takes a spate of injuries or a bad signing or two to take them back down. Increasingly all of Europe is moving to the German model, something Financial Fair Play reinforces: only if the superclub or superclubs fail is there a competitive title race. In fact, it could be argued that the relative competitiveness of the Premier League is precisely the reason for the relative recent underperformance in Europe.

That becomes a serious issue as the nature of support changes. Once teams were supported largely by people who lived near the ground. The games weren't televised, so the only way to see football was to go in person and watch. That meant that the clubs became rooted in the local community and an expression of that community; they were the men in cloth caps streaming over Wearmouth Bridge. Football gradually became about self-validation; a means, in England at least, for provincial cities to put themselves on the map, to get one over on the capital. Power, in those days, came from gate receipts and small-scale investment, the local businessman putting something back into his community (or seeking to raise his profile by being associated with the club). That's why no London team won the league between its inception in 1888 and Arsenal's first title in 1931.

Once the notion of football clubs as an expression of identity is accepted, a second phase of fandom can open up, when a certain section of society feels itself disenfranchised, usually for economic reasons. The disenfranchised, with little else to cling to, turn to football clubs as a means of defining themselves. This process often goes hand-in-hand with a vague right-wing nihilism that lashes out against anything perceived as 'Other' – be that other fans, other social classes, other nationalities or other races. That is what lay behind the hooliganism that marred English football in the seventies and eighties and continues to blight the game in, for instance, parts of South America and eastern Europe.

Then there is phase three, which is where English football is now. In an age of globalisation, fans are drawn from all over the world. Many won't even have visited the city where the club they support is based. They consume on television and online. The sense of community is far less pronounced. At the same time, football within England has become so pervasive that it seems absurd if anybody in the public eye doesn't at least feign allegiance to a team. It's much easier for those from towns and villages without major clubs to follow a big team. The internet is awash with bloggers on Manchester United or Liverpool or Chelsea who've never been to Old Trafford or Anfield or Stamford Bridge. In phase three, success tends to be drawn more directly to money – that is, financial centres or those traditional clubs who have successfully transformed themselves into global brands. That's why London now plays a weightier role at the top end of English football than ever before.

For the new wave of supporter, football is often primarily an entertainment: they demand goals and deride defending. For phase one and two supporters, the loyalty of phase three fans often seems ersatz. There is resentment of them: resentment if they don't go to games and then resentment if they do, because "tourists", as they will be dismissed, dilute the atmosphere and drive up prices. It's those phase three fans who have made the Premier League so apparently determined to take matches around the globe, to make the tournament not even a global league that happens to be played in England (and Wales) but a simply a global league. And once that happens, frankly, you may as well invite Real Madrid, Barcelona, Bayern Munich and Paris St-Germain rather than trying to convince people in Beijing or Doha to stump up for games involving Burnley or Stoke or Sunderland. And once you've done that, probably persuading them to join the new league with a pot of cash and insulation against relegation, how different really would an elite league of 12 or 16 superclubs be from a franchise?

When I was about seven years old, I marched into the kitchen where my mam was preparing lunch. "Mam," I said, "I wish I'd been born in Liverpool."

She looked understandably surprised. "Why?" she asked.

"Because then I could support a team that wins," I replied. Sunderland, at the time, were in their fourth straight season of battling relegation. I'd been too young to understand the promotion of 1980: scrapping against relegation was all I knew and so too was Liverpool success. Their reign seemed eternal and my instinct in those days was to equate with them any good foreign side who happened to appear on television: Aberdeen, the Liverpool of Scotland; Bayern Munich, the Liverpool of West Germany; Independiente, the Liverpool of Argentina. They even all wore red: the world in those days was a pleasingly simple place.

Three decades later and two things strike me about that conversation. The first is the categorical acceptance that you supported the team from the town where you were born. I was from Sunderland and so I was a Sunderland fan. There was no thought that I could just choose to support Liverpool. At birth, you were dealt a hand and you played it as best you could, and the team you supported was one of those cards.

The second is a profound sense of relief. Supporting a successful side seems a tremendous burden. I go to most matches expecting Sunderland to lose: anything else is a bonus. The best experiences are the unexpected victories, the sense of overcoming the odds. Goliath faces David and completes emphatic victory over him thanks to superior physique and weaponry isn't much of a story: what joy, really, could Goliath's fans have taken from that? The Ryder Cup, perhaps, is a case in point. In 1985, Europe winning seemed an epic achievement because it was the first victory for Europe (or GB & Ireland) since 1957; winning this year felt mundane because it was an eighth win out of the last 10 matches. Success comes to be expected and so what is memorable is failure.

There is little glory in expected victory. In 2008, I visited the Japanese national football museum in Tokyo. They showed a documentary about qualification for the 2006 World Cup and it, farcically, portrayed Japan as heroic underdogs overcoming extraordinary odds to secure their place in Germany. In fact, Japan had won three of the previous four Asian Cups, were overwhelming favourites to qualify and did so by winning 11 of their 12 matches. The need for narrative, for a satisfying arc, overcame any sense of reality.

In fact, I'd go as far as to say there are only really two satisfactory victory paradigms. One is the underdog story and the other is that of the ageing or ailing champion, combatting not only his opponent but also the fallibility of his own body to rekindle past glories. Golf, again, perhaps provides the best example: the greatest of Jack Nicklaus's major victories was his last as, aged 46, he shot 30 on the back nine at Augusta on the Sunday to win by a shot. Many of his other 17 majors felt routine: that one, defying his creaking body as well as Tom Kite, Greg Norman, Seve Ballesteros and Nick Price, was gloriously unexpected.

In that sense, I'd probably enjoy being a Liverpool fan now more than I would have done in the eighties, precisely because there is always that battle with their own past, because the sense of expectation has been diminished. When José Mourinho criticised Chelsea fans for their lethargy in the win over Queens Park Rangers in November, it prompted a brief flurry of soul-searching about ticket prices and exactly who goes to games now. They're valid issues, but there's surely also a sense in which Mourinho is to blame for having made Chelsea to relentless at home. That hilarious defeat to Sunderland at the end of last season was the first he'd ever suffered in the league at Stamford Bridge. I've been through that myself: in 1998-99, Sunderland scored 50 goals in their 19 home games, losing only once at the Stadium of Light on their way to promotion. They won Division One by 17 points, taking 55 points from the last 61 available. In some ways, it felt an appropriate reaction to the 4-4 draw and penalty shoot-out defeat to Charlton Athletic in the play-off final the previous season – "You want us in this division? Really? Because this is how much too good we are for you" – but in other ways home games that season stopped being much fun. I remember seeing a Sunderland crowd boo the team off at half-time when they were 2-0 up. Yes, it was partly ironic, but only partly: a sense of entitlement creeps up quickly and the worst thing about entitlement is how it saps the joy for things that ought to be good.

I suppose in part that's my conditioning as a Sunderland fan speaking. I remember explaining to a Boca Juniors fan that I hated it when Sunderland went ahead because it meant agonising for the rest of the game over the victory we might be about to lose. She looked at me with pity and said, "Small club mentality." Which it probably is.

But that's what I have and it's what seems to me most fun in football. It's why thousands of Sunderland fans took over Covent Garden last season the night before the Capital One Cup final. It had been 22 years since we'd last been in a final and it might be even longer before we're next in one: it was an occasion to be relished. Did Manchester City fans – even City, who were promoted from Division Two in that 1998-99 season, whose past was essentially comparable to Sunderland's, however different their present may be – feel the same sense of glee, the same joy at simply being there? There's a reason that, on the morning of the final, Sunderland fans were gathering on Olympic Way at 9am and City fans arrived much later, and that is familiarity.

In 2007, I was commissioned to write a book about Sunderland's first season under Roy Keane. That promotion seems to me a hugely under-rated achievement. Outsiders talk about the money he spent as though that made success inevitable; they underestimate, I think, just how low the club was when he arrived. The previous season Sunderland had broken their own record for Premier League ineptitude, taking just 15 points, and they'd begun the campaign in the Championship with five successive defeats, the last of them in the League Cup to Bury, 92nd in the league pyramid at the time and reduced to 10 men for the final minutes.

I decided to structure the book around a walk from the old Roker Park to the Stadium of Light, partly to create a sort of symbolic pilgrimage from the past to the present and partly for sentimental reasons. I'd been living away from Sunderland for more than a decade by then and, although I go back to the North-East regularly, it seemed necessary to reacquaint myself with places I hadn't been to in years, to try to establish some sort of geographical context for Sunderland. After all, for all the Irish fans who follow the club because of Keane and Niall Quinn – and before them Charlie Hurley – Sunderland remains fundamentally a team whose support is geographical. Some older supporters, perhaps, were drawn by the glory of 1973, but you need a pretty good reason to support a club like Sunderland. They're not a team you follow on a whim.

It became a journey into my own past and that of the city, and into a particular type of fandom. I hadn't been back to that part of Roker since 1997 when I went with a few friends to watch the demolition, thinking we could maybe pick up a souvenir or two. It had been impossible, though. All the good stuff had already been auctioned off so, unless you fancied an anonymous brick, all we could do was wander disconsolately around and wonder if going to matches would ever be the same again. All my life I'd been going there at least once a week, whether to watch football or to visit my gran, who'd lived about 200 yards behind the Roker End. But she'd gone 18 months before the stadium, moving into a home in December 1995, on the day Sunderland beat Crystal Palace 1-0 to go second in the table, and dying a few weeks later.

I was in the North-East covering the England v West Indies Test match at Chester-le-Street. Because my parents were on holiday, I ended up staying in a hotel in Durham and had to get a cab to Roker at 6am so I could make it back to the Riverside in time for the first ball. That gave the walk a weird feel, partly because the streets were empty and partly because I was being dropped in Roker, rather than, as I usually would have done, wandering the couple of miles south from my parents' house. I'd feared the driver might think it was a little strange going to visit an old football ground a decade after it had been knocked down, but Bobby from Chas's Cabs seemed almost more excited by the trip than I was. It turned out he'd missed only one home game since 1965 and that because he'd been in hospital.

We turned left off Roker Avenue, past the Cambridge, where the pub sign still shows an immaculate Roker Park gleaming in the floodlights, then swung right down Roker Baths Road, past the Roker Pie Shop with its red and white frontage. "Yer can 'ear it," Bobby insisted. "Yer can still 'ear it, man. Listen to 'em." Maybe he could, but I couldn't. I often feel a chill in empty stadiums as though some shadow of expended emotional energy remains and I wanted desperately to hear some echo of past chants or roars or the ageless programme seller with his shopping-trolley and his indecipherable nasal roars but all I could hear were the shrieks of the gulls and the gentler twittering of the odd blackbird.

Bobby dropped me off where Town Centre Garages had once stood and I tried to get my bearings. The New Derby, where in later years we'd go to clear out the quiz machines after night matches, was still there and so was the newsagents at the end of Brandling Street, but nothing else was the same. I turned up Grantham Road, which would have taken me along by the Main Stand. Back when I lived in Sunderland, the route of my longest run would take me down there here, completing the loop off Fulwell Road before turning back for the long pull up alongside Roker Park – the park – and past St Andrew's church before dropping down to the sea-front. I probably ran it once a week on average for about four years but I could barely recognise it.

On the other side of the road is the Wimpey housing estate, covering the old car park. It was there that you'd queued at the ticket-office, there that you caught official buses to away games, there that Lawrie McMenemy was mobbed on his arrival in 1985. The stand, designed by Archibald Leitch and featuring his trademark latticework, had once been one of the finest in the country – would have been finer, if Rangers hadn't purloined his original design for Ibrox. By the nineties, though, it had begun to look shabby. The paintwork was faded, the concrete stained and even the style of the lettering that spelt out 'SUNDERLAND AFC' looked dated, almost as though, as many Sunderland fans wished it had, time had stopped in 1973.

I wandered round, looking at the street-signs: Turnstile Mews, Midfield Drive, Clockstand Close... it was all desperately banal. This surely was a chance to pay tribute to the greats who had played on the spot, to celebrate Carter, Shackleton and Hurley, but perhaps that would have been too much like showing off, and that, in the North-East, is pretty much the unforgivable sin.

Wimpey also built the new houses on the old Ayresome Park in Middlesbrough and they too suffer from an uninspired naming policy. There, though, there are at least physical reminders of what the area used to be. A bronze ball marks a penalty spot, a sculpture of a child's coat hangs where the goalposts used to be and, most movingly, there is also a low, stud-scuffed bronze mound on the spot from which Pak Doo-Ik scored the goal with which North Korea beat Italy in the 1966 World Cup. Forty years on, local residents looked out of their windows one morning to see half the North Korea squad standing to attention around the sculpture, singing their national anthem. Why couldn't Sunderland have similarly marked Jozsef Szabo's dramatic goal-line clearance for the USSR against Hungary in the quarter-final of the same tournament? Or even a great Sunderland moment: Trevor Ford hitting a shot so powerfully on debut in 1950 that it uprooted a post, Vic Halom's screamer against Manchester City in 1973, or Gordon Armstrong's headed winner against Chelsea 19 years later?

I retraced my steps, passed the newsagents and turned left down Givens Street. The streets here are typical of the early twentieth century, imposing and sturdy, unwaveringly respectable, with between them the backlanes that allowed for coal and such-like to be delivered. I passed Cooper Street, where George Reynolds, the notorious safecracker and former Darlington chairman grew up, and then the back lane where, between the walls topped with shards of broken glass, my dad had taught me to ride a bike. Then I came to Appley Terrace, where my dad grew up and where my gran lived until her death. From her back garden – even from inside the house if the crowd was big enough or the wind was right – you could hear the roars from Roker Park so clearly that there was no need to check the final score. In the old days, as she would regularly tell me, she'd open the doors of the garage so fans could park their bikes inside, leaving a box on a shelf for them to drop in sixpence as a fee. We'd regularly go up there for tea on a Saturday and after a while my dad started taking me to watch the last 20 minutes of games, sneaking in when they opened the gates to let people leave. The first piece of action I saw live in a football ground was Steve Williams stroking in an equaliser for Southampton in October 1982, Ally McCoist having put Sunderland ahead with an overhead kick in the first half. It was more than a year later that I first saw Sunderland score, Gary Rowell plunging in to head an equaliser against Leicester.

Even after I started going to games with mates, heading for the Fulwell as my dad took his usual spot in the Roker, we'd meet up at my gran's afterwards. A match wouldn't have been a match without an over-milky coffee and some homemade ginger biscuits to follow.

My gran died shortly after Christmas and was cremated on January 6. That day, Sunderland played away at Manchester United in the third round of the FA Cup. In the afternoon following the funeral, my dad drove me back to university and we listened to the game on the car radio. Nicky Butt put United ahead but in the second half, in quick succession, Steve Agnew and Craig Russell scored. For a while it seemed football may be handing out a sentimental favour but Éric Cantona equalised with a late header and

United won the replay. As we lingered on the terraces following the 3-0 victory over Everton eighteen months later, my dad in the Roker and me in the Fulwell, it wasn't just a football ground to which we were saying goodbye.

At the end of Park Parade is the Booze Buster that, when it was still Blayney's, was drunk dry as thousands of fans queued overnight for tickets to the 1992 FA Cup semi-final and over the road at the end of Bede Street is Armstrong's Aquatics, still selling turtles and other pets. Opposite is the Methodist church, where you used to be able to get tea or coffee and homemade cakes before games. I turned down through the park, past the bandstand and through the ravine to the Cat and Dog Steps down onto the beach. The name supposedly derives from the fact that when dead cats and dogs were flung into the river, it was there that the bodies were washed up but these days in summer it's probably the most popular part of the beach. In 1963, Brain Clough slogged up and down through the sand by the steps as he tried to regain fitness after rupturing his knee ligaments.

I turned right, past two crows fighting over a polystyrene tray of half-eaten chips, past the marina and on to the old North Dock. Through the aspen and the hawthorn the path climbs Look Out Hill. At the top is a sculpture of a telescope, pointing straight into the shrubs, and alongside it, carved of stone, a stool, a Gladstone bag, a picnic hamper and diary, part of the Sculpture Trail that dots the north bank, memorialising the past in trying to create a present. Two centuries ago, a gun battery stood near here, defending the port against naval attack, initially from the privateer John Paul Jones, who carried out raids in support of the Americans during the War of Independence. A similar battery stood across the river, and it was there, local legend has it, that a soldier on watch duty, startled by the mewing of a black cat after falling into a drunken sleep one moonlit night, insisted he'd been approached by the devil incarnate. From then on, it became known as the Black Cat Battery and the black cat took a central place in the folklore of Wearside and, particularly, its football. The nickname was formalised by a vote after the move to the new stadium in 1997, but Sunderland players had incorporating black cats into their team photos for almost nine decades before that.

From Look Out Hill, the path drops back down to the river. The area is thick with bushes now and although the South Dock still bustles it's hard to believe that half a century ago these banks were home to Britain's most productive shipyards, and had been for more than 100 years. In 1834, the Lloyd's Register recorded that Sunderland was "the most important shipbuilding centre in the country, nearly equalling, as regards number and tonnage of ships built, all the other ports together". Between September 1939 and the end of 1944, 249 vessels totalling over 1.5million tons were built on the Wear, 27% of the UK's output over the period. To put that in context, the output of the entire United States in 1938 was only 201,251 tons. The loss of shipbuilding dealt a grievous blow to the city, not only in terms of jobs – as the pits closed as well, unemployment reached a peak of 22% in the eighties – but also to its pride.

Carrying on, I passed by the National Glass Centre, a nod to the glass industry that until very recently had remained strong in the town since Benedict Biscop, abbot of St Peter's, had first brought over craftsmen from Rome in the seventh century. St Peter's, where the Venerable Bede took his vows, is still there, a squat, robust building, and in front of it, where once the ballast from ships formed ever shifting mountains, is the main campus of Sunderland University.

By the river is a metal tree on a plinth, one arm arcing out from the trunk towards the river. The obvious association is the tree of knowledge, extending its reach further and further, but then you notice the odd patterning of the paving stones stretching away from it. Viewed from the bridge, or in a mirror set in the sculpture, it becomes apparent that the shape formed is that of a hammerhead crane, industry's shadow reaching out from knowledge, the past reaching back from the present.

Under the bridges, the banks are supported by brick ramparts that once formed part of the shipyards. A brick chute – once used to drop coal down from the colliery to the river – cuts through the tangled grass to the right. The Stadium of Light is up there, no more than 60 or 70 yards away, but obscured by the steepness of the bank. Behind the West Stand, beyond the car park where the land falls sharply towards the river, are a series of sculptures by Graeme Hopper, strange silver stickmen done in the style of the artist LS Lowry, who visited the city regularly from the early fifties until his death in 1976. They may be a nod to the miners who once worked the site but as they strain to push an enormous silver polyhedron – manifestly a rock – up the bank, the more immediate reference, appropriately enough, is to Sisyphus.

And for a club like Sunderland, Sisyphus is the perfect metaphor, forever striving towards achievement, only to be relegated or to sell their best players, forever building again. And for what, exactly? Perhaps one day Sunderland will win something again, but what then? My dad always spoke of the strange sense of sadness he felt when the final whistle blew at Wembley in 1973. Sunderland had just completed perhaps the greatest fairytale in the history of football, going in six months from being sixth-bottom of the Second Division to beat Manchester City and Arsenal before overcoming Don Revie's great Leeds United in the FA Cup final. They'd just won their first trophy in 36 years. They'd just become the first second-flight side since the Second World War to win the Cup. And he knew, in the moment of consecration, that nothing in football would ever be that good again. I wouldn't say I was relieved when City came back to beat Sunderland in the League Cup final last season but there was a part of me that thought that if Sunderland are going to win only one trophy in my lifetime I'd rather it was in another 30 years: young enough, hopefully, still to enjoy it, but old enough not to suffer the 30-year hangover my dad and others of his generation went through.

But what of other teams, bigger teams, those for whom winning a trophy isn't some great culmination but just another notch? That's where European competition used to be so valuable: it offered exoticism and a chance for a club to test itself against teams whose very foreignness gave them a sense of mystery and menace. Even for the truly great sides, Europe was an adventure and a challenge. That feeling is being diminished. Familiarity has dulled the sense of the unknown and such are the economic divisions in European football that a virtual franchise system now exists, with half a dozen sides habitually reaching the quarter-finals. Winning the Champions League is still, of course, a great achievement, but it feels less like an epic quest, as it was when, say, Manchester United or Liverpool first won the European Cup, and more as though, for the superclubs, if they hang around long enough, it will eventually be their turn. The romance has been diminished and, in its place is a self-perpetuating elite supported around the globe that is extremely difficult for smaller clubs to penetrate. And the global nature of that support, necessarily, means the connection between the club and its immediate community is reduced.

Just across the car park, outside the main entrance of the Stadium of Light, there is another statue. In bronze, it depicts a family of the thirties – standing behind two children, a mother holds up the arm of a flat-capped father as though she were a boxing referee and he had just won a title bout. His face heavily lined, he holds aloft a sphere made of three interlocking hoops. A plaque in the plinth makes the point overtly: "All generations come together at the Stadium of Light," it reads. "A love of 'The Lads' has bonded together supporters for more than 125 years and will for many more years in the future... Supporters who have passed away have their support carried on by today's fans, just as the supporters of today will have their support continued through family and friends."

It is a touch saccharine, perhaps, but it taps into something quite profound. Perhaps, in this age of quasi-franchises and superclubs, when the structure of the competitions and the nature of globalisation makes the rich richer so they exist at an impossible remove to the rest, this is all that remains of the traditional mode of support: football not as an expression of provincial industrial pride, but as a reminder of it.

# The Great Betrayal

*Mike Ashley and the cheapening of the Newcastle United dream*

**By George Caulkin**

**Along Stowell Street and up to Gallowgate, hemmed in by the illicit, everything mam would scold you for; men weaving through traffic, a chuffing of tabs, the fucketty-twat, rat-a-tat swearing, pie-flecked gobs crooning mayhem. A half of orange squash at fart height outside the Strawberry and it is ten to three and tears are prickling and panic clenches and you cannot swallow but the rush is on and you bolt it.**

Moved and buffeted, onto tiptoes, Dead Sea swimming, but a sea alive, afroth with yanking current, past the walls to the turnstiles though pockets of meat smells, piss and ale. Step-dad on one side and a neighbour on the other – his tickets, his offer, an eight year old's queasy nod – but nobody had told you it would be this affront to childhood, to responsible parenting. This obscenity, this stench, this first time, this only time, this cesspool.

A struggle up some steps and then a struggle to comprehend, a long field of emerald bordered by grey, fringed with concrete, by black and white. Glorious green in a monochrome landscape, vivid and out of context, too vivid to wrest your eyes from. It is what you remembered stuffed between the adults, packed so tightly that you rose when they did, arse-down when they sat. The rest of your view: the back of someone's parka.

No teams, no scorers, no specific date, just a pressing of eyes and that flash of green. Nothing else brought you back, nothing else made sense, certainly not the invisible, middle-distance game you did not witness. Nor the shouting or the scuffle for the bogs at half-time, the leaving five minutes early and the dull, distant cloud-burst of two late goals (you would never do that again). Just that big grey city green.

That was how it began and that is how it remains; arrive at a stadium and search out the grass, man-made but natural, defying the stanchions crowding in on it. There would be human heroes – Keegan as a player, Beardsley and Gascoigne, with his chip-fat shine and bagatelle feet – but the tingle of that feeling, eyes wide at the incongruity of an urban savannah, the darkness of encroaching terraces, is what burrowed inside.

It is what Newcastle United meant. That oasis inside St James' Park. In a city as foreign as Marrakech, manic and polluted, nothing like home, like Durham, with its university skin and pit-village veins, but the green and the football and Keegan's return and then the promise of energy pulled me to it after college. 22

years later – 35 since the first time – it keeps me there, bound to it by work, relationships, a shadow of love.

The job makes it different. You get closer to the club, but the boundaries extend to Sunderland, Middlesbrough and elsewhere and there is a professional reserve which prevents your embrace. There was no reserve with Keegan, that defiance of a bedraggled history, that have-a-go fluidity, and love is expressed in different ways; players became friends.

Slaughtered at Gretna Green (another green), with one of them your best man, you say a woozy yes.

Now (never more so) there is a yearning to give assent again, to renew vows with a place that has both grown and retreated, but this is a team which does not win – although that, in itself, is not so unfamiliar – a dry, joyless club which operates like the footballing wing of a retail empire. A club where cups are everything, the essence, the futile goal, those decades of waiting, but where cups are now nothing, no longer a "priority". It's business, just business.

No coal, no ships, no steel, but a legacy of hapless football, of pygmies with reins around mammoths, urging them towards irrelevance. From ambition burnt out by vanity and pawning the future, to silence from the boardroom, relegation, Joe Kinnear, the Sports Direct Arena, press bans, Wonga, the sieving of emotion, the Premier League tribunal which described Newcastle's evidence as "profoundly unsatisfactory". Profoundly unsatisfactory: make that the club motto. Crap football is one thing. Mediocrity was once a mantra, the selling of players a recurring habit, until Keegan arrived, fumigated the first-team dressing-room and lit a spark beneath a city. There had always been fury and frustration and stumbling backwards to a precipice, but there was always hope, too, no matter how skinny or misplaced. A chance. Newcastle is now a monument to the death of hope, a club which exists with the sole aim of existence.

Stop the clock, turn back and ask, "What was it again? What brought me here? Why?"

Michael Martin, fan, editor of *true faith,* the fanzine, representative of the Newcastle United Supporters Trust:"It's a local thing. It's a community thing. It's a way of looking at the world from a North-East angle, from a corner of a country often forgotten, it's the cap badge of our Geordie identity. It's family, friends, the street, the estate, the village you were brought up in. The club should stand side-by-side with the aspirations we have for the North-East, wanting to be better, to give us pride and recognition.

"The 1974 FA Cup run is the first thing I remember really well, the Leazes End at the end of the Forest quarter-final, Supermac, Jimmy Smith, Moncur. My old man having a bit crack with Jackie Milburn on Grainger Street and Milburn calling my old man 'son' and asking me if I played and then walking off into the crowd and no-one taking much notice.

"And it's Keegan, so much is Keegan, believing and making us believe we can do better and must do better. Massive shows of support all over the country – the San Siro with 12,000 Mags pinching ourselves we were really there. Sir Bobby, with so much of the Milburn way himself but more cunning, unaffected, comfortable in his own skin and tough but not hard (there's a big difference). It's the away end at Roker Park during the miners' strike applauding the NUM lads with the banner from East Durham. It's us alone, Geordie and fuck the rest of you."

Chi Onwurah, fan, MP for Newcastle upon Tyne Central: "I've been an MP for four years now and have met many important and even very important people, but it was only recently when I met Malcolm Macdonald that I had cause to imagine my nine-year-old self arriving at Hillsview Primary School playground and saying that I would one day be arm-in-arm with Supermac and then looking at the faces around me. It would not be jealousy there or even disbelief but absolute awe that I should raise my sights so very high.

"That's what Newcastle meant to me as a child and although since then I spent many years living away from Newcastle and watched the team play mainly in London grounds I still stand in awe of them, for all I hate the Wonga name emblazoned across their shirts.

"For me, the arrival of Ruud Gullit as manager was very important. He didn't bring the club much success, but as a child I would avoid Gallowgate and the ground because of the National Front presence, so to see fans honouring him with dreadlock wigs made me realise how much had really changed (thanks in part to the work of Show Racism the Red Card and other groups).

"Then there were FA Cup finals, Sir Bobby, Kevin Keegan managing us up from the bottom of the second division, being in the Premiership race, Shearer scoring ...I can't really talk about silverware but I'm looking forward to that changing."

Max Roberts, fan, artistic director of Live Theatre, Newcastle: "At the age of 18, when I moved to Newcastle to become a student, I was a stranger in a strange place and a long way from home but I liked the band Lindisfarne, the McEwan's Best Scotch was cheap and thanks to my lecturers and a couple of inspiring mentors (writers CP Taylor, Tom Hadaway) I quickly grew to love the North-East and its rich social history and radical traditions.

"Unbeknown to me it was a great place to begin shaping a sensibility that would inform my work as a theatre practitioner. The North-East's identity and culture were distinctive and vibrant. Newcastle United seemed to be etched into the heart of that culture and so it wasn't long before I became a regular on the Leazes End. They got to the Cup final the year I arrived and while the league form was erratic, I loved the maverick personalities and talents.

"Little did I know that such fluctuating fortunes were to become the norm, but I still enjoyed the bus journey into town, the walk up the hill and a good luck pint in The Trent House. I always travelled in hope rather than expectancy in common with the vast majority of true football supporters."

Roberts talked of Jimmy Smith, Terry McDermott, John Tudor, Pat Howard, Terry Hibbitt, Tommy Cassidy, Alan Kennedy. Of Supermac, Keegan, Chris

Waddle, Beardsley and Peter Haddock ("an average footballer, but I loved the name.") Of Mark McGhee and Micky Quinn who, "like many players from working-class backgrounds simply 'got' Newcastle and entered into the spirit of the region's identity and culture."

Keegan as manager, then later Bobby "brought some of the best games it was possible to witness,"and the players –local or otherwise –"seemed to genuinely connect to the club, the city and its supporters ...You genuinely believed they wanted to play for the club and shared their managers' passion. They seemed to recognise the club's significance to the city, the North-East as a whole and, most importantly, the lives of its supporters. They also won more times than they lost."

The hearing of it helps, the hearing of it hurts and not simply because the winning has stopped (the winning barely started). It cannot just be generational, cynicism corroded further by time, because although things have been more perilous than this, it has never felt so empty. The Newcastle United of autumn 2014 is no longer leaking money and it is in the Premier League (just about), but bonds have strained and snapped. A club should attract and nurture bind; this one is cold.

Michael Martin: "There isn't anything I like about it at all. The strip is shit, a great modern stadium is defaced with appalling advertising, the manager is a puppet, shouldn't be there and the players are all making a move to get somewhere else, somewhere better. Mike Ashley just wants Newcastle to advertise his horrible cheap shops and to keep the TV money rolling in.

"It's dead-eyed, zombie football, meaningless, the antithesis of what sport should be about – getting better, striving, dreaming, stretching – it's none of those things. The fans who remain like me are powerless, defeated, apathetic, fucked over, empty."

Chi Onwurah: "As an MP, I don't regard myself as a proper fan anymore. I don't get to go to, or even watch, every home match never mind the away matches and I can't name every attendance and every squad member, but I am still a supporter and I still stand in awe of the team and United, match days, St James' Park, the black and white, the sense of unity, that in this city, unlike Liverpool or Manchester or Glasgow or Birmingham, if you are into football then Newcastle is your team. They all mean as much to me as before.

"But I also feel saddened and shamed by the link with Wonga, another sign of the ownership's total lack of respect for the fans and for the city. I'm often out knocking on doors around Newcastle at the weekend and the sight of five year olds playing in the street with Wonga shirts, innocent placards for 5000 per cent interest rates, breaks my heart.

"Almost equally bad is the sight of some of the richest young men in Newcastle telling some of the poorest that they should go to Wonga. I've said I won't go to St James' Park for matches while the team is sponsored by a legal loan shark. Some of the club's actions like renaming St James' Park and bringing back Joe Kinnear seem explicitly designed to play with the fans' emotions. I have no idea what the club's ambition is, but it is certainly not to be at the heart of the city. Sometimes it doesn't even seem to include footballing success."

Max Roberts: "For the most part, the club has been owned by idiots; greedy bastards who lacked the wit, wisdom and most tragically of all, the final ambition, to achieve greatness. They were all blinded by avarice and the possibility they could make millions in their fortuitous roles as temporary custodians of the club as the game's finances rocketed out of control.

"And as for the present ownership? In 2008 and 2009, Live Theatre created a play about the plight of the club and its new ownership. Ashley's tenure was the biggest story in town and it seemed like a tale that had to be told. The first production was called *You Couldn't Make It Up*. It was so successful we had to bring it back in an updated version as the club's fortunes plunged further downward and we were relegated on that sad afternoon at Villa Park. We called the sequel *You Really Couldn't Make it Up*.

"It's difficult to rationalise or justify why I remain a supporter and season ticket holder – the club I support has been transformed 'into a glorified advertising hoarding', as someone wrote, 'a works team largely bereft of joy'– but as I'm the same fella who watched Chester FC through thin and thinner and have avidly followed my eldest son's experiences through grass-roots football, I obviously require my live match fix. Like many people I find such simple pleasures a brilliant antidote to my professional occupation.

"I live and work in a great city, in a region of sublime natural beauty with some of the finest landscapes in Europe. It has great universities, restaurants, museums, cinemas, art galleries and theatres. You can see world-class art, some of it created here, with a universality and quality that touches hearts and minds, nationally and internationally.

"So surely it's not much to ask for a half-decent, attractive-to-watch football team that recruits world-class players and augments them with locally-nurtured talent? Surely we can aspire to follow that team in Europe or to the final of a cup competition? And surely that team should connect directly to its community and its supporters? I don't think that's asking too much of a club that's the third-best supported team in the country.

"The current transfer strategy and youth development programme at Newcastle can never produce the loyalty, commitment and connection to the place where they perform and the fans that come to see them. The club is now completely enveloped by the owner's indifference and ruthless economic strategy. It's faceless. I'll try to be more succinct – it sucks. Am I concerned? Yes, passionately and angrily."

It is not just to supporters and the media that the club are closed to (for more than a year, three local newspapers, who should be family, have been prevented from attending press conferences and sitting in the press-box); they have locked and barred their doors to other institutions, to politicians. The club's Foundation is a worthy body, but the dots are not joined and stories are untold, in a place where there is a desperation for pride.

Michael Martin: "The Supporters Trust is banned from a pointless 'fans forum' which, on reflection, inflates the profile of the Trust because they fear it and are aware it has the wherewithal to expose the crass manner in which they run the club. As for *true faith*, I've no interest in having any kind of relationship with any of the current mob in the current situation. I have no respect for them, no regard, no faith, no belief, no trust in anyone who works for Ashley. I've no interest in being lied to, patronised or misled by Ashley's saps."

Chi Onwurah: "I have had no engagement with the club – the club, that is, not the Newcastle United Foundation – beyond a joint appearance at one Wonga event. I wrote to Ashley to invite him for tea in Westminster. It was a very nice letter and I took a long time over it but the only response was a note from Lee Charnley (the managing director) not to bother Ashley again.

"They do not encourage dialogue and instead I have engaged with NUST and with the Sports Minister, the Shadow Sports Minister, the Labour policy team and other MPs –such as Alison McGovern –who are concerned about the state of football today more generally. Labour's policy on fan engagement is one of the fruits of that engagement. It is said countries get the politicians they deserve, but no-one would argue United fans have the ownership they deserve."

Max Roberts: "It would be great to think that the club actually cared about where it resided and who came to watch it – but under Ashley it simply does not. It would be fantastic to think that an institution like Newcastle United in the heart of the city might be keen to promote understanding and awareness of issues that, as an arts organisation, we feel we have a responsibility to explore with young people.

"It seems the club is simply not interested. Even if we felt it worth having a crack, I'd be at loss as how to establish a partnership that might develop such projects. Our first port of call might be via the local media, who we enjoy a strong and important relationship with, but as the club has severed its dealings with the local press that would be a non-starter. It feels clear that the club has no desire whatsoever to engage."

On a recent Saturday, that journey again, shorter now, bereft of uncertainty, each step well-trodden by repetition. Along Stowell Street, inhaling rendered duck fat and soy, a hopscotch exhaling around last night's kebab puke, spray-painted near the casino. Slower for the hill, through Gallowgate car park to the side of the Strawberry, turn left and skirt the club shop. Too early for seething waves of people, never too late for discounts, reductions, roll up and pay up.

Fingertips on the bottom of Sir Bobby's statue, staring south to Durham and then parallel to Barrack Road, beneath the Milburn Stand, a sharp right and inside. Kick-off is delayed because a new jumbo screen is untethered in the wind and the ground is empty and the breeze gusts through it and you march towards steps, that sensation of knowing unknowing, like those anticipatory seconds in the car before the sea fills the horizon and the sea will be there, but you haven't seen it yet and so you cannot quite be sure.

You climb slowly towards the sky, the stands darkening the view, each stride bringing light to the black, not feeling panic, no coughed back tears, but waiting to remember, waiting to feel anything but dread, anything but this stomach-fist of sadness. And then it opens and is there, that same long field of emerald, but the eyes flicker to it and away, tempted by rivals, beckoned by blue and red, by the words and the logo scrawled on a noble space, by the sirens of nylon and acrylic. The moment dissolves. There is a sale on at Sports Direct.

# The Van Basten of Hartlepool

*Adam Boyd and the glory of a talent that flickers without ever catching light*

**By Harry Pearson**

**During the 2004-05 season, Adam Boyd mesmerised League One defences so thoroughly you'd think he had only to click his fingers to make them strip naked and quack like ducks. As the striker's goal tally mounted, his Hartlepool United teammates started to call him Dennis Bergkamp.**

Up in the seats of the Mill House Paddock, my mate Ed cackled with delight as Boyd sashayed past defenders, hips wiggling like some old-school gigolo. "Boydy,"he laughed madly, as the forward smacked a volley into the stanchion of goal, "Boydy is what Van Basten would be like, if he'd been a Poolie."

Like many English people, Ed sees the Dutch as cultured, sophisticated and restrained. These are not traits always associated with the North-East of England. And even within the North-East, Hartlepool is viewed as a place apart. You know your town is rough when people from Middlesbrough look down their noses at it, and we do.

Adam Boyd was born and raised in Hartlepool. He watched Pools from the terraces. When – or so we imagined – Marco van Basten was visiting art galleries, eating steamed greens and discussing the boundaries of freedom, Boydy was downing pints and going to grab-a-granny nights in clubs with two-for-one offers on blue Bacardi Breezers and fights in the car park.

Boyd made his Hartlepool debut as a teenager, coming off the bench to score against Shrewsbury. He was hailed as a prodigy, then struggled to make an impact – fifteen goals in four seasons, a loan spell at Boston United that added little to his value and several inches to his waistband.

The Pools boss Neale Cooper told the local press that Boyd was overly fond of pies. The Poolies laughed and said that, oh aye, sometimes on Saturday nights Boydy had so many pies he could barely stand up from the weight of all the gravy. It was not the sort of thing the Milanese said of Marco.

Adam Boyd was six foot two, with long, black hair, a sunbed tan and a twinkle in his eye. I didn't think he was a League One Bergkamp or an East Durham Van Basten, I knew he was the Frank Worthington of the 21st century – a view that was re-enforced when the tabloids reported the Pools forward fled semi-naked across a "posh estate" after the ex-boyfriend of the woman he was in bed with turned up drunk from a stag night and attacked him.

I'd seen Worthington play for Huddersfield Town when I was eight – a night match at Ayresome Park, the Terriers on their way to claiming the Division Two title. In the Bob End behind the goal, my grandfather and his coevals, incensed by all modernity, railed against the visitors' number nine: "Get your bloody haircut, you big pansy, you look like a ruddy girl." I did not hear them, nor did I care when Worthington tucked away the penalty that won the match and, smiling broadly, waved in our direction. I was wide-eyed, smitten. It was a rare encounter with charisma.

In the summer of 2004 Boyd shed nine pounds, linked up with Joel Porter, and started to find the net with regularity. Pools ascended. Word spread. Middlesbrough and Sunderland sent scouts to the Victoria Ground, Newcastle and Liverpool too. There was talk of a £1 million price tag. Boyd was 23. He had Worthington's small-town lothario swagger, his flicks and tricks and his bravado. They shared something else too. Or rather they shared a lack of it: pace. In the 1970s that didn't matter quite so much as it did in this millennium. There was little doubt in my mind that had Boyd been able to cover 10 yards even a split-second faster than a fully laden brewery dray, he'd become very famous indeed. In possession Boyd was elegant, devastating, but he ran as if his knees were welded, leaning backwards like a nervous child on a skateboard. The big clubs looked. They shook their heads.

Boyd was unlucky. He hit 29 goals in 2004-05. Pools made the play-offs but lost in the final in front of nearly 60,000. Boyd had offers but, "sucked in by the excitement" of Pools' promotion push, determined to stay. Early the next season he injured a knee in a collision with the Yeovil keeper. The knee joint became infected, the blood poisoning so bad he nearly died. He missed five months. He lost confidence. A spark went out of him.

A £500,000 move to Luton Town, then in the Championship, ended with a single goal, relegation and release. He joined Leyton Orient, scored on his debut, and stayed for two listless seasons. He drifted back to Victoria Park where the occasional flash of brilliance served only to remind watchers of what had gone, and the impatient old men who fill the terraces of lower league grounds bellowing, "Show some passion, you lazy get," at any player who does not literally bleed for the team, were driven to frothing fury by his languid grace.

Hartlepool released him without ceremony at the end of the 2011-12 season. I thought then of a Friday night seven years before. Ed and I drove through pouring rain from Tynedale to Victoria Park in his vintage camper van. Buffeted by the wind, we aquaplaned on the A19 and nearly died by Easington services. The game was against Sheffield Wednesday, a key moment in Pools' promotion battle. We arrived 10 minutes before the start, hysterical from cold, terror and anticipation; dizzy from the sugar rush of all the Haribo Tangfastics we'd chewed.

The pitch was waterlogged. Great puddles lay across it, shimmering beneath the floodlights. The rain kept on falling, remorseless as if Hemingway himself had written it. Twenty-one footballers struggled to stay upright. The other one was Adam Boyd. He not only kept his footing, he waltzed across the sodden surface. He struck a hat-trick, each goal better than the last. For the third, Boyd collected a pass on the edge of the Owls' penalty area, drifted to the right, stopped dead to send the pursuing Wednesday full-back splashing. He faked to shoot and watched another opponent slide past engulfed in spray. He looked up then, and seeing David Lucas marginally off his line, toe-ended a chip so delicate it ran down the back netting of the goal soundlessly, soft as a playboy's fingers along a showgirl's spine.

There was collective release of breath. The man beside us in the Mill House Paddock tilted back his head and bayed in incoherent joy, his Burberry baseball cap blown off by the force of it. The Poolies yelled and sang and smashed their fists against the corrugated iron at the back of the stand until it rocked your fillings loose.

I have watched the goal twice since on YouTube and never will again. To replay the video highlights of our lives over and over, each time another drop of the joy and surprise drained from them, is a besetting vice of our age. To see a thing like that unfold before your eyes is a thrill you never can recapture.

Adam Boyd is now 32 years old. He turns out sporadically in the Northern League and, though he appears unnaturally pale and just a little jowly, can still bring smiles with a volley, a back-heel, a drop-shouldered shimmy – a little bit of wonder in the fading winter light.

# Bob Paisley and the Red Kennedys

*The north-eastern influence that underlay Liverpool's period of domination*

**By Michael Walker**

**The remains of the day were slipping away over the brown stone walls of the squat, cold Liverpool graveyard where Eleanor Rigby lies buried. The happy screeching children from Quarry Street playground had gone in for tea and across the road from St Peter's Church, in the fading white winter dusklight, the verger was winding down the silent afternoon.**

It had been busy, lots of pre-Christmas parish work. And for him there was the usual line of excited tourists bustling down to Woolton in the south of the city regardless of the season or the weather. They arrive at St Peter's in a state of religious expectation. It was here in July 1957 that John Lennon first met Paul McCartney. The very place.

Nine fabled years after the Quarrymen skiffle group appeared in this little landmark church, the Beatles penned "Eleanor Rigby". Although Paul McCartney has said that the song's title and its dismay did not originate from a greying head-stone in the grounds of St Peter's, there is one here marking the life of a woman named Eleanor Rigby.

Maybe it is coincidence that the man who raised John Lennon, his uncle George Toogood Smith, is also buried here, though Beatlemaniacs will think not. They will feel it is magic or fate or whatever, and there is indeed something unusual, special, in the fact that the greatest English football manager, Bob Paisley, is another who lies here close to Eleanor Rigby.

Paisley was the first of only two managers in history to win the European Cup three times. Carlo Ancelotti equalled his record in 2014.

Paisley said his finest hours were spent in the shadow of St Peter's, but it was Rome's St Peter's he was talking about. As Gunner Paisley he helped liberate the Italian capital in the Second World War and it was in Rome in 1977 that Paisley became the first English manager to lift the European Cup. "My first glimpse of Rome in 1944 was through the dusty windscreen of an army truck," he said. "My second visit was rather different."

On the latter occasion it was Liverpool 3 Borussia Mönchengladbach 1 and Paisley joked it was the second time he'd beaten the Germans in Rome.

In Liverpool, St Peter's was also the name of the Paisleys' chosen church and if that were not enough coincidence – or magic – the verger who deals with the daily line of tourists has the surname Paisley. He is Graham Paisley, son of the father.

On this late afternoon, a match day 17 years after Bob Paisley's death, there had been some football footfall in Woolton. Graham tidies pastoral paperwork and says, "At St Peter's we have a mix of the Beatles and my dad, a mix of music and football.

"My dad still attracts people here – today there was someone from Chicago and someone from Israel. The taxi drivers always like it when Liverpool are at home because people come here as well as Anfield. Liverpool have this worldwide following and I'd like to think a small part of that pays testimony to the success when my father was here. He helped make them a European and world name. So, sometimes he becomes part of the Beatles tour."

The Beatles never declared which club, if any, they supported. McCartney's preference was for Everton but he was not an avid fan and the Beatles' most direct connections to football are red. Matt Busby is mentioned in the song 'Dig It' – Busby played for Liverpool. And on the cover of the album Sergeant Pepper's Lonely Hearts Club Band, there is one football face in the 61 crowding around The Beatles.

That face belongs to Albert Stubbins. Stubbins, too, played for Liverpool.

Albert Stubbins came from Wallsend, Newcastle. He was Bobby Robson's early hero. As a teenager Stubbins joined Sunderland on the understanding that if his hometown club wanted him he could go there. In 1937, when he was 18, they decided they did. Stubbins played 30 times for Newcastle United before the Second World War; during it, he scored 244 goals. His goalscoring exploits led Everton and Liverpool north across the Pennines in 1946. Newcastle were prepared to sell, for money and to accommodate a young player, Jackie Milburn. Stubbins was at a cinema in town when he was summoned to the boardroom at St James' Park to meet the Merseyside clubs. He did not know who to speak to first. He tossed a coin, spoke to Liverpool and that was that.

Liverpool paid a club record fee of £13,000 and Stubbins joined a man back from the war, Bob Paisley, at Anfield. Together they helped Liverpool win the first post-war league title, Paisley at left-back, Stubbins at centre-forward. Stubbins scored 24 goals in 36 games and became a local hero.

Paul McCartney once sent Stubbins a telegram that read, "Well done Albert for all those glorious years of football. Long may you bob and weave."

John Lennon was seven when Liverpool claimed that title and presumably heard the playground rhyme "A-L-B! E-R-T! Albert Stubbins is the man for me."

On the 1967 Beatles' album cover, Stubbins is next to Lewis Carroll. Carroll was the inspiration behind another Lennon creation: "I Am The Walrus". Carroll spent a lot of time in the North-East near Sunderland, where today there is not a statue of Albert Stubbins, but there is one of a walrus.

"A small part" was Graham Paisley's reference to his father's contribution to

Liverpool's global status. The modesty must be genetic.

Alan Hansen once said that Bob Paisley's autobiography would contain just two references to Bob Paisley and Graham offers further evidence. When Paisley was announced as Bill Shankly's successor in June 1974, news that shook the world, Graham heard it not from his father but "on the radio".

Paisley was football's definition of discreet genius. "If I can walk down the street and nobody recognises me, I'm delighted," he said.

His unease with publicity and his desire to avoid the media deterred him from seeking the England job. As he said, "It's a specialist job and you've got to be a bit more of a diplomat. If there's one thing I preach, it's knowing your strengths and weaknesses. I might have been caught out from a verbal point of view."

Liverpool's players have countless tales of Paisley's idiosyncratic language, when every sentence contained "doings" or "an' that". In the case of Newcastle's Stewart Barraclough, Kevin Keegan said Paisley would warn, "Watch that fellow Wheelbarrow."

Paisley probably knew the mirth he was creating – in his office he had a clock that went backwards – he just didn't shout about it.

Discretion was a trait Paisley traced back to his roots. He was humble in the days before humility became part of football's ostentatious parade of personal promotion.

The son of Sam Paisley and Emily Bones, Bob Paisley was born in Hetton-le-Hole, County Durham in 1919, six months before Stubbins was born 12 miles away. Paisley's father was a miner who worked at the Hetton Lyons colliery in the town and on the occasions when Paisley was prepared to look back on his life, he said of Hetton, "The population was about 12,000 and it was just mad about football. When I was a youngster, about five years old, when the New Year was coming in I kicked a ball on New Year's Eve, and in the North-East this was a sign: that if you kick a ball through New Year, you'd be kicking a ball through the rest of your life."

There was the pit and there was the ball, or a pig's bladder from the butchers where Paisley's Uncle Alan worked. As a boy, Paisley witnessed the effects of the General Strike of 1926 and with his father he scoured coal tips to bring home crude fuel.

It gave him perspective. He said in 1978, "The poverty was there to be seen but the people were happy, they accepted their lot. It grieves me now to hear people say what a state the country's in when you look back to those days. Yet you were happy, and you didn't have anything at all."

And Hetton gave him something deeper: "Character, to be modest, to be thankful for small mercies. This was the upbringing, what I was taught. The character, reluctant to be pushed down. Perseverance, reluctance to give in."

In 1935 Paisley's father almost lost an arm in a pit accident and reacted by withdrawing his son, who had not yet gone underground. "I was sorting coal from stone, what they call 'on bank', on top of the pithead," Paisley said. "I'd little interest in this.

"It was either going down the pits or being a footballer. This is where the North-East was in pre-war days, and why there were so many footballers. It was such an incentive. I was at Hetton Lyons colliery for three months. The colliery closed down and my father had been badly injured. He wouldn't let me go to another colliery."

Paisley got a bricklaying job 12 miles away in Blackhall, cycling there and back. But professional football would intervene. Paisley had been a prolific medal-winner at Eppleton school and was looked at by Wolves when he was 13. He was rejected, then by Sunderland, which hurt more: "Sunderland was my team, the team I supported. These were the days of Jimmy Connor, Patsy Gallacher, Alec Hastings."

Paisley joined Hetton Juniors, with Harry Potts, who would go on to play for Burnley and Everton and to manage Burnley and Blackpool, and then the great amateur club Bishop Auckland. The Bishops knew what they had uncovered: they would send a Rolls-Royce to Hetton to pick up their new youngster. Although amateur, there are numerous stories of how Bishops paid more than Football League clubs and the Paisley family needed it. Samuel had not worked since his accident.

But Bob Paisley always credited luck in his life and he had proof when one of his brothers, Hughie, got 14 of 15 predictions correct on his football pools coupon and won £315, nine shillings and a penny, a fortune in the 1930s. The Paisleys could relax financially and matters improved further when the Liverpool manager George Kay went to see Bob to offer him a contract at Anfield. "Sunderland had turned me down because I was too small," Paisley said. "They came back again but I'd promised to come to Liverpool. We won the Championship in 1946-47. That had to be my highlight as a player."

His last Bishop Auckland game was in the Durham County Cup final at Roker Park. Considering what Paisley was to achieve, just as a player, never mind coach and manager, Sunderland's error ranks as historic ineptitude. It was 1939 and Paisley's time at Anfield was brief. He was soon in the Royal Artillery, serving in North Africa and Italy. Part of Montgomery's Desert Rats, Paisley's brother Hughie said that Bob temporarily lost his sight during the battle of El Alamein – "Bob was in the trenches and a plane came over and sprayed them with bullets. His eyes were full of sand and he thought he was blinded."

On demobilisation, Paisley finally got his Liverpool career moving and played 33 times as Liverpool won that 1946-47 League championship. Peculiarly, that success is less well-remembered today than Paisley's subsequent omission from the 1950 FA Cup final team.

Stubbins saluted Paisley's contribution as a player: "Bob Paisley offered so much energy in the course of a game that I often thought he would be stretchered off when the final whistle sounded."

Learning he had been left out of the 1950 Cup Final two days before Wembley, was a heartache that would never go. "I felt sick, really sick," Paisley said, while his wife Jessie said that when the news reached County Durham "he had the whole of Hetton up in arms. Dear me, there was nearly a riot. They were very loyal."

But it taught Paisley a lesson about selection and non-selection, about ruthlessness. It was a concept to which the avuncular Paisley would return with incisive success, a knife inside a cardigan. Lawrie McMenemy once said of Paisley, "Canniness in Yorkshire is carefulness, canniness in the North-East is niceness. A canny lad is a nice lad and that's what he is," whereas Brian Clough said of Paisley, "Sometimes his smile is genuine. Sometimes it hides his true nature. He's as hard as nails, and crafty."

Kenny Dalglish recalled Paisley observing, "I'm only a modest Geordie, but back me into a corner and I'm a vicious bastard."

And Paisley himself understood, "Where I come from in the North-East, we were all brought up with the need to better yourself. That, and the belief in football as a religion, produces a certain kind of driving force for this job. It gives you that little spark of ruthlessness, that need to win."

Paisley had left Hetton in 1939 and stayed in Liverpool for the rest of his life, but his son Graham says, "He never lost the accent. The North-East was very much a part of who he was. Even though he left when he finished playing for Bishop Auckland, those were his roots. He came from a coalmining community. He lived the major part of his life in Liverpool but the North-East was still very much home to him."

---

If the world of football thought David Moyes had a difficult job succeeding Alex Ferguson in the summer of 2013, imagine how it reacted in 1974 when Bill Shankly stunned Liverpool with his impromptu retirement on the day he signed Ray Kennedy from Arsenal.

Few considered Bob Paisley to be the man to follow a legend. Shankly was a giant of the game, a national figure, a messianic character. Paisley was a former Liverpool player, a physio, a coach, a quiet assistant. He was not the man to front a football club. So it was thought.

Paisley changed that notion. "I never applied for the job, I wouldn't have applied for the job," Paisley said. "It came at us overnight. Bill decided to retire and I thought if I don't take it, I'd worked with backroom staff, if someone new came in... thought I've got to make a go of it to keep this. There's such a family spirit at Liverpool. I thought I'd give it a go. It was for the staff.

"There's no doubt about it, Bill was a great manager an' that, so well liked, everybody held him in such high esteem. Everywhere you went [he was there]. Bill wasn't unique for nothing. I don't use that term loosely when I say that Bill was unique as a manager. I mean, his very presence, all the rooms seem to be filled, you opened a drawer and you felt Bill was there an' that. Aw, it was a tremendous sort of pressure and something I'd not given a thought.

"There's no way anyone imitating can be great. You've got to be yourself. If that's not good enough, you've just got to accept that. I couldn't go on and say things like Bill did. But I could do them – in a more cunning sort of way."

In his first season as manager of Liverpool, Bob Paisley won nothing. Liverpool were out of Europe before Christmas, they lost to Middlesbrough in the League Cup and to Ipswich in the FA Cup. They had been the holders. Liverpool finished second to Derby County in the league. Never again, in Paisley's time, would a season go by without silverware.

There was no revolution, Paisley changed odd positions, such as bringing in Phil Neal from Northampton Town at right-back. In Paisley's second season Liverpool won the league title and beat Club Brugge to lift the Uefa Cup.

Paisley was on his way to three European Cups, six league titles, three League Cups and one Uefa Cup – 13 trophies collected between May 1976 and May 1983. Paisley's understated intuition, his cool, ruthless decision-making – his "cunning" – saw him improve the fine team he had inherited.

It is probably over-simplification to say that Paisley's genius was simplicity but it was the idea he preached. "We don't want purists or theorists at Liverpool," he said. "Football is a simple game but one of the hardest things in soccer is doing the simple things regularly. Take concentration. That's too easy to bother most so-called deep thinkers, but is it? Geoff Boycott stayed at the very top so long because of it. They decry him and say he's too professional but if Geoff Boycott were a footballer, he'd be welcome here."

When Paisley took over, he gradually changed players and earned a reputation for for his ability to renew the squad. Status, and age, did not protect a player from Paisley's continual assessment. "A birth certificate doesn't tell me a player's age," he said. "The training ground and match day does that. That's how I knew when to unload. A player isn't necessarily finished when he leaves us, he's just finished here."

Of the team that won the FA Cup in 1974, only Ray Clemence, Phil Thompson and Emlyn Hughes started the European Cup final of 1978. Phil Neal, Alan Hansen, Jimmy Case, Graeme Souness, Terry McDermott, David Fairclough and Kenny Dalglish were all added by Paisley.

By the 1983 League Cup final, only Neal, Hansen, Souness and Dalglish started. Bruce Grobbelaar, Alan Kennedy, Mark Lawrenson, Sammy Lee, Ronnie Whelan, Craig Johnston and Ian Rush had been brought in. "It's always fascinated me how Liverpool have let players leave the club without causing even a little ripple," said Brian Clough. "A star drops out but the team keeps on winning."

Clough sang loudly of Paisley's achievements, but while Paisley was voted Manager of the Year five times by his peers – and received and rejected a job offer from Real Madrid – there was a broader sense that he was under-valued. Every season the *Rothmans Football Yearbook* nominated six people or clubs for awards. In his nine years at Anfield, Paisley was not nominated once individually. When knighthoods began to roll into football, Paisley was again overlooked. On Merseyside, there was a failed petition to have him posthumously honoured.

But Brian Clough knew. "There is no magic formula, there is no mystery about Anfield, it's just down to pure talent," Clough said as Paisley approached retirement in 1983. "Bob Paisley epitomises that and I am amazed that people in football, who ought to know better, do not just accept the fact.

"He is on the same level as Sinatra in his field and nobody should question his talent. It's not the fact that he's got a bigger band or sings on bigger stages, it's just down to ability. The man oozes talent and he talks more common sense than 10 of us other managers put together. He probably works harder than the ten of us put together as well."

Clough was particularly smitten by one unforeseen Paisley decision: his conversion of Ray Kennedy from striker into left-sided midfielder: "An absolute masterstroke."

Even the unassuming Paisley was prepared to note, "Ray Kennedy was one of the best moves I ever made."

Ray Kennedy was a graceful tank of a player. He had balance and power. Kennedy had won the double with Arsenal in 1971, when he was 19, and in 1974 had become Shankly's last signing at Anfield. He arrived on July 12, the day that Shankly left, but Shankly was not worried what his sudden departure would do to the player. Kennedy, Shankly said, "reminds me of Rocky Marciano."

Paisley inherited Kennedy who was bought to play up front. When Paisley eventually got round to his autobiography after leaving Liverpool in 1983, he wrote, "Apart from all the other problems I had to contend with so soon after succeeding Bill Shankly as manager, I was left with the legacy of harnessing Ray Kennedy's talents to Liverpool's pattern of play."

Kennedy was supposed to rival John Toshack as Keegan's partner but Paisley quickly discovered that "Ray had really lost his appetite for playing up front."

Kennedy came from Seaton Delaval, north of Whitley Bay. His father Martin, a miner, worked at the local pit, then at Longhirst Drift pit near Morpeth. Paisley reached back into North-East past to speak to a schoolteacher of Kennedy's and "learned that he had played midfield as a schoolboy." Paisley added that Kennedy "was surprised I had found that out."

Kennedy was impressed, too. He was not an easy man at times, according to others at Anfield who had nicknamed him 'Albert Tatlock', after the grumpy Coronation Street character. But Kennedy played superbly well for Bob Paisley. Converted to left midfield, Kennedy missed five league games in five seasons and won five league titles, those three European Cups, the Uefa Cup, League Cup and 17 caps for England.

"In my view he was one of Liverpool's greatest players and probably the most under-rated," wrote Paisley. "At England level he was totally misused."

This is scorching criticism from someone like Paisley. "At Liverpool things were built around him, and we played according to his abilities, which were recognised throughout Europe – except in England. He never received the acclaim he deserved in this country and at international level England wrongly asked him to 'pick people up'."

Not receiving due acclaim may have felt familiar to Paisley. "I had a lot of time and respect for Ray," he wrote. "With both of us being from the North-East we could talk to each other and we had a good rapport – something that is not too common between a manager and a player."

Paisley's affection for Kennedy flows off the page. But when Kennedy's form began to dip, the rapport did not prevent Kennedy being moved on to Swansea City. No one knew then that Kennedy was suffering from the onset of Parkinson's disease.

Kennedy joined Toshack at Swansea, then returned to the North-East, moving to Hartlepool United in 1983. Kennedy made his Hartlepool debut in a 5-1 defeat at Reading's Elm Park, scoring Hartlepool's goal.

The club was on the brink. Finishing second-bottom of the old Fourth Division meant another bout of seeking re-election. Kennedy travelled to London to help make Hartlepool's case. They won and the club's official history records, "He played just over 20 games for Pools, but his respect and standing in the game probably kept the club in business during the re-election vote."

Kennedy had been diagnosed with Parkinson's by then. He took over a pub in his native Seaton Delaval and remains in the area.

Kennedy's 1982 exit from Anfield meant that he missed Paisley's final season at Liverpool, who won the league by 11 points and the League Cup at Wembley against Manchester United. Alan Kennedy, no relation to Ray, scored Liverpool's opener that day.

At the final whistle, the Liverpool players, knowing it was Paisley's last Wembley appearance, broke with tradition and pushed him up the 39 steps to receive the trophy ahead of the captain Graeme Souness. It was Souness's idea. Paisley looked flattered and embarrassed, but he took off his cap and skipped up those steps to collect the trophy and shake hands with the occupants of the Royal Box. "The honour was theirs," observed Dalglish.

---

The man who scored the only goal of the 1981 European Cup final came from Sunderland.

Alan Kennedy was born and raised in Shiney Row, on the city's southern outskirts. Kennedy was playing for Liverpool, managed by a man from nearby Hetton-le-Hole, and to score his historic goal, Alan Kennedy received a throw-in from a lad from Seaton Delaval, Ray Kennedy.

Given what Bob Paisley said to Alan about his erratic Liverpool debut in 1978 – 'They shot the wrong Kennedy" – he might have called this goal a North-East conspiracy.

It was the 83rd minute in the Parc des Princes, Paris, 27 May 1981; Real Madrid were the opponents. As the Real defender Vicente Del Bosque looked on,

Alan Kennedy did what came naturally. Until his late teens when he was converted to a left-back, Kennedy had been a left-winger. Now he raced into the Madrid area and scored from a tight angle to give Liverpool, and Paisley, their third European Cup. It was the third in five seasons.

Three years on, back in Rome where Liverpool had won their first European Cup in 1977, Liverpool and AS Roma drew 1-1. The 1984 European Cup final went to penalties.

Liverpool led 3-2 and needed one more successful kick to reclaim the trophy. Joe Fagan had become Liverpool manager but he had the left-back signed by Paisley. Alan Kennedy stepped forward and scored. Once again he had produced the decisive strike in a European Cup final.

Kennedy came to mean a lot to Liverpool and Bob Paisley. There had long been one-way appreciation and it began before Alan Kennedy was born. Conforming to a Paisley pattern, it started in Hetton-le-Hole, where Alan Kennedy's mother and her six sisters grew up.

In an upstairs restaurant at Anfield called the Boot Room, Kennedy recalls his North-East childhood: "My mother knew Bob Paisley back in the 1940s – I was aware of him probably from the early stages of my life. He lived in the same village as my mother and her sisters and many a time I'd hear my mother say, 'Oh, I remember Bob Paisley.'"

Sarah-Anne Donnelly, later Kennedy, worked in Worlock's fish and chip shop in Hetton and would see Bob Paisley, then an aspiring player, on a Friday. It is uncanny – or canny – that decades later Paisley would sign her son for Liverpool. "There wasn't much to Hetton," says Alan Kennedy. "My uncle used to go into the local bar and have a couple, and inevitably the talk would be about football, and about Bob. 'Oh, Bob did this, Bob did that, Bob made good.'

'They were very proud of him and what he did at Liverpool – though they would have loved it to have been done at Sunderland or Newcastle. My grandmother used to talk about him playing for Bishop Auckland. But Bob decided that his future was away. It was tough back then to get a job. So they understood. In the area – Easington, Hetton-le-Hole, Houghton-le-Spring – they were proud of him. These were all mining people, my uncle was a miner. They were hard, rugged people but good, honest and homely. That was epitomised in that village.

"Around the time I got into the youth team at Newcastle, I used to go back to Hetton to see my grandmother. She still lived there and two of her daughters still lived there. By then everything was about Bob Paisley, what he was doing, and I felt pride about him coming from Hetton-le-Hole, very much."

Kennedy had still not met the man he heard so much about, and would not until, remarkably, they shook hands at Wembley Stadium.

The 1974 FA Cup final which ended Liverpool 3 Newcastle United 0 provokes many and varied memories: Kevin Keegan's two strikes against the club he would later save, David Coleman's "goals pay the rent" commentary, the fact it turned out to be Bill Shankly's last match in charge of Liverpool.

Alan Kennedy, as with all Newcastle's players, had reason to rue the team performance. He had reason, too, to rue the purple tracksuits and the pre-game photo-op of him dressed as a zebra in a Durham wildlife park. But it was also the day he met Bob Paisley. Kennedy was 19.

"Of all things, I got to meet Bob Paisley and Bill Shankly at Wembley in 1974," Kennedy says, impressed still. "It was amazing to me that this man from Hetton, who my mother had talked about, who'd played football and gone on to do well at Liverpool, that I'd be meeting him at an FA Cup final. We didn't realise then that he was going to be the Liverpool manager."

Neither Paisley nor Kennedy knew in 1974 that one would be signing the other. But in August 1978 a north-eastern journalist, Bob Cass, turned up at Kennedy's parents' council house to tell him Liverpool wanted to sign him. Kennedy still lived at home and for 18 months Terry McDermott lived there with them.

Kennedy, by then an established Newcastle United player, had his TR7 parked outside: "It was white with a go-faster stripe. I bought it in Newcastle. Cars were very important in those days."

Yet while Alan Kennedy had a TR7 and his older brother Keith had also made it as a professional at Newcastle, then Bury, the Kennedy home did not have a telephone. Kennedy had the number at Anfield of the chief executive Peter Robinson, but no phone.

"Some people probably had phones in their house then, but I didn't know anybody who had," Kennedy says. "We're talking 1978. We were in a council house. It was a case of finding the nearest telephone box, which was at Barnwell shops, and going down there and phoning up Anfield. I was shaking like a leaf, I really was, like.

"I remember the number, it was 051 then, not 0151. I remember dialling slowly and thinking, 'Who's going to be on the line, like?' The secretary came on and I asked: 'Can I speak to Mr Peter Robinson, please?'

"Peter then said the deal was more or less done but that I would go into training with Newcastle the next morning as normal. Then I would go down to Liverpool. It was amazing how it happened. Bob Cass knew Liverpool were interested in me. I thought I was going to Leeds United, they were number one to sign me – or so I thought. It wasn't like that. Liverpool came along, offered the money.

"The Barnwell shops at Penshaw: my mother worked in the fish-and-chip shop there. Before that she'd worked in the fish-and-chip shop in Hetton.

"I walked down to the phone box, 60 or 70 yards – this is a true story. There were three or four people in front of me using the phone. I was standing there, like, telling people Liverpool want to sign me. They're going, 'Huh?' I was trying to get them to hurry up, but their telephone calls were important too. I must have waited an hour. It must have been an hour.

"If you remember, at six o'clock it used to get cheaper, didn't it? Half-price, something like that. You'd be there with your 2ps.

"That was about your background and Liverpool knew that. We couldn't afford very much, we lived in a three-bed council house. We had a washer, an old-fashioned one, then you'd use your mangle. We'd a coal fire. We lived basic.

"But it was great. And everything was about football. We were on the River Wear, it was close, near Penshaw Monument. Plenty of hills. We actually played football on a hill, it sloped away to the river. I'd go on cross-country runs, miles.

"The shipyards were too far away to see, it was more rural. I felt more of a country lad than anything else. Yet everywhere around us was work, work, work. There was an ironworks near us, a factory that made iron. I could see it from my bedroom window. It glowed at night, every night, until they closed it down. We'd get wood from the local joinery about half a mile away. I'd push my barrow down, get the cut-offs, wheel it back up. The things you did – but it was physical, all physical.

"In County Durham there were lots of little villages, all linked by one road. There was Shiney Row, Philadelphia, Newbottle, Houghton, Hetton, Easington and on. I've run that road. It'd cost tuppence on a bus, and you didn't have tuppence."

The £330,000 transfer was concluded within 24 hours of his 2p phone call. Kennedy was thrilled to be joining Liverpool, the European champions, and also to be leaving Newcastle United.

"The players at Newcastle felt the problem at the club was the directors interfered too much. They appointed Gordon Lee as manager, who came with Richard Dinnis. He wasn't up to it and we knew that. We lost 10 of our first 11 games. The club was going nowhere. After Dinnis, they said they'd get a trouble-breaker in – Bill McGarry. I was off. I didn't like McGarry. He didn't like me. The club wanted a lot of money for me."

Newcastle's demand caused a delay in Kennedy's sale. Increasingly frustrated, he chose to express himself in an unusual fashion. There was no knock on the manager's door or the chairman's. Alan Kennedy describes what he did next: "I grew a beard.

"'Look at me! I'm a rebel, I'm tough. I've got a beard on.'

"When I came to Liverpool I'd a beard. I looked 36, I was 23."

Kennedy's facial hair did not put off Bob Paisley. He collected his new signing from a Liverpool hotel the next morning and drove him to training.

"We didn't talk about the North-East, he talked to me about getting into the team. I remember Bob saying, 'I can't promise you anything. Work hard. I've got Joey Jones and Emlyn Hughes still here. But I've brought you here to make that position your own. If you can't do it, we've got two others. Although we won the European Cup three months ago, no-one here is guaranteed their place.

I've changed it around before and I'm looking at better players all the time.'

"You were immediately under pressure, that first day. That was in the car from the hotel in town where he picked me up. That's pressure. Straightaway. I'd not had that at Newcastle. There, I knew I'd be playing.

"I'd had a bad injury in 1977 and Liverpool were a bit sceptical as to whether they should take me. But the knee was fine. I didn't know then, but it was the best day of my life."

Kennedy would go on to play for England, but what he and Paisley had in common – knowledge of Hetton-le-Hole and Kennedy's mother – did not translate into favouritism.

Kennedy says Paisley had "a soft centre" but he saw other characteristics.

"When I first arrived at the club in '78 he wanted to look after me. I looked at him, cardigan, tie, jacket, hair brushed back – he was like a fatherly figure, a grand-fatherly figure. I was 23. He was nearly 60. But he didn't care how he dressed and he didn't say much until you talked about football, then you'd see his eyes light up.

"When he first talked about Liverpool to me, it was like he was telling a story about his family. It was about the love of Liverpool Football Club. It was his, though he had so many good lieutenants around him, it was family-run. Bob was the reluctant leader thrust into the limelight. He wouldn't like it today.

"He was an intelligent man but he didn't like speaking too much. He didn't want to speak to the media. He always said the players did the talking. He would speak to fans one-to-one but in front of people he looked uncomfortable."

At other times Kennedy experienced Paisley's toughness. That was a reference to the day in 1982 when Sunderland needed to win at Anfield to stay up and did so, Stan Cummins scoring the only goal. Paisley's support for Sunderland was quiet but there was champagne in the away dressing-room and the rumour was it had been sent in by the home manager.

Kennedy was there and he says it wasn't like that because "Bob Paisley wasn't sentimental when it came to things like that. Listen, Bob loved the North-East, he loved the people, but when it came to business, he would want to win the game. He'd always pick his strongest team. He picked a strong team that day."

Kennedy already had direct experience of Paisley's hardness. It came three months after scoring that winning goal against Real Madrid. That was the last game of season 1980-81. For the first game of season 1981-82, Kennedy was dropped.

"I'd scored that goal in Paris and I was in every newspaper in the North-West, pictures of me with champagne, whatever. We'd won the European Cup but when we got back to training we'd a practice match at Anfield. It was the younger players versus the older and established players. I was in the young team, so was Ronnie Whelan, Ian Rush. Others. We beat the first team 6-1.

"As far as I know, the manager summoned the coaches and said, 'That wasn't good enough. We're going to get rid of him and him and him.' Gradually they all went.

"I was left out for a while. Mark Lawrenson came in. Mark was a great player. He could play anywhere. When I came back into the team he was at left midfield in front of me. Then Bob decided to play him at centre-back. I knew then that if I missed a game I'd never get back in the team. I didn't miss a game for four years – 205 games."

Alan Kennedy stayed seven years at Anfield. He won five league titles, four League Cups and two European Cups.

After Paris in 1981 he took his medal back to Sunderland. "I was very proud. I was in the Penshaw, the local CIU working men's club – I was a member. I showed the medal off and the look on the faces: 'God, is that all it is?' They went back to talking about greyhounds."

After Liverpool, Kennedy joined the doomed Lawrie McMenemy experiment at Roker Park which ended with Sunderland in the Third Division.

Kennedy had returned to the North-East, as he had done "most weekends" while at Liverpool and though he briefly later played for Hartlepool, Kennedy would re-settle in the North-West.

And he recalls one North-East to North-West journey after a victorious Liverpool trip to St James' Park. "Bob was very proud. He told the driver to go by Penshaw Monument. We didn't go into it but Bob was pointing at it saying, 'That's where I used to roll me eggs down.' He'd also organised [the scout] Alex Smailes to sort out sandwiches. Ham and pease pudding. The lads were looking at them thinking: 'What's this?'

"I was loving it. We're driving by Penshaw Monument eating ham and pease pudding.

"Bob said, 'This is it.'"

*This is an edited extract from* Michael Walker's *book* Up There: The North-East, Football, Boom & Bust, *published by BackPage Press.*

# 42

## Strikers

"You've got to be beyond reproach, even when you're playing in the back garden, in front of your cousin."

# A Season in Turin

*Man-marking, training without the ball and a car crash: Denis Law on his year in Serie A*

**By Dominic Bliss**

**The fifties were difficult years for Torino. Having dominated Italian football throughout the previous decade, the *granata* had lost arguably the country's greatest-ever club side in a devastating air disaster in May 1949.**

The *Grande Torino* had been on the verge of winning their fifth consecutive *scudetto* when their plane crashed into the hillside at Superga on the outskirts of Turin as they travelled back from an exhibition match in Lisbon. It was a shattering way for an era to end and in the years that followed the club's beleaguered president Ferruccio Novo desperately tried to rebuild a squad capable of contending for honours. It proved an impossible task.

Initially, several talented players joined Torino out of solidarity and in the hope of being part of something special, while various sporting associations loaned the club money to aid the reconstruction process. But it just wasn't possible to recreate the team they had lost. The *Grande Torino* had been a one-off and no amount of money could have helped the club to reclaim their mantle as the nation's best.

In the years that followed the crash, the *granata* faithful looked on ruefully as the likes of AC Milan, Internazionale and – most painfully of all – their city rivals Juventus became the dominant forces in Italian football. Meanwhile, Torino bobbed between mid-table and the lower reaches of Serie A for much of the fifties before their deep decline was confirmed. In 1959 – 10 years after the Superga disaster – Torino were relegated.

Perhaps it was the indignity of demotion to Serie B or the realisation that a new approach was required; maybe they were simply too big for the second tier. Whatever the reason, Torino achieved promotion at the first attempt and their young squad, which included two club legends in the making in Enzo Bearzot and Giorgio Ferrini, also managed to retain their place in Serie A in 1960-61.

Yet the new board wanted more. They wanted to challenge Milan, to challenge Inter, *to challenge Juventus!* To do this they needed to make a splash in the transfer market and, over in Britain, Torino's sporting director Gigi Peronace had seen just the men to thrust his club back into the spotlight.

Peronace, a former goalkeeper from Calabria, had started out in the game by arranging matches between British Army teams and local Italian sides during the latter stages of the Second World War.

By 1961, he had become something of a prototype superagent as he negotiated deals taking British players and managers to Italian clubs. His connection to Torino began after he had smoothed the way for Englishman Jesse Carver to become the club's coach in 1953.

Peronace had previously worked with Carver at Juventus, where he had been prominent in the negotiations to bring John Charles from Leeds in 1957. He had been taken onto the Torino pay roll, although he remained open to a bit of freelance business. He was a key figure in the transfers of Jimmy Greaves to Milan and Gerry Hitchens to Inter, but he saved two big names for his employers, as Denis Law and Joe Baker joined Torino ahead of the 1961-62 season.

Baker was just 21, but had already passed the 100-goals mark for Hibernian and was considered one of the most promising young centre-forwards in the British game, while Law's thrilling play at inside-left had inspired Manchester City to break the transfer record when buying him from his first club Huddersfield in 1960. After scoring 21 goals in his first year at Maine Road, Law had come to the attention of Peronace, who believed the Scotsman could make the difference between mid-table obscurity and a top-of-the-table challenge for Torino.

More than 50 years later, I visited Turin to research a book about the manager of the *Grande Torino,* Ernő Egri Erbstein. I met Corrado Golè, a local artist who had supported *Toro* since those turbulent post-Superga days, and he spoke enthusiastically about Law, asking me if I might be able to put him in touch with the great man. Law was equally keen to talk about his time in Turin.

***When you arrived at Torino in 1961, the club had just achieved promotion from Serie B and were looking to re-establish themselves as one of Italy's top sides after a decade of struggle. How was the move sold to you and Joe Baker?***

Well, we didn't really know any of that. It is very different today in terms of what you would know about foreign teams. It was more like, "Torino. Who are they?" and when we got there, we realised that the history of the club was just incredible. You had Juventus and Milan, whom you knew about, but not Torino, so it was a big shock to discover they had this great history. I later joined Manchester United, who of course were recovering from the Munich air crash, but I didn't realise until I arrived in Italy that Torino were involved in a crash as well and they lost all their players. The team they lost had been fantastic. Most of the Italian national team were killed in that crash, but we didn't know anything about that. If it happened today, everybody would know about it. So going to Torino was an experience that I thoroughly enjoyed – not particularly the football side, but the life, the different language, different people and everything that was different. It was an experience to go there.

***How did the move come about?***

Gigi Peronace was like a scout who was doing a lot of stuff in England at that particular time and he came to City for me. Several years before, John

Charles had gone to the other team in Turin and that was the beginning of something because the maximum wage in England back then was £20 a week. Then, all of a sudden [in January 1961] it changed, but the wages still weren't in the category of those being offered by the teams in Italy. It was just an adventure, it was something to do. If I had my time again, I would still have moved there, even though I didn't particularly like the football.

***I imagine playing at inside-left in Serie A during the early sixties was a whole lot different from playing the same role in England.***

Completely. Two guys were marking me and two guys would be marking Joe when he got the ball at centre-forward, but then two of our guys would be marking each of their strikers as well. So the game was more about who makes the mistakes or who lets you get away from them and I learned a great deal from that. When I came back to England it felt like nobody was marking me at all – it felt like I had so much space. I picked up a lot from having to try and get away from two guys all the time. We were kicked all over the place by some of these guys and when you go to a different country, you don't know who they are. These days you'd know them, but it was different back then and we would look at some of them and think, "Oh dear," particularly when we went to Sicily. You just thought, "Nobody's going to win here; nobody's going to get off the pitch!"

***So you noticed the regional differences?***

Well, the accents were so different from place to place. It's like if you take someone from Cornwall and someone from the Isle of Skye – they don't understand what the other one is saying half the time. It was the same in Italy. You had a different accent to get used to in Turin, in the north, and in Sicily, which is obviously way, way down south. It was like a different language altogether.

***Just how physical were the man-marking specialists in Serie A at that time?***

Well, you don't mind them kicking you when the ball's there. It's when they were kicking you while the ball was in the other half. Then you're thinking, "Well, this isn't right!" So you had to learn, there was a different atmosphere on the pitch. But we gave a bit back, don't you worry. Once we got to learn the rules of the game, we gave a bit back. The thing is, if people keep hitting you or kicking you and you don't give anything back, they will keep doing it. That was another thing I learned – look after yourself.

***You scored a few goals, though.***

Well, I didn't really. I scored some.

***You managed 10, which made you Torino's top scorer and was a decent return by Serie A standards of the early sixties, especially as you weren't playing centre-forward.***

By their standards, yes. I don't know, but it wasn't too many. I suppose 10 was quite good, but it was an experience. I look back on it and I wish I had enjoyed it a bit more.

***Why didn't you enjoy it? Were they more tactically advanced in Italy at that time?***

No, it's just that the *catenaccio* style meant they were so defensive. Nobody wanted to concede a goal and whoever scored first always looked like they would win the game. It didn't always happen that way, but that was the way it felt. So they were more defensive than anything. They were ahead in terms of the training situation, though. They were far ahead of what we were doing in Britain at that time, so I enjoyed that side of things. We used to do all these laps round the pitch in England – well, they didn't do that in Italy. We trained with a ball more or less all the time. Whether you were running or whatever it was, you always had a football, so that was something we tried to bring back with us when we returned.

***Presumably, you preferred training with a ball.***

Well, I didn't like running – not without a ball. So the fact that you had a ball at least made it interesting. It wasn't like running down the steps in the stand, it was proper training.

***How did you cope with this 'proper training' when you first arrived in Turin? It must have been a shock to your system.***

Oh, absolutely, yeah. It was a different lifestyle altogether. When we first went over there, we trained in the mountains and we were away for two or three weeks. We had a good laugh, though. Mind you, the first day I went there, I went to go to the toilet and there it was – a hole in the ground! You think, "Oh dear! What do I do?" So that was a big shock. You come to a big Italian club, who are spending fortunes and, I'm not kidding you, the toilet was a hole in the ground.

***Was it difficult for you socially when the team went into* ritiro *for pre-season training or ahead of big games?***

Well, it was, because a lot of the guys in that part of Italy didn't speak any English. It wasn't like Rome or Milan in that sense, so we had to try to pick up Italian as good as we could and we could only have conversations with a couple of guys, with Gigi interpreting. He couldn't do that all the time, though, so it was a bit difficult to begin with. But they were football players and they were good guys and I liked them all. I eventually got very friendly with Enzo Bearzot, who was terrific. He spoke quite good English and we became good friends.

***Did you pick up the language at all?***

Yeah. I don't speak Italian, but I could understand it and I spoke it reasonably well – not grammar-wise. When you are young, you pick things up, though, and the guys would tell me to say things. Obviously, too far down the line, I realised they were teaching me to say things like, "Why don't you fuck off?" and they were telling me to say this to the press! So there were plenty of laughs as well. A few of the guys went on to become big players actually – there was Roberto Rosato, who played for Italy for quite a while. He was only a young boy at that time, but he was a good player. Then there was Giorgio Ferrini, who played for Torino for a long, long time. The club were just coming back into Serie A, still recovering from the plane crash, and it was a lot of young guys who really didn't have a lot of experience, but we were all young together.

***What was it like to play in the Stadio Filadelfia, which Torino fans wax lyrical about to this day, despite the fact that it has been nothing more than a ruin for many years now?***

Well, at that time, I think Torino were one of the only teams in Italy to have their own ground. Most of the others were owned by the city or whatever. The Filadelfia was Torino's own ground and the atmosphere was fantastic. Wherever we went in Italy, it was like that, though. Football was like a religion really.

***Some people at the club when you were there in 1961-62 would have worked with the* Grande Torino. *Did you feel that the Superga disaster was still relevant?***

Oh, without a doubt. The longer we stayed there, the more we knew about the crash and the team that had died and, of course, we went to the site of the crash at Superga, which is just outside of Turin. Oh no, it was huge. It was huge. It was huge all the time we were there. The conversation was all about the crash. If we'd had the internet, like today, we'd have gone straight on there and known everything about Torino before we went. Turin was unlike the other cities in Italy, with all the industry and Fiat and the shroud as well. There was all sorts to learn about it, a big history, but don't forget that we were only young men and we didn't know a great deal. I was learning as I went and it was really quite interesting. I was quite good at geography, but I thought of Italy as this nice, warm place – I had no idea Turin was just at the bottom of the Alps and was really quite cold at times. I wasn't expecting snow in Italy, I was expecting sunshine. So I learned a lot and of course we went to Rome and we went to Venice and saw all these wonderful places.

***You mentioned that training was different, but I imagine the Italian diet was a bit of an eye-opener for you as well.***

The food was excellent. Ah, yeah. When I came back to Manchester, Italian food wasn't a standard thing at that time, but after we came back there were a lot more Italian places opening up suddenly. So we brought that back with us as well. People were like, "Spaghetti? What's this?" The guys back in England liked a pint of lager, but they were into their wine and we got to like our wine as well. That was new for us because the guys back home only drank beer. So, yeah, we brought a wee bit of class back with us.

***Did you and Joe have much contact with the other British players who were out there at the time? As well as John Charles at Juventus, there was Gerry Hitchens at Inter and Jimmy Greaves at Milan, while Jesse Carver was coaching Lazio that season too.***

We did, yes. John spoke Italian by then, of course, and he was living in Turin as well, so he became a close friend to us – a father figure almost. That was great because, don't forget, the two teams were big rivals. The Torino-Juventus thing was enormous. When we beat them, the fans were going down the street with a coffin in Juventus colours and everything. I thought it was fantastic, a different world.

***Joe missed a run of matches towards the end of the season following a terrible car crash, in which you were a passenger. Do you remember what happened?***

Joe had just picked up a brand new car, but up until then I had been doing all the driving in a little Fiat 600. Then Joe picked up an Alfa Romeo and, because he hadn't been driving while we were out there, he came to a roundabout and he started to go around it the English way. I said to him, "Joe, you're going the wrong way!" but as he turned the steering wheel he clipped the curb on the roundabout, which was about a foot high, and I can't remember what happened after that. Apparently the car went over a few times – and don't forget we had no safety belts in those days. Joe was thrown out of the car, I was thrown into Joe's seat and my brother – also called Joe – was in the back. When I saw the car afterwards, I looked at where I had been sitting originally and the roof was completely flattened to the dashboard, so if there had been safety belts, I'd have been dead. I'd have been killed.

I didn't have any injuries really, just a couple of stitches in my hand. My brother in the back didn't have any injuries either, but Joe had landed on the road, smashed his face and broken his jaw. He was in a coma for a few days, but he made a marvellous recovery. He was fortunate, really, that his legs were not damaged in any way because he was able to carry on his career – and very successfully as well.

***Did the shock of that crash make you feel that it was time to go home to Britain?***

Yes it did. Absolutely. Don't forget, we had very little communication with home back then because we didn't have television or internet and we only had the phones in our room to contact home. Nowadays, it is nothing to go anywhere in the world and hop on a plane home whenever you want to, but it was different then and that moment brought back a few things – you miss your friends, you miss your family.

***What were the circumstances of your departure from Torino? Is it true that the club wanted to sell you to Juventus but you flew home to prevent the move from going ahead?***

Yeah! [Laughs] There was no way I was going anyway! I just got on a plane and flew home to Aberdeen. I left all my stuff behind. I just said, "I'm not going". What can you do? I had no interest in staying in Italy. I'd had enough – but only because of the football. I wanted to go back and enjoy my football at home but it was in the newspapers that I was going to Juventus and as soon as I saw that, I'm on my bike. I probably did it in a way that, looking back, I shouldn't have done, but I just got in a taxi, got on a plane and flew home. I didn't tell anybody, and I left some great friends there as well. I went back when Torino had their centenary a few years ago and it was nice to see some of the guys because I was pals with a lot of them. I enjoyed everything else about living out there and I learned a lot, but the football just was not for me.

# The Lost Weekend

## *Spending two days with Faustino Asprilla on his ranch in rural Colombia*

**By Jim Davies and Juan Felipe Rubio**

**"I don't know why there's so many traffic lights, this is Tulua, not New York!" grumbles Faustino Asprilla as he simultaneously jumps a red and sends a text while drunkenly driving my hire car around the streets of the small Colombian town he has always called home.**

Despite having re-scheduled and re-confirmed my request to come and spend a weekend as Tino's guest numerous times, he seems surprised when I do finally arrive at the ranch at 4pm on Friday. "I'm supposed to be in Barranquilla tonight at a party for my friend's mother. I'm going to get killed for this story!" he complains before leaving my photographer and translator, Juan Felipe, and me in his kitchen with his bodyguard and personal friend, John.

John was ex-army and had seen a lot of active service. He had the demeanour of Rambo at the start of the movie: brooding restlessness. Apparently he was de-mobbed after an over-zealous revenge killing of a jungle guerrilla unit. I ask about Tino's gun collection and he hushes his tone before reeling off a list of weapons that would make Snoop Doggy Dogg swoon. Tino later told me that he no longer kept his collection at the ranch and that John had left the army after stealing a horse. I never found out where the truth lay with regards to Rambo; he seemed to prefer it that way.

Ice-breaker required. I spy empty bottles of *aguardiente* (literal translation: 'fire water'), Colombia's national tipple. "I love *aguardiente,*" I lie enthusiastically as Tino returns. "But I haven't seen this *Blanco* brand before." Tino smiles (a relief for me): "It's a speciality of the valley, would you like one?"

Tulua is home to Tino's sprawling ranch and lies in a vast, flat valley. The ranch itself is big: eight bedrooms, pool and poker areas and various TV rooms. Outside are a swimming pool, sauna, games room and a pool-side disco equipped with a booming sound system which I soon learn provides the constant salsa soundtrack to Tino's life.

This complex is surrounded by football pitches, stables, grazing paddocks, a training ring for his dancing horses and field upon field of sugar cane – farming is the family business. It's a beautiful, relaxing place to be and Tulua is hot, bloody hot, the type of place a man could develop a permanent thirst.

It certainly has that effect on Tino, who pours us both a large measure of firewater. I down the noxious aniseed-flavoured spirit in one and Tino looks impressed. "You play pool?" he asks and with that the ice definitely begins to crack. Tino shouts to a maid who promptly arrives with three cold *Poker* beers, another local brand: Tino's home town obviously holds a special place in his heart, and as I later discover, he keeps his cards pretty close to it too.

He enjoys kicking my arse three times on the bounce and impressing us with his collection of English swear words, recited in a Cockney, rather than the expected Geordie accent. "Keith Gillespie was one of the best pool players I ever knew," he reveals. "Did you see him when you went back to Newcastle last month?" I punt. "No, but I was with Sir Les [Ferdinand] and Shearer. I didn't get to Manchester to see Falcão either, but we talk on Skype and we'll make a documentary together next year on Colombian players in England, he will be a big success at United." He disappears upstairs, leaving me and Juan Felipe grinning across the table at each other like excited schoolboys.

Tino built the ranch, Santino, immediately after leaving Newcastle United in 1997 and it feels as though it hasn't changed since. There are many family photos hanging on the walls, including one of his son, Santiago, whose room in particular looks as though it hasn't been disturbed for a decade. There are also many photos of Tino throughout his career, but most eye-catching is an oil painting of a smiling Tino and his mother. The importance his family play in his life is plain to see.

Horses too feature prominently in life and décor: in gold on the front gates and in a mosaic on the house's exterior wall facing the pool. Tino soon has us outside for a display of some pint-sized dancing ponies which he skilfully encourages to prance and canter around him, tethered by a rope which he twirls around his head.

It's all very impressive, but that firewater has definitely kicked in and I suspect the best way to overcome it is to request another. Tino approves and we knock back a few more before heading into Tulua and Tino's local, the Poker Club. "I'll drive," he insists. "Only I know the way." And with that he takes possession of my car keys for the weekend. Here it's Tino's rules, just accept a fresh beer and enjoy the ride.

Cards, insults and poker chips are flying around the table. Tino has a freshly shaved head and the joke is that the trim is actually the result of a vicious parrot attack. "Gonorrhoea!" he shouts, making use of a popular Colombian expletive, before switching to one of his favourite English expressions: "Fuck off, you wankers!" These are Tino's people: loud, macho, competitive and very funny. Tino and I are both wiped out and we depart to a chorus of horse impressions from his friends – something I later learn means "losers".

It's time to hit the local salsa club. We are greeted by infectious Latin rhythms and a sea of beautiful bodies, black, white, brown, all moving to the music. My head is spinning as Tino hooks up with a crew of guys by the dance floor and two more bottles of firewater appear.

I'm debating with myself whether I should approach a woman standing close by for a dance lesson, when I feel

Tino's hand on my shoulder: "There's a girl of mine here. She knows I have another girl waiting at the ranch, so we must leave now."

The drive home is a blur. Reports about Tino's past car crashes spin through my mind and my stomach churns as he swerves around the dirt track leading to his home. "I have a convertible BMW, but I lent it to a friend who drove it into a pothole and set off the air bags which got jammed in the roof," he explains as we finally go through the gates to his ranch. He immediately retires to his room to attend the guest waiting in his bed. I collapse onto mine and the first night with Señor Asprilla is well and truly over for me, though I suspect his is just beginning.

Saturday dawns and I run to the bathroom, where I sink to my knees, vomit violently, hold my head in my hands and question the meaning of life. After a couple more hours in bed, I stroll through the ranch toward the spiral staircase leading to the kitchen, coffee and redemption. I pass Tino's closed bedroom door en route and am distracted by a jaw-dropping sight. There, to my left, smoking over the balcony adjoining Tino's room is a woman wearing a G-string that reveals a huge, surgically enhanced bottom. The bottom and its owner soon join us for breakfast. She seems a trifle annoyed and I guess her and Tino have had an argument. Shortly after, Tino appears in his usual shorts and designer T-shirt to announce, "Just taking the car to run a few errands." And with that he promptly disappears for six hours.

The day is baking hot. I grab my trunks and thrust my carcass into the cold water of the swimming pool. By the time I haul it out again a couple of lengths later, the woman arrives poolside. She is drinking a large glass of the single malt whiskey I'd given to Tino the night before and smoking a joint of pure *creepi* (Colombian skunk). She seems dangerous and I'm relieved when Felipe arrives shortly after our conversation begins. "Have you been Tino's girlfriend for long?" I ask, taking an immediately mind-numbing hit and passing the pure rolled blunt back to her. "I'm not his girlfriend. Tino has girls everywhere!"

Before we know it, it's 4.30pm and the sun will soon be fading. There's no alternative but to call Tino: it was imperative that we get some portraits done before sundown.

"Relax, I'll be there in five minutes," says Tino and, thank God, he is as good as his word. "I have to get rid of this chick, there's a party here tonight!" he adds as we bundle him back into the car as soon as he arrives, taking his replica of the Uefa Cup with us and heading to a nearby football pitch, cut into the midst of a huge plantation of sugar cane.

The photos are done in an hour and a half and we manage to incorporate a kickabout. First Tino hits a few crosses to me and laughs at my attempted Mark Hughes-style diving headers and then we switch roles and I get my weekend highlight: hitting crosses to the legend. I'm swinging balls over to the far post and Asprilla is banging them home! I'm no longer 38 years old: I'm 14 again and in football heaven – could life get any better? "Fancy a penalty shootout?" I dare to ask. "Why not?" replies Faustino Asprilla, and life just did get better.

I managed to save one penalty but Tino won easily. I shake him by the hand. He can't resist selling me one final dummy and gestures to swap shirts before waving me away with a hand and a smile. "Who would believe this fatty scored a hat-trick against Barcelona, eh?"

Most of the poker crew had been witness to my valiant penalty defeat and now more people began to arrive for the party. Tino was keen to get rid of yesterday's woman and get the gambling underway. Soon the place is packed full of friends and family, the women in the kitchen and around the barbecue and the men around the pool table.

Eventually I am summoned for another poker game and I start surprisingly well. After 40 minutes or so, I pull off a master bluff and amass quite a tidy pile of chips. Tino looks at me with a subtle wink, "You play good," he says and I feel so proud I suspect that I blush. Not long afterwards I am flat broke again. It's well into the wee hours and despite the temptations of the dance floor I head up the spiral staircase to the safety of my bed, a chorus of whinnying ringing in my ears. The poker boys are not impressed.

Sunday morning comes and goes and Tino eventually surfaces mid-afternoon. Today's girl is young and beautiful, but I have little time to admire her as I still have one final request to make. "Do you still have the coat you wore when you arrived at St. James' Park? We have to get a photo if you do." He laughs: he is in a good mood and I'm not surprised. "The Newcastle boys love that coat. Sir Les was always asking me about it! I'll eat and we'll go to get it from my sister's."

Back at Santino we are introduced to more family members before getting a real treat as Tino's dad saunters down the staircase to join us in the lounge. He is clutching a huge bundle of shirts Tino has collected for him. This inspires Tino's sister to grab some magazines featuring her brother, including a Full Monty on the cover of Colombia's biggest-selling magazine, *Soho.* A sly joke about Photoshop manipulation causes the whole family to fall about in laughter. Tino is as full frontal in the photos as he is in real life.

Tino decides that this is an opportune moment for departure as he is keen to show us the Río Frío ('Cold River'), one of his favourite childhood haunts. Tino's on fine form; driving, eating corn, selecting photos of hot girls on his Blackberry all while simultaneously scouting for any eye-popping bottoms he might spy. It's a fun drive to the riverbank as Tino sings along to the radio between conversations. Chicago's "Making Love Out Of Nothing At All"is a particular highlight.

The water is fast-flowing but shallow and Colombians are out in force, sunning themselves, picnicking and playing in the rapids. Tino is immediately recognised and people begin to flock to him, bumping knuckles and waving camera phones. The two of us go for a refreshing paddle and he tells me of his previous camping trips in the BMW packed with women and followed by car-loads of friends and family.

We accept an offer of a few shots of firewater and hit the road together for the last time. The conversation soon switches back to women. I ask, "What's the most extravagant thing you ever did for a woman?" and he tells of how he once requested to leave the Colombian World Cup training camp in order to spend time with Lady Norriega, a famous actress/model/singer with whom he had a high-profile relationship in the nineties. "Risking national football for a woman is big!" he adds.

He expresses a preference for Newcastle lasses before handing the World Cup to the Brazilians. Best player of all time award goes the same way, as he names Pelé despite my putting forward a strong case for Maradona, Tino sums up neatly, "No player will ever again play in four World Cups and win three of them."

I can't resist asking him about his new range of fruit-flavoured condoms that he has just launched and has been busily promoting in Medellín. "As a poor Catholic country, Colombia has many problems with teenage pregnancy. I wanted to promote safe sex and my own range of condoms seemed the perfect way. The fruit flavours are sexy. I particularly recommend the guava flavour. We had a guava tree in my garden when I was a child. I had many good times in that garden and always found the smell of the fruit romantic." There's a discernible twinkle in his eye. I wonder if he ever worries that he is a sex addict? "No, not at all, sex is just a part of life," he says, shaking his head before retorting with his own question "Why did you not fuck anyone at the party last night?" I tell him that the reason is because I love my girlfriend in Bogotá and don't want to be unfaithful which makes him laugh and shout, "Fuck off, you wanker!" He amuses himself, and us, each time he delivers that line. "Are you ever faithful?" is the best comeback I can muster. "For me it is not possible," he admits, grinning.

I smile too. If I've learned anything about Tino Asprilla this weekend it has been that he is, at heart, a man of simple pleasures. Most Colombians maximise any opportunity for enjoyment and Tino is no exception. Under Tino's rules, all you can do is grab a cold beer and enjoy the ride.

ARMANI
EXCHANGE

7

GUES ANGELES
INETEEN EIG

TIM
COMPASS

ARMANI

£5 Bank of Newcastle United
FIVE
Pounds

# A Game for Individuals

*Thierry Henry reflects on how football has changed in his 20 years at the top*

**By Thierry Marchand and Philippe Auclair**

**AS Monaco had started the 1994-95 season catastrophically. Beset by injuries, Arsène Wenger's team had been hobbling from defeat to draw to defeat when OGC Nice, their fiercest local rival, visited the Stade Louis II on 31 August 1994. Rumours of the manager's sacking were already circulating, even though he'd just turned down an offer to coach Bayern Munich out of loyalty for the Monegasque club he'd joined in 1987 and taken to the French League title, a European Cup Winners' Cup final and – only a few months earlier – to the semi-finals of the European Cup. With his star striker Sonny Anderson unavailable, Wenger turned to a young forward from the Parisian *banlieues* who'd racked up goals at an astonishing rate with ASM's reserve and youth teams over the previous two years. Thierry Henry had celebrated his 17th birthday two weeks previously. Monaco lost 2-0 against the Niçois. They lost again in the following round, 1-0 to Le Havre, when the teenager came off the bench to no great effect. Wenger was soon gone and it would only be two seasons later that Henry, under the prudent tutelage of Jean Tigana, exploded onto the French football scene. But one of the most prodigious careers in modern football history, certainly in terms of honours and longevity, had been launched on 31 August 1994. *France Football* thought it right to mark the 20th anniversary of Henry's debut with a special issue, although not everyone in France would have thought it necessary to celebrate this milestone with such fanfare.**

**PA**

The shadow of Knysna 2010 still obscures the perception the French public has of their national team's record goalscorer. Many feel he could have prevented France's very public meltdown at the World Cup in South Africa. Only he had the prestige, the status and the authority to put an end to the farce that was played out live on the world's TV networks: players refusing to train and taking shelter in the team bus while their hapless manager Raymond Domenech was delivering an absurd statement on their behalf to the assembled media. Henry could and should have nipped that pathetic rebellion in the bud, but he chose to keep his own counsel. What made him retreat into silence is a secret he has kept from everyone but his closest friends, who have kept silent themselves. When he returned from the World Cup, it was to be whisked away to the Elysée palace, escorted by a phalanx of police motorcycles. What he told President Nicolas Sarkozy in the hour-long talk which followed, no one knows but them. An interview he granted to a French TV station several days later only added to the mystery surrounding the whole sorry episode, as Henry refused to answer the question everyone was asking in France: what on earth happened? Why did he do nothing? Why had he chosen to ignore the best chance he'd ever been offered in football?

Still, despite Knysna, despite the *Hand of Gaul* scandal in the World Cup qualifying play-off against the Republic of Ireland, Henry's position in the French football pantheon, behind only Michel Platini and Zinédine Zidane, is assured. Alone among the *Bleus* of his generation, he has chosen to carry on playing well past his 35th birthday in a genuinely competitive league – and as a striker, when his most potent weapon had always been sheer pace, with or without the ball at his feet. The lesser demands of MLS suited his ageing body, that's true, but that did not and does not mean that the prime reason behind his move had been to freewheel towards retirement. Even in what should be his last season, he can still be decisive. The USA was another box to tick in the career plan he'd drawn for himself when he was still at Monaco. Done. This too was worthy of celebration. But we had a problem: how could we hold the party without the birthday boy himself to blow out the candles? Apart from routine press conferences and a few sponsors' engagements, Henry had not spoken at length with any journalist for more than four years. It was decided that my colleague Thierry Marchand would fly to New York on a wing and a prayer. Henry has always been unpredictable. He might just – if approached at exactly the right moment – agree to talk to us, even after politely declining all the approaches that had been made to him previously. Fortune smiled on us. Henry was taking part in a shirt-signing session in a Manhattan sports shop. The journalist queued with the fans, the player recognised him and welcomed him like a long-lost friend. It was agreed the two would meet a couple of days later at the New York Red Bulls training ground, where the conversation that follows took place.

***When you look back and think of your first game as a professional, do you say to yourself: 'it is so long ago' or 'it seems like yesterday'?***

[He hesitates] A bit of both. But what I tell myself, above all, is that not everything [that happened] was always set in stone. At the same time, I'm always aware of the road I've followed, and of the work I've had to do to stay on course. Especially that it's not a given in my kind of position. I insist on the word 'work', as it is the basis of everything. You may have a gift, but if you don't work... It wasn't a sacrifice for me. I do what I wanted to do. I loved working and I wanted to be the best at everything: the way I headed the ball, free-kicks, reading of the game...

***In your case, what was that "gift"?***

I was quick. I had to have 10 chances to convert one into a goal – but at the same time, I kept creating these chances. Then I told myself, "You won't have these chances all the time. You must stick them into the net." Then, to avoid over-thinking in front of the keeper, you work on your finishing, so that it all becomes automatic, so that you don't think anymore. The hardest thing for an attacking player? When he has time to think. So, with Claude Puel, who was then a fitness coach at Monaco, I went through session after session with dummies. I wasn't born with a gift for goals. As I started my professional career on the wing, I also worked on my crossing – which helped me understand the role of the guy who passes the ball. We give praise to the guy who scores and, as a result, we're too quick to forget the guy who bust a gut to cross the ball behind the defence.

***And that's unfair, in your opinion?***

No, that's the way it is. How many times did I save games in which I'd been poor by scoring the winning goal? But it helped me to understand things better when I played in the middle again. I've often been told, when talking about Dennis Bergkamp or Robert Pires, "These guys have fed you." – No, *we* fed *each other*. It's a team game. The goalscorer shouldn't have all the glory and I'm not humble-bragging. I've often been unhappy with games in which I'd scored.

***What difference is there between the joy of scoring and the joy of providing the assist?***

To me, the most beautiful thing is making the pass when you are in a position to score yourself. You know you're good enough to score, but you give the ball. You share. And you see that joy in the eyes of the other guy. You know, he knows, everyone knows. People have never understood that when I do that [Henry mimics a gathering gesture, his hands above his shoulders], that's not to say, "Come and see me, I've scored!" but, "Come here, so that we celebrate together, so that we savour it together."

***But haven't celebrations become a show, a game in themselves?***

I've often been criticised for not smiling or even for putting on a long face when I celebrate my goals. It's often because I'd missed something just before. I'd got the ball back a few seconds later and scored – but I was still aggrieved by what I'd done wrong. Those who know me will tell you that it can take me 10 minutes to get over a mistake. Even if we lead 7-0. Because in my head, I tell myself, "It could have been the only chance of the game, I should have dealt with it better."

***Are you constantly looking for perfection?***

It enables me not to rest on my laurels, to keep going forward. I've always been like that and I like being like that. My teammates will tell you that I have to be on edge to be good. Pat [Vieira] knew it and kept pestering me. It's when I'm bothered that I play well.

***What's the secret of longevity for a player?***

First, to avoid injury [he touches wood]. I've also had a fairly healthy lifestyle. I've never been someone who drank or partied regularly. I've been doing it – reasonably – for two or three years, but before that, never. I went home, I re-played the game in my head. I pictured all the chances I'd missed and told myself, "Next time, make sure you don't miss that pass." You've got to be beyond reproach, even when you're playing in the back garden, in front of your cousin. I call that pride. If we play a one v one against each other, I have to make you feel that I'm stronger than you are. It's as simple as that. Lilian Thuram taught me that. I've always wanted to be the best at home. Playing cards, playing marbles... Then I wanted to be the best in my street, in my neighbourhood, in my city, in my *département,* in my country. The aim is to be the best you can be. What matters is not to get there, but to want it, to have that desire.

***So that "gift" is desire?***

Exactly. Then it's up to you – up to you to work or not, end of story. When I see guys turning up late for training, when we train an hour and a half a day... It happened to me once, in Monaco, and it wasn't my fault. Jean Tigana made it clear to me that it would be the last time this happened and he was right. If you're late for training when you're driving a car, you'll be late in the game when you'll have to use your legs.

***Have you ever questioned your worth throughout the 20 years of your career?***

Every day! I've always wanted to be judged on the next game, not on the one I'd just played. What's happened is behind me. It's up to you journalists to comment on it.

***But you've won everything, with your clubs and with the French national team. Have you never felt you'd reached the absolute top?***

No. You should never feel satisfied. Aim higher, always.

***How do you do that when you're on top?***

Every game is a mountain. Each time, you climb down, better to climb it again when another game comes. And each of these mountains is different. Sometimes, you stop and take a deep breath in. At other times, you don't climb at all, because you're crap.

***But you don't play a World Cup final every day...***

What helps you to get back to earth after a World Cup final is when, three months later, you find yourself playing for the Under-23s in Ukraine, in front of 200 spectators [as happened to Henry in 1998]. People have erased this chapter from my story – but I'm proud of it. I won't say it was easy to swallow, but it helped me question myself. I was part of that generation of players who played in the 1997 Under-20 World Cup in Malaysia – Silvestre, Gallas, Luccin – players who'd helped me go further. It hurt me to go back to the *Espoirs,* but I couldn't look down on these guys. So I played. I was good on some occasions. On others, I was not. People said, "His heart is not in it." But three months earlier, I had been lifting the World Cup trophy. Once, as part of the *Espoirs* team, I travelled with the A team. I was at the back of the plane when, just a few weeks before, I'd sat 10 rows further up. I even played in a B international against Belgium, in front of 202 spectators. Two more than in Ukraine. I haven't forgotten that.

***What was going through your mind then?***

That I had to work and that things would get back to what they'd been before. It was a pain in the arse, but I did come back.

You grow thanks to others. You're nothing without your team, whoever you are.

***Is longevity the toughest thing to achieve in football?***

Yes. But it's also the ultimate accolade – especially when you're a striker, with all the young guys coming through. It's not just a question of staying power, it is also an obligation to perform. There is no more beautiful trophy than longevity. Maldini, Zanetti, Zizou, Tutu [Thuram], Desailly, Liza, Blanc, Deschamps, Lama, Platini, Giresse, Tigana, Luis Fernandez... To stay at the same level, when people are expecting so much at each game... Ronaldo, Messi... Are people really aware of what they do, of their consistency of performance? Do they realise how tough it is to be always at the top?

***What does it take to stay there? Energy?***

And not a little bit. An awful lot of energy. People don't realise that when we need rest, it's not our bodies which need resting. When a World Cup is over and you're given 10 days' holiday, it's tough. Yeah, I know – we're well paid. But, mentally, it's not that easy to start again, almost immediately. Tiredness has got nothing with what we earn in a month. I can count the games I've played at 100% of my capacities on the fingers of one hand. And I've played a few. Look at the Germans. They're the world champions. And they have to start again from scratch. Nothing exists anymore – the achievement is behind them. They'll only be able to savour it in 20 years time, when they have retired.

***The sportsman, the star, has erased the human being...***

That's true, but that's part of the game. "If you're on the pitch, it's because you *can* play." I say that often. People don't have to know whether you feel good or not. I've often come back to the dressing-room, telling myself, "Fuck it, Thierry, you just couldn't do a thing today!" ... But if you know how often I've scored a goal in those games... I remember a Champions League game with Arsenal, against Sparta, in Prague. I was just coming back from an Achilles injury, I'd only started training again on the eve of the match. The manager told me, "You're travelling with us, but you'll stay on the bench." Then José Antonio Reyes gets injured after a few minutes. I wasn't even looking at who was warming up, as I was certain I wouldn't be asked to do it – and the manager tells me to get on. I do so, I score twice and I beat Ian Wright's record of 185 goals with Arsenal. Even when you're not feeling good, you always believe you can help the team.

***Do you have to say no, sometimes, in order to last?***

I've never been able to do that. Never ever. And all the great players do the same. Take Vieira. You had to knock him out to prevent him going on the pitch. He's played games when he was unable to walk before or afterwards. And he wasn't crap.

***In which country, which league, is it easiest to last that long?***

It depends on your playing style. I've never been sparing in my own game – but it was always the same style of play. Let's just say the Premier League is tricky. Not just because of the physical intensity of the game, but because of the lack of a winter break. We play the most when others are having a rest.

***Were you given advice when you started as a pro that you've never forgotten?***

What Thuram told me, which I mentioned earlier. Tutu was very tough with me, but I thank him for that every day. My dad too, above all others. Christian Damiano, Gérard Houllier, all my youth coaches. But Tutu was tough, during the games, at training... His words were tough. It helped me. When you join the national team for the first time, you must impress Desailly, Liza, Zizou, Djorkaeff... At Monaco, when I didn't cross a good ball in front of goal for Sonny Anderson or Mickaël Madar, they kicked it high above the wire fence of La Turbie [Monaco's training ground]. And guess who had to go and fetch the ball? David Trezeguet and me. There was no artificial lighting at La Turbie in those days. In the middle of winter, we were training late in the afternoon, we couldn't see a thing when we had to get the ball back. I can still picture myself. [Shouting] "I got one, David!" "Me too!" What else could I have done? Say, "The older guys talk badly to us, it's a lack of respect?" But what kind of respect are we talking about? What had we achieved? Who were we? If Sonny asked me to cross the ball, I crossed it. When he asked to cross again, I crossed again. Even after I'd become a world champion, Tigana asked me to carry the kit bags. There was a woman and a couple of kit men who wanted to take care of it, but he said, "No, no, it's up to the youngsters to do it."

***Do you do the same with the young Red Bulls players?***

Very often... but when you're the only one to say it...

***A question of education, then...***

When I was a young player at Monaco, there were no names on the lockers. I waited until all the pros had arrived to find a place to sit. In the team bus, when we left at 10am, I turned up two hours earlier to make sure I wouldn't miss it. I stood there for two hours, waiting. I didn't sit until I was told I could.

***How does it feel to see these values disappear from the game?***

It's a pity. We're losing something. Becoming a pro is not something that is owed to anyone. It shouldn't be a reason to celebrate or an attainment it itself. When I was younger, I went to all the pros to say hello to them. Nowadays, it's almost the other way round. I started getting massages when I was 21, 22. If Tigana saw us on the massage table, he said to us, "What are you doing here? Where do you hurt? Your back? You've played five seconds in Ligue 1 and you hurt? [He mimics Tigana's voice and accent] Go train, go run, and leave your place for Franck Dumas or Enzo Scifo!" He was right.

***You seem to get worked up about these kind of things...***

Yeah. Too much, by the way. I lose it when a guy is late for training. Look around you. What is it that prevents the young guys coming and training this afternoon? Six years ago, the San Antonio Spurs provided Tony Parker with a shooting coach. Tony Parker. It wasn't a lack of respect – just so that he could improve a part of his game which could be improved.

***Is it this kind of adjustment which enables a footballer to last beyond his physical limits?***

Me, I worked on my passing game. When I was young and I was playing on the flank, then when I played down the middle at Arsenal. And the slide-rule pass from the wing is a very different thing from the appreciation of the game you have in an axial role. But it's just work.

***What were the most striking changes that you noticed in the game itself over the past two decades?***

Take Ronaldo – the Brazilian Ronaldo. He did things nobody had seen before. He, together with Romário and George Weah, reinvented the centre-forward position. They were the first to drop from the box to pick up the ball in midfield, switch to the flanks, attract and disorientate the central defenders with their runs, their accelerations, their dribbling. Who'd done that before? Gerd Müller? Paolo Rossi? No. George Weah was a big influence on me. I copied his game, maybe. But how many guys can claim they have reinvented a position? Not many. One of the consequences has been that there came a time when media and marketing people started to individualise football performance. People stopped highlighting the collective dimension of the game, how a goal was constructed, how a phase started. Maybe you remember the catchphrase of a kit supplier: "ten plus one". It meant, "If you have a gift, you can win." But Ronaldo is the only one who can do what he does. Then everyone wants to show off technical skills, *sombrero* tricks and so on. Everything has been geared towards the individual. We are not talking about football anymore.

***Physically speaking, Müller, Onnis, Rossi and Bianchi did not have much in common with Weah or Ronaldo...***

Sure. But we shouldn't believe that's the norm. Who's got Cristiano Ronaldo's body? Lionel Messi's game? They're one-offs. But if you want to educate players, if you want to talk about the game, you can teach a youngster what Xavi does. Xavi, yes, you can do it. Ronaldo... not so sure. What's true is that if I am shown step-overs and nutmegs on a loop, I'll want to execute those on the pitch. When I was a kid, I wanted to be Boniek – on the end of a pass by Platini. Ronaldo executed a skill to go past an opposition player, not gratuitously. Not everyone is Zizou, Messi or Cristiano Ronaldo. I'd like to have an explanation of the fact that no Spaniard has won the *Ballon d'Or* over the last four years. The game is too focused on the individual. Stars are fine. But within the team, not without.

***That's a very American perspective...***

I'll tell you: I grew up with Michael Jordan, who scored up to 60 points in some games at the beginning of his career. He scored fewer when Scottie Pippen and Horace Grant came to Chicago, but he started winning titles too. That's the truth – he was a star within a collective. When you're not at your best, the others conceal your weaknesses.

***How does a footballer know when it's time to call it a day?***

[Lengthy pause] I don't know. The love of football will always be there. But I think it's when you start to force yourself to do it. I cannot say or think, "I must go to the training ground." When you breathe, you don't think about the act of breathing. It's natural. Same with football. I'm not talking about a reticence that would be linked to a physical problem, I'm talking about the heart that's not quite in it anymore. When you don't feel like it, repeatedly.

***What's left when that happens?***

The fundamentals. I didn't learn football, I was educated. Not the same thing. At Clairefontaine, *messieurs* Dussault, Mérelle, Damiano, Filho educated us. Whether we lost or won, we had an identity. We had to play a certain way, we had to respect football. They put that in my veins. We all reflect the education we received. When my parents sometimes complain about my being hard, I answer, "Who educated me?"

***And you think you're hard?***

Yes, I'm hard, demanding, a pain in the arse, especially when it's about football. But always in the name of love and respect for the game.

***When you talk of 'identity', what do you mean? A club, a style of play?***

They go together. Barça have an identity. The most beautiful thing I've ever heard from a coach was Guardiola's talk before the 2009 Champions League final. He said, "Guys, all I want is that, at the end of the game, people tell me that Barça played football. The only thing I don't want us to lose tonight is our identity. Have a good game." And that was that. It was the same at Clairefontaine. [On one occasion] Francisco Filho told us, "I do not want to see a back pass." That was the theme of that particular game. But we also had to win. Another time, he forbade us to tackle for a whole game – he only wanted interceptions. In other words, he wanted to teach us how to read the game.

***Isn't that forgetting the game's ultimate objective – to win?***

No, because victory is forged in identity. It is when you forget the principles that winning becomes difficult.

***Can this identity still exist in modern football?***

Yes, at Barça. Win, but win playing well. Even the managerial changes haven't altered the identity of the club.

***What about you? If you were to become a manager, could you go anywhere?***

The important thing for a manager is to affirm his identity, whatever it is. If your identity is defending, no problem. You can win that way. But you shouldn't change it if you lose. In 2009, Guardiola didn't talk about the result. The same goes for Arsène [Wenger] before the 2006 Champions League final. They are aesthetes, they want everything to be beautiful. You act that way when you love your work. When you paint a picture, it is so that people look at it and like it.

***How do you feel now, twenty years after that first game?***

I think a lot about the extra training sessions – work pays off. I kept telling myself, "If I don't do this [right], someone else will do it instead of me. Maybe that guy's already doing it. And if this guy wants to nick my place, I'll be ready. Hats off to him if he's better than me. But I'll have prepared myself." And I'd love to be remembered by people when my career is over. I've always dreamt of leaving a trace.

***As a manifestation of respect?***

Towards the quality of my work, yes. I'm immensely proud to have been part of these winning generations, with the *Bleus,* with Arsenal, with Barça. It's also the proof that I wasn't lied to.

***By whom?***

Tutu, who told me, "Work so that you can show you're the best." My father. Tigana, Puel and his demands, Damiano, Domenech with the *Espoirs.* All the people who were with me when I was becoming myself. I'd love you to give their names: Laurent Banide at Monaco, Paul Piétry with the U17s at Monaco as well, Jean-Marie Panza at Palaiseau... Lippi and Ancelotti in Italy. These people didn't lie to me.

***What if you had to pick one memory from those 20 years as a footballer?***

[long pause] The first time that my father saw me on a football pitch. Because everything started there. The rest of the story, everybody knows it.

***Will Thierry Henry, the manager, be as demanding as Thierry Henry, the player?***

I'd certainly want people to respect football. It's impossible to have a great career and be out partying at midnight. I've done it, like everyone else. But a mistake shouldn't become a habit. For me, the pleasure lies in improving and being demanding with yourself. I cannot play a game to have fun. Either you play, or you don't. Winning is only the end credits sequence of that particular film.

*Interview by Thierry Marchand, text and transcription by Philippe Auclair.*

# 79

## Davids and Goliaths

"They play the game without love."

# The Boys who Never Grew Up

*South Africa are African football's greatest underachievers. What's gone wrong?*

**By Luke Alfred**

**There is a well-rehearsed period piece going back about four or five years that encapsulates South African football's oddness. The story concerns Gavin Hunt, the then coach of SuperSport United. SuperSport had just won their third league title in four years and Hunt was called into the office of Imtiaz Patel, slightly confusingly the head of the *other* SuperSport, the pay-per-view station that probably shows more live English and European football than any other station in the world. Instead of being congratulated as expected, Hunt was berated. SuperSport (the television station) were in the business of selling decoders, he was told, not winning championships. Winning like this was bad for business because SuperSport, as they both knew, were not the biggest or best-supported local club. Far better, Patel added, that one of the traditional powerhouses, a club like Kaizer Chiefs or Orlando Pirates, win the title because they have far more supporters– more fans translates into more potential customers. SuperSport cannot win on two fronts –better they win commercially. Best to go out in future and lose the title.**

When he's not pounding the touchline or scowling for the cameras, Hunt is a handy golfer. Depending on his schedule he spends at least a morning or two a week shuttling from hole to hole in one of Modderfontein GC's many golf carts. He's no poet but the airiness of the fairways and the dance of the leaves brings out the raconteur in him. He often tells the story of his meeting with Patel and shakes his head as if to say: "Do you see the kind of bullshit I have to put up with? Can you imagine the head of Sky telling Sir Alex or Moyes or the wild-eyed Van Gaal to stop winning the title because Sky owns the fucking club?" Afterwards, gathering himself, he bends down over his putter and, unerringly, slides it wide.

In his day Hunt was a left-back for Hellenic, the much-loved but now defunct Greek outfit from the Western Cape. I never saw him play but his manner – grumpy, suspicious of frippery, unsentimental – suggests that he wasn't scandalously gifted. I imagine he would have been hard and unsmiling and liable to kick the shit out of you if you gave him half a chance, which is why, along with his prickliness and strangely old-fashioned penchant for truth-telling, he possesses an authority like few others in the local industry. Despite having a compelling claim, he's never coached the national side, being seen as a public relations time bomb, but he's done well for himself and the clubs he's coached, although he has struggled slightly at his new club, Bidvest Wits. He's been there for a season and a bit and shows little sign of steering the ship in the way he steered SuperSport. Then again, with the wealthy Brian Joffe at the helm of Wits, a man who has made his money in services and catering, at least he's not going to be asked anytime soon *not* to win the title. In turn, this could have a knock-on effect on his short game around the greens. In a nice little coda Hunt might even point out that since he left SuperSport United, they haven't come close to winning the title again.

Depending on how you look at it, Hunt had either the fortune or the grave misfortune to be coaching SuperSport United at much the same time that the Premier Soccer League brokered the biggest TV rights deal in its history. Before that, domestic football was shown by the national broadcaster SABC and certain domestic and international matches were defined by the regulator as being in the national interest so had to remain where they were. The PSL was becoming increasingly frustrated with the SABC, however, complaining that the quality of their service and the product left much to be desired. They gave the SABC the opportunity to bid for the rights when the deal came up for renewal and, when they failed to do so, they went to market, market in this case meaning SuperSport. It is safe to say that football in South Africa has never been the same since.

As elsewhere in the world, much business in South Africa is conducted on the golf course. Some have pointed out that Patel and Irvin (pronounced Ivan) Khoza, the chairman of the league, play golf together, although – as far as I know – they don't play on the same course as Hunt. While there's nothing strange in this, it is a local peculiarity that Khoza wears too many hats. As well as being chairman of the league he is the owner of Orlando Pirates, one of the biggest and most powerful clubs in the country, and it is difficult to know whether he and his board of fellow PSL governors are ever really able to make decisions for the betterment of professional football rather than the betterment of themselves and their clubs. Two years after SuperSport won the title for the last time, Pirates won the league and cup double. Ruud Krol, parachuted in from Egypt to coach Pirates, was promptly given his marching orders.

There are not only corporate governance and conflict of interest issues bedevilling the league. The league's detractors point to a dependence culture where the distribution of the broadcast rights monies at the clubs means that they receive R1.5million (£85,000) per month, whether they are sponsored or not, and do little to develop or grow their club. Indeed, many clubs in South Africa don't own their own stadiums. Merchandising by British and European standards is poor or non-existent, and watching the second tier of professional football –say Polokwane United against Free State Stars –feels rather too close to non-league football in the UK for comfort.

Khoza is proud of the fact that teams no longer have to travel by bus to far-flung venues in what is called the *platteland* in South Africa, saying "we're now an airborne league, everyone flies to away fixtures". And while this is true, the monthly grant to the clubs also means that the players are comparatively well paid in local terms. This has led to an absence of desire to pursue options elsewhere – another expression, perhaps, of the dependence culture. Eventually players tend to stagnate locally, and, with most of the players chosen for Bafana Bafana coming from the PSL, this has impacted negatively on the national side. There was a time when South Africa used to qualify for World Cups, as they did in 1998 and 2002. Not any more, unless they sneak in via the back door by being hosts. "I played in Europe [in Germany and Norway] so I understand their mentality,"says Mame Niang, a Senegalese striker who plays for Mamelodi Sundowns. "There is talent here, for sure, but no hunger. The two big academies in Senegal have put 35 players into Europe in the last three years alone."

It seems a distant memory but fairly recently South Africa used to export good players in numbers to Britain and Europe. Fifteen-odd years ago, it was producing players like Lucas Radebe, Phil Masinga and Shaun Bartlett (all born between 1969 and 1972) and, of a slightly younger generation, Benni McCarthy, Mark Fish and Quinton Fortune (all born between 1974 and 1977). These players all came of age during the dying days of apartheid, when South Africa was economically, culturally and geographically isolated in a way that it isn't today. It is difficult to know for sure but the deprivations of apartheid might have sharpened these players' hunger. Playing overseas would have been enormously attractive. Heading north was generally advisable for an ambitious young football man, even if few had any clear idea of what Europe entailed. Those who moved to Europe played in robust, relatively well-organised amateur leagues before turning professional. (The only possible exception to the list of six above would be Fortune. He was at Spurs from a very young age, so in many ways would have escaped some of the hardship and social unrest experienced by the others, particularly the older players like Radebe and Masinga). Football then was seen in the black community as carrying the flame of black identity. Rugby was the white man's game; football was the black man's sport and a form of opposition. With the cutting of development budgets and the refusal of teachers in township schools to coach the sport after hours, some of the traditional wellsprings of football have dried up almost completely.

Nowadays the best of the export crop are Thulani Serero at Ajax Amsterdam and Kamogelo Mokhotjo at FC Twente, both having been dropped into Europe from South African clubs with strong Dutch connections. Serero's Ajax Cape Town are twinned with the mother club in Amsterdam while Mokhotjo came from SuperSport, who once had strong links with Feyenoord but have since established a less satisfactory relationship with Spurs. Elsewhere in Europe, South African players here and there are scattered across Belgium and Scandinavia. In England, South Africans are playing at clubs like Bournemouth, Doncaster Rovers and Crystal Palace. This, it is fair to say, is hardly the glamour world of European football.

So why should South Africa, winner of its first African Cup of Nations tournament at home in 1996, beating a good

Ghana side en route to the final before accounting for Tunisia, have declined so markedly? Can the comparative financial health of the players really account for such a marked drop in standards? Or is South African football suffering from a sporting equivalent of cultural cringe, the idea that now South Africa is once again a member of that global community, able to receive European football in vast quantities on television, able to host a World Cup, that the magnitude of what needs to be done to become competitive again is simply too intimidating? The shrinking of borders and horizons has not led to a 'can do' attitude but rather its opposite: the idea that with the world being so close, it is indeed a far more frightening place than was first thought.

If there isn't a pathological element to South African under-achievement, there is certainly a lack of confidence and insecurity in front of goal. In the PSL in 2013-14, Bernard Parker, the leading goal scorer in the league, scored 10 goals in 27 matches for Chiefs – and this is a man with *Eredivisie* experience. This might charitably be explained by the fact that with the monthly grant at stake and the threat of relegation so real for poorer teams, mediocre sides' first aim is not to lose. Defences are deep and counter attacking-football (often badly played) is the norm. Hunt might have put his finger on it best when he said,"In my day at poky Hellenic, players like Grant Young and Gerald Stober were banging in 20 goals a season. Defences have become better and teams more compact but the quality of the service is poor and the strikers make bad runs."

As I write this, Amajita, the South African under-20 side, have just qualified for next year's African Youth Championship in Senegal, beating Cameroon 3-2 home and away. The side is a talented one but qualification of this kind is not a regular occurrence. The McCarthy, Fortune and Aaron Mokoena generation took South Africa to the Sydney Olympics, beating Brazil 3-1 before losing their final group game to Slovakia and failing to progress to the knockout stage. Sometimes we qualify, more often we don't. This might be the fate of our national sides in a nutshell: capable of magic on their day but strangely skittish when it comes to consistency. Niang thinks consistency is a problem, deriding the 'Johnnie Walker syndrome' that afflicts many of the league's more glamorous players. "They can have a really good midweek game, "he says, "then they arrive drunk or hungover at the next practice or play the next game badly. When a European scout comes out what he's looking for is consistency. He wants return."

Black youngsters tend to play soccer on poor pitches and are often coached by well-meaning but under-qualified coaches, something the association is slowly attempting to turn around. As one of their development evangelists, Robin Petersen, told me: "In Spain the ratio of highly qualified coaches to players is 1:17, here it's more like 1:200. We have to change that by judicious use of the monies we raise and that are in our coffers from the World Cup ticket sale profits."

There might, of course, be a deeper, more abstract answer to why South African football seems wedded to under-achievement. Township youngsters often receive little parental support, a fact noted by Khoza and many others. Despite the advances of democracy – electrification, universal schooling, improved public transport – the legacy of apartheid is still very tangible for many of South Africa's poor. The township game, once glowingly referred to as 'piano and shoeshine', looks anachronistic when compared to the quick, selfless and highly athletic modern game of today. Perhaps crucially, from the children's point of view, there is frequently no mom to bundle you into the estate car after practice or on hand with an energy drink and an encouraging word. The apartheid legacy expresses itself in obvious ways but has also deformed what the Europeans would call 'mentality'. South African footballers' confidence is fragile. They play the game without love. Therein comes a sadness and a peculiarly South African form of melancholy.

Neither Serero or Mokhotjo are regulars under the new Bafana coach, 'Shakes' Mashaba, an old-style coach with an edge of sniffy pride to his parochialism. 'Shakes', it is probably fair to say, is rather proud of the fact that he isn't going to be seen anytime soon sipping a skinny latte in a patisserie in Knightsbridge conversing with an agent in a continental European language. Fears abound among the more discerning that he might ultimately take the national side backwards. Early results have been impressive. In the opening two rounds of qualifiers for the Africa Cup of Nations early next year, his side banged three goals past a very ordinary Sudan in Khartoum. A couple of days later in chilly Cape Town, the Super Eagles were held to a 0-0 draw. The Nigeria game showed a more bumptious Bafana than had been seen in a while, although such confidence didn't translate into a goal against the African champions. Under Mashaba, Bafana are relentlessly busy and that approach brought four points against Congo. The murder of the goalkeeper Senzo Meyiwa has hit the squad hard, but they finished qualifying with another win over Sudan and a 2-2 draw in Nigeria that eliminated the holders. Given they were 2-0 up after three-quarters of the game, there was frustration that South Africa couldn't hold on for a first competitive win over Nigeria, but still, they head to Equatorial Guinea with an unusual sense of expectation.

# When FFP Goes Wrong

*Luzenac's promotion to the French second flight should have been a joyous fairy-story but it killed the club*

**By Robin Bairner**

**The ball seemed to hang in the air for an age but Idriss Ech-Chergui studied the flight perfectly. As the lofted diagonal cross from the right touchline dropped at the edge of the penalty box, the 29-year-old journeyman midfielder drew back his left foot and sent a volley skipping into the corner of the Boulogne net. It was the goal that should have secured Luzenac AP promotion to Ligue 2 but instead it sentenced them to death.**

After the 1-0 win, the dreadlocked midfielder Guy Ngosso led the celebrations in front of the modest home support at the Stade du Courbet and in the dressing-room champagne was raucously sprayed. This should have been one of the most remarkable achievements in French footballing history. Luzenac, hailing from a village with a population a handful over 600, were set for the second flight. The club was well set financially, with the president Jérôme Ducros bankrolling the side sufficiently to prevent any debt accruing and planning on building a professional base in the Pyrenees to challenge Toulouse – the only side of note within 100km.

Five months later, the Amateur Football Association of France (AFFA) wrote the obituary of the club, explaining the unexpected and rather brutal hardship that followed. "Luzenac are a symbol of amateur football sacrificed on the altar of contempt," read the statement from Éric Thomas, president of the AFFA. "Today, a certain idea of football, that of morals, ethics and justice, is dead, murdered by those who are supposed to defend its values.

"The mission of the Professional League (LFP) was simple: to make it possible for Luzenac to attain professional status by helping with their structure. Everything has been done to prevent this promotion! Therefore, the AFFA demands the immediate resignation of the president of the LFP."

That statement was released on September 11, fewer than 24 hours after the final nail had been hammered into Luzenac's coffin. They were indeed offered the opportunity to play in a new league, but it was not Ligue 2 as hoped. Instead it was CFA2 – the fifth rung of the game, two divisions lower than they had spent the previous season. Luzenac may have won their battle on the field, but those in power in French football proved unmoved by their romantic tale.

Ducros had worked hard to put together a formidable staff from which to build his project. A successful businessman who earned his fortune building houses, his vision was to construct a club for the south-west region, not one simply reliant on the small local population. This was reflected in a name change in 2012, when US Luzenac became Luzenac Ariège Pyrénées. The former Marseille, Manchester United and France goalkeeper Fabien Barthez, attracted by the prospect of such a team near his hometown of Lavelanet, was drafted in as sporting director. A series of (relatively) big names followed. Among them were the top-scorer Andé Dona Ndoh, who would lead the goal charts by eight at the end of the season, and Nicolas Dieuze, who made more than 150 appearances in Ligue 1 for Toulouse.

There was also the former USA Under-20 goalkeeper Quentin Westberg, who had been part of the Evian side that had shocked Marseille in the Coupe de France in 2011. He had come through the famous Clairefontaine academy, where he had worked with Hatem Ben Arfa and Abou Diaby, and had been part of the USA squad for the 2005 U20 World Cup.

It may have been modest, but it was a strong foundation from which the club could rise further after becoming the smallest team ever to play in the third tier when they won promotion in 2009.

On the evening that promotion was clinched, Luzenac topped the standings but they were overhauled by Orléans on the penultimate weekend of the season. That disappointment was soon forgotten.

All seemed satisfactory on May 30, when the fixture list for Ligue 2 was produced. There were Luzenac, scheduled to play Troyes at home on the opening day of the season, although admittedly it was not yet known where 'home' was going to be.

Even before a top-three finish in the Championnat National was secured, officials from the LFP had visited Luzenac's temporary home in Foix and had judged it unsuitable for the professional ranks. The village's Stade Paul Fedou was completely out of the question, despite holding nearly three times the population of the settlement at 1,600. A deal, however, seemed to be struck quickly with the rugby union side Stade Toulousain, under which the Stade Ernest-Wallon would be used as a medium-term fix.

But on June 5 the financial watchdog of the French professional game, the Direction Nationale de Contrôle et de Gestion (DNGC), denied the minnows entry into Ligue 2. Ducros, who had saved the club from extinction only a couple of years earlier, steadfastly declared he was "confident" an appeal would be successful. Nearly a full month passed before that was heard, conveniently under the cover of France's World Cup quarter-final against Germany which took place the following day.

That the FFF had rejected Luzenac's budget once more was met with overt frustration by the club's president. "It's a simple story of cash," he told the local paper, *La Dépêche*. "I didn't even get a letter informing me about the decision. I had to hear about it in the media and on the internet... it is shameful to treat us like this."

There was less than a month until the season started and, with LAP filing an appeal to go to the CNOSF, France's sporting court, there was still some distance to run. Another fortnight passed before Luzenac were again rebuffed, with the club "shocked and stupefied" by the decision. An accountant had demonstrated that there was "no hole in the budget" and that "balanced accounts had been validated by an auditor".

"People high up didn't want to see Luzenac in the second division," Westberg explained. "Everything was good, the finances were good, everything was ready... Everything was falling into place and it just felt like there was some Luzenac bashing. We really felt we were being cheated.

"We felt like we had everybody against us. It was hard to believe at first. We didn't know what to believe from a player's perspective. We wondered if our president and our club were doing the right thing.

"The president told us: 'It's incredible what's happening to us. It's really political. We meet all the criteria to play in Ligue 2. We need to show them that the club has done everything we can to play in the second division. I will go all the way to have justice prevail.'"

When Ligue 2 kicked off on August 1, it did so in confusion. Luzenac had, hours earlier, won their final appeal at the Administrative Court of Toulouse and Ligue 2 seemed poised to go ahead in a bizarre 21-team format after the DNGC finally ratified their budget the following Wednesday.

But hope was short-lived and, within 24 hours, LAP had their dreams dashed again by the politicians at the LFP, who appeared keen to avoid the embarrassment of an inflated league after David had overcome Goliath in the courtroom. "The club does not have a stadium meeting the regulatory safety standards," the League decreed after an emergency meeting. "The club has not taken the necessary steps to play in such a stadium throughout the season."

"They don't want Luzenac among the pros," Barthez claimed in an interview with *L'Équipe*.

Ducros was more forthright. "Frédéric Thiriez [president of the LFP] is a liar," he said on August 8. "From the beginning he did everything he could to prevent Luzenac playing in Ligue 2. He never wanted us."

In the meantime, the city of Toulouse was doing its best to accommodate the village team. While upgrade work was carried out on the Stade Ernest-Wallon, permission was granted on May 30 for Luzenac to ground-share at the Stadium Municipal with the city's Ligue 1 side.

But three weeks into the season the club still did not know in which league they would be competing. This also worried Les Amis du Stade Toulousain, the owners of the Stade Ernest-Wallon, who understandably were unwilling to sign a contract for any upgrade work until the future of LAP was made plain.

Government officials began to take an interest, leading the Secretary of State for Sport Thierry Braillard to say, "It is a kind of hypocrisy from the League that prevents a team ascending from the amateur world to the professional one."

Meanwhile, *L'Équipe* published a statement from an anonymous source "close to the case", who asked, "What does Ducros want? The money from television rights – that's all!"

Ducros had previously put money into Toulouse's Ligue 1 side, helped fund Barthez's successful post-football motor-racing career and also backed Aviron Toulousain, a rowing club. While some outside the club sought to disparage the ambitious owner, who had been at the centre of a registration scandal in a previous stint with Toulouse Football Croix-Daurade, those closest to him spoke only in the highest terms. "Jérôme is honest, passionate and emotional. He can sometimes get carried away because he loves the club and its players," Barthez had said.

The 46-year-old investor admitted he was after television money, but insisted it was not for nefarious purposes. "Without television rights, half the clubs would disappear," he said. "The money will be used to fill the increased gap between the payroll and the other sources of income."

It proved to be a source of revenue Ducros would never see.

On August 27, a decisive blow was landed. Without a concrete plan for a stadium in place, the LFP once again turned down the club's appeal to be involved in Ligue 2. The CNOSF, who had on August 22 supported Luzenac on this issue, performed an about turn, arguing no deal for the Stade Ernest-Wallon had been finalised.

Without assurances of Ligue 2 football, though, this was impossible for Luzenac to achieve. Catch 22.

The rugby world also had its doubts about the groundshare. Although the LFP had ensured in the preliminary fixture lists that Toulouse and Luzenac were never at home on the same weekend, Stade Toulousain's calendar produced by the national Rugby Federation had not been so considerate and had thrown up four fixture clashes even before potential cup matches were placed in the equation.

"The problem with Luzenac is extremely simple. How can you participate in a professional league without a stadium?" Thiriez argued."Their current stadium does not meet safety standards and the alternative they offered, the Stade Ernest-Wallon, does not meet the safety standards of the LFP and FFF. And anyway, they still have no agreement with Stade Toulousain.

"The first obligation of the League is to ensure public safety. We could not make any other decision.

"I am sad for the Luzenac players, who won the right to play Ligue 2 on the field, but they have to question the management of the club, which has been unable to fulfil its responsibilities."

Strangely, the stadium had previously been deemed fit to host France's Under-21 side when they drew 1-1 with the Netherlands in November 2013 (the fixture attracted 4,867 spectators – significantly more than LAP could hope to attain with regularity) and copes with a rugby public of nearly 20,000 on a frequent basis.

Luzenac insisted they had done everything required of them to win promotion and accused the LFP of "misleading" the public. Predictably, the claim fell upon deaf ears.

Accusations of amateurism were fired at the club, who would later admit they were not necessarily "prepared for their sudden arrival in the spotlight".

There was to be another twist. With the second flight also well underway before the procrastinating of the appeals process was finally over, Luzenac would not even be offered their previous place back. Instead they were cast to the CFA2. Their crime? Unspecified.

Automatic promotion would not even be guaranteed back to the National after a season, and for Ducros and Barthez that proved too much.

On the evening of September 10, they called a meeting with the club's professionals and announced that they were all released from their contracts. Although it is possible for those players to join clubs as free agents outside the transfer window, the financial reality is that most teams, having already built their squads in the summer, do not have the budget to invest any further.

Luzenac, however, did not die completely. The team lives on in the reserves, who play in the obscure Division Honneur Régionale.

Understandably, the FFF and the LFP have come under fire for their approach, particularly when it was set against the backdrop of bigger teams earning what appeared to be unjust reprieves.

Valenciennes, fresh from top-flight relegation, were very nearly liquidated over the summer. However, an eleventh-hour pitch saved the club and allowed them the opportunity to start the season in Ligue 2. That they had only 14 professional players – one of whom was out with a long-term injury – days before the season started and had therefore been unable to play any pre-season matches seemed of little concern to the powers that be.

An even more controversial case came in the form of Racing Club de Lens, a former powerhouse of the French game from the north east. Having won promotion to Ligue 1, their budget was rejected by the DNGC, who advised that there was a €10 million deficit that needed to be covered by the owner Hafiz Mammadov, an Azeri business man who also has a stake in Sheffield Wednesday.

The president Gervais Martel hinted in an interview with *France 2* that the gap may never be bridged when he said, "Mammadov is very annoyed by the request of the DNGC."

Ultimately, the money did not arrive and Lens were forced to put forward a new budget of only €38m, which was grudgingly accepted by the CNOSF at the appeals stage. Despite the reprieve, such was the state of Lens's finances that they were placed under a transfer embargo until a payment of €4m was received by the League, which still holds at the time of writing. Indeed, Lens could not even have a new contract ratified for the centre-back Alaeddine Yahia, who subsequently left the club for SM Caen.

Grave doubts over Mammadov had been earlier voiced by Olivier Richard, president of the DNGC, to Radio

Monte Carlo. "There is a good chance that Lens will have viability problems before the end of the season if there is no new investment."

"You have serious concerns over the financial capacity of Mammadov today?" Richard was asked by the interviewer.

"Oh yes," came the stern answer.

The kicker for Luzenac, however, is that Lens did not even have an agreement in place over their stadium plans. Forced out of their Stade Félix-Bollaert due to renovation work being carried out, no deal for them to play at Amiens's Stade de la Licorne was finalised until five days after they were admitted to Ligue 1. An independent credit review published in October by the US-based markets and risk specialists McGraw Hill Financial gave Lens the poorest score of 44 publicly listed clubs in the whole of Europe.

It's a shambolic situation that seems to fly in the face of the DNGC's safeguards, which they were so keen to uphold in the Luzenac case.

Lens had trump cards that LAP didn't. Although they hail from a town of fewer than 40,000 inhabitants, their crowd is renowned for being one of the most passionate and colourful in France. Indeed, the Félix-Bollaert holds 41,000, is regularly close to full and, crucially, will host games at Euro 2016. To damage such a club by denying them promotion would be a dangerous political stance for the league.

Luzenac had little such muscle behind them, although their plight was embraced countrywide as the nation's football supporters very publically questioned the *'égalité'* clause in the national motto of France. "It was a piece of cake for them [Lens] to win their appeal," Westberg lamented. "The DNGC is sanctioned by the FFF and the LFP, and they just make their decisions together. We didn't have the same treatment at all. It was pretty crazy for us to see that Valenciennes were saved after they almost exploded but for us everything was an incredible struggle."

The Rennes defender Cheick M'Bengue and the Bordeaux winger Nicolas Maurice-Belay both voiced support for the club in post-match interviews and fans of other clubs were sympathetic. Toulouse's 'Indians' supporters group was one of many in the professional ranks to show their solidarity with Luzenac by unfurling banners hitting out at the LFP's actions.

"Firstly, it is a matter close to our heart on a purely sporting level," Yves, a leader of the group, explained."Then there is the scheming and tricks [of the LFP and FFF] that we want to show we denounce. Football is a mafia hungry for profit; it does not respect sporting criteria."

Thiriez has rejected suggestions of favouritism towards more marketable teams. "This accusation is unacceptable," he said. "Each year, we have small clubs that go from the Championnat National to Ligue 2 and we apply the same treatment to them all.

"US Orléans are a good example. They work in compliance with all the safety standards.

"Why are Luzenac unable to comply with conditions accepted by other clubs?

I reject the argument that there are different standards being applied."

Westberg acknowledges that his club could have been better prepared but believes Luzenac have been treated extremely badly. "Not everything was necessarily done well," he confessed. "But you have to know if the penalty is fitting for your mistakes."

And of the players' belief in sporting integrity? "This is the greatest paradox for me. Those people who put the spoke in our wheels are the same ones who complain about the image of the players at the top of the ladder. These are the people who criticised what happened in 2010 [when France's World Cup side staged an infamous revolt against the head coach Raymond Domenech] and these are the people who create a scandal when a player wears headphones.

"Especially here in France, people criticise footballers for their lack of loyalty and their lack of attachment to their club. That's the opposite here. We really fought for the club and stood by the club. The club did everything they could to stand by us, too. [The leaders of the game] talk about the image and values of sport, but they are able to deny us promotion on more or less arbitrary points. For me, sporting integrity has been done no justice.

"I've got the impression it's increasingly hard [for small clubs] to find a place in the sun. In 15 years as a club, Guingamp managed to climb to Ligue 1 because there were not as many economic and structural barriers. Now they are a Ligue 1 club in a town of only 6,000 inhabitants. Today, that would maybe be impossible."

Guingamp's unlikely rise was achieved in the 1990s, their side graced by players of the calibre of Didier Drogba, Florent Malouda and Laurent Koscielny, and as they compete in the Europa League this term they stand as a monument to what Luzenac wished to achieve.

Meanwhile, Paris Saint-Germain were one of a handful of high-profile clubs deemed to have flouted Uefa's differing set of FFP rules over the course of the last year. Their punishment has been far more manageable and, in Westberg's eyes, there is a two-tiered system that counts against smaller clubs."I knew football had become political since so much money came into the game," he admitted. "Any club that has good politics and fine lobbying will find that things are going to fall into place for them, whatever the rules.

"We had the system against us and we set an example towards the rest. You have to fight for what you want and you must never give up, although the system might be crooked at some points. What we experienced definitely wasn't a fair deal."

The Luzenac saga should, however, produce a crumb of good as it will force the FFF to establish a swifter judicial process with fewer levels of appeal and far swifter turnaround times."It is necessary to simplify the chain of litigation," the politician Jean Glavany wrote. "Recent economic situations have shown how the duration of the appeal proceedings, mediation and litigation is hardly conducive to the sustainability of structures, the interests of the players or the resources of local communities."

Remarkably, that passage comes from a report dated January 2014: it predicted such problems as Luzenac suffered. Had the Sports Minister Valérie Fourneyron not resigned in April, a safety net may have been put in place in time to save LAP.

Now there is a push for a three-tiered reform system. Thierry Braillard is lobbying for club budgets to be completed at the end of March, as opposed to June, while it has also been suggested that clubs should know whether they have the right to promotion before the preceding season is finished. Finally, a streamlined appeal process is likely to be established.

Westberg, meanwhile, is counting the human cost of the Luzenac tale. Like many of his teammates, he is unemployed and receives financial support from the French government and admits that with a young family he is ready to listen to any offers. "We know very well we're not in a position to choose," the goalkeeper said. "We're not at all in control of our destiny.

"I wish no football player to experience what we've been through. It's like you're taking away the nice results. It's like a bunch of white collars decide what they want to do with their league. It's totally unfair but it's exactly what happened. We had special treatment – and it was not good."

Luzenac's experience must serve as a lesson that FFP is not a panacea. Livelihoods far more vulnerable than those enjoyed by multimillionaire players are sometimes at stake.

# Defying the Odds

*How tiny Eibar have taken their place in the Spanish top flight*

**By Will Unwin**

**Eibar's home league meeting with Villarreal this September was a meeting of two tiny clubs. You could fit the population of both towns into the Nou Camp and still have room for another 24,000 fans. Mist shrouded the hills around the town, adding to the sense of unreality: this sort of thing isn't supposed to happen in modern football, not in the top flight of one of Europe's major leagues.**

Locals still can't quite believe that Eibar won a second straight promotion last season to reach the *primera* for the first time, but the Basque side can draw encouragement from the example of Villarreal. Before their promotion in 1998, Villarreal had never played among the elite, but they've had just one season out of the top flight since.

Three hours before kick-off I was ticketless, but there was no rush: there was no chance the game would be a 6,000 sell-out. As the TV crews set up their cameras in the ground, I nipped through an open door to witness the pitch being marked after the nets were put up. No one showed the slightest concern that a stranger had entered: this was a million miles away from the tight security of British stadiums.

Inside the basic Ipurua ground that sits at the top of Eibar, 4,231 supporters witnessed the club's third home game in the topflight. A few dozen of them were wearing the boisterous yellow of Villarreal. Flats that overlook the stadium offer a view for another few hundred non-paying supporters. Bars around the ground are draped in the blue and purple colours of Eibar.

Having seen the quaint surroundings, I moved to the club offices to buy a couple of tickets. When the young assistant realised there was no change, he went to his own wallet to get a €10 note. It's not something that's likely to happen at Old Trafford or the Emirates.

I sat behind the goal, watching as the *socios* made their noise for the whole game. It was hard to believe this was one of the world's most watched leagues, only the adverts for betting companies and holidays in Dubai providing a reminder of the context.

A wander around the ground throws up a few surprises, including a 'Scotland the Brave' emblem on the wall where the Basque flag and Saltire are pictured side by side, 20 yards from a temporary stand installed to cope with the increase in demand. In 2001, a group of Eibar fans went to Murrayfield to watch a rugby international and were so taken by the home support that they founded the Ezkozia La Brava fan club.

That in turn prompted an interest in the club in Scotland. Eibar needed all the external support possible during the summer of 2014, as they had to raise €1.7million to comply with La Liga regulations that teams must have capital equal to 25% of the average expenses.

The head of Ezkozia La Brava, Jose ba Combarro, believes his club were paying for the errors of the bigger clubs. "I am grateful to all those who paid to support the club to avoid us suffering an unjust demotion," he said. "Eibar have never had any debt nor owed money. We were having to pay for the financial mismanagement of Barcelona, Real Madrid and Deportivo La Coruña." They received donations from 48 different countries, much of it from people who had never heard of Eibar before their remarkable promotion. Supporting Eibar became a gesture of defiance against the corporate machine of modern football.

The striker Mikel Arruabarrena, in his fifth season at the Ipurua, opened the scoring early against Villarreal. Gerard Moreno equalised but the visitors struggled to break down the well-organised home defence, which has become a theme of Eibar's games.

Three days after the draw with Villarreal, Eibar would once again show their doggedness as they earned another point away to Athletic. They took almost 5,000 fans to Bilbao, the majority sitting with home supporters in a show of Basque unity. Before this season, a Copa del Rey win at the San Mamés in 2012 was the highlight of club's existence – Arruabarrena also scored that night.

"We very much appreciate all the help we have had," the club president Alex Aranzábal said. "It has been surprising for us, a small club in a small town in the Basque mountains. We have discovered that we have a story to tell and that people want to hear stories like this, that we are fighting against this rule and we have achieved something big."

This has certainly brought a new audience to Eibar, but the club remains rooted in the town. Eibar was founded on the arms trade, having made weaponry since the 14th century – hence the club's nickname, *'los armeros'*. The area has suffered during the recession. It's industrial and there's no huge wealth, which has perhaps increased the club's importance as the centre of the community.

Villarreal, with a population slightly over twice that of Eibar, was founded by James I of Aragon in 1279 to consolidate his conquest of eastern Spain from the Moors, but despite its name meaning 'royal town' there's not much to excite tourists beyond a couple of churches. Villarreal offered free season tickets to out-of-work fans when unemployment peaked in the town before the 2009-10 season as the pottery industry went into decline. Just four years earlier, with a team managed by Manuel Pellegrini and featuring Juan Román Riquelme and Diego Forlán, they reached the semi-final of the Champions League.

Humble as Eibar is, World Cup-winners have worn their shirt in the past: both David Silva and Xabi Alonso have spent time on loan at the Ipurua. Silva was part of a team that finished fourth in the second flight, their highest finish before last season's promotion."I had a marvellous year in Eibar," Silva said. "I made many friends there and I am grateful to all for their help at that time."

To grasp the scale of Eibar's achievement, it's worth noting that the smallest town to have produced a team to have played in the Premier League is Burnley, with a population of 73,000. The Clarets were noted for their prudence, yet they spent over £8m on transfer fees alone after ascending from the Championship.

Eibar's summer incomings barely added up to €160,000 and no player will earn more than €500,000 during the year. Javi Lara, who scored the club's first goal in La Liga in their opening-day victory over their Basque rivals Real Sociedad, had bought himself out of his contract with the Segunda B side Ponferradina. "We want to demonstrate that in football, the small club, when it handles things well, can beat the powerful," Aranzábal said. "This year, it will be a lot more difficult because the differences are gigantic."

Despite their lack of top-flight experience, Eibar allayed fears they would be cast adrift by taking eight points from their first six games. Even finishing outside of the relegation zone won't guarantee survival, though. Eibar's stadium does not meet La Liga criteria, meaning they are proposing an increase in capacity at the Ipurua. That has not pleased local residents, with many protesting against the plans, threatening the club's future.

Reaching the elite will bring financial rewards for Eibar. Barcelona and Real Madrid will get up to €150million, with *los armeros* expecting to receive around a tenth of that figure. The Premier League's bottom club last season, Cardiff City, picked up more than £62million for their efforts on the pitch and are entitled to another £60million in parachute payments to ease the burden of relegation.

Playing the loan market with expertise has served Eibar well in recent years: last season four Real Sociedad players shone at Eibar, including Yuri Beriche who has been a regular starter for Sociedad this season. The imminent adoption of collective negotiation of television rights will make that less of a necessity, providing Eibar will a sustainable model if they do finish above 18th. "Staying in the Primera Liga, that is to say, not being relegated, this would be a success this season," said Combarro.

Things are stacked against lower-league clubs in both England and Spain. Ticket prices are constantly on the rise as boards desperately try to eke out every last penny from those loyal enough to support their team on a weekly basis. Eibar fail to fill their stadium, which Camborro puts down to price: "The tickets, costing €30 or €50, are just too expensive. It's a little sad, but this is something that all football fans are facing."

Over the coming season Leo Messi and Cristiano Ronaldo will visit the Ipurua in knowledge that their annual income is greater than that of the squad they will come up against. They may not appreciate the surroundings, but they will remember the experience of visiting Eibar. There will be around a tenth of the people in the ground for that game than there were when Ronaldo was unveiled at the Santiago Bernabéu.

Eibar didn't chase the dream, they stumbled upon it, but now they are in the middle of it, they will savour every single second.

# Fifa's Exiles

*For Pacific islands, football development can be a haphazard and fragile process*

**By Paul Watson**

**'Fifa develops football everywhere.'**

**If you watched even one game at this summer's World Cup, you will have seen that slogan nestled among the world's most costly advertising hoardings every time the ball crossed the halfway line. Fifa's showpiece event is the ideal opportunity for the game's governing body to revel in the scale of its operations. As the greatest players in the world do battle for the amusement of a billion, it's almost impossible to imagine that anyone has been forgotten.**

Fifa has 209 member associations, a staggering number when you consider that there are only 193 members of the United Nations. This anomaly is easily resolved when you bear in mind that many football 'nations' such as the Faroe Islands and Guam are actually dependent territories. Then there are cases like Palestine and Taiwan, recognised by Fifa but not members of the United Nations. A little closer to home, there's the thorny issue of England, Northern Ireland, Scotland and Wales playing independently in spite of forming the United Kingdom. Remove the territories, dependencies and other awkward entities and you are left with a total of 188 independent countries in Fifa. Through a simple process of subtraction, that leaves eight nations that aren't represented. The two Europeans on the list are fairly simple to work out. Vatican City does have a league and a cup competition, the Clericus Cup, which pits teams mostly composed of Swiss Guards and administrative staff against each other. There was even speculative talk a few years ago about Giovanni Trapattoni taking the reins and trying to enter the Vatican in Italy's professional leagues. Fairly unsurprisingly that has never happened and the Vatican instead settle for occasional fixtures against Europe's other non-Fifa nation, Monaco. A small group of passionate players remain insistent that Monégasque players should have the chance to represent their nation, but for the foreseeable future Monaco will have to make do with one of France's top club sides.

The other six Fifa exiles have longer, more complex tales to tell and they all hail from one region of the world where football development is stuck in limbo – the Pacific Islands. It's probably safe to say that most people in Europe would struggle to locate any of Kiribati, Marshall Islands, Nauru, Palau, Tuvalu and the Federated States of Micronesia on a map, but they would be best served looking for the largest expanse of blue on the globe. The Pacific six are some of the most remote islands on earth and home to inhospitable climates and high obesity rates. The time difference from Fifa's base in Switzerland is ferocious, email contact is at best sporadic and flying there can break the bank.

**Nauru and the Marshall Islands: football's final frontier**

Fifa probably shouldn't lose any sleep over the state of football in the Marshall Islands and Nauru because, put simply, there's not much to develop. The world's smallest island nation, Nauru, is a tragic riches to rags story. For a brief period in the late 1960s and early 1970s, Nauru's phosphorous stocks, envied and needed by Australia in particular, made it one of the wealthiest countries on earth by GDP. The island was over-mined, leaving its centre desolate like a moonscape and the wealth was squandered and misappropriated. Today, Nauru is poverty-stricken and home to Australia's controversial immigrant processing camps. Aussie Rules has always had a stronghold, but Nauru excels at weightlifting where the islanders' short stature and strength make them a force to be reckoned with. Wikipedia used to claim that Nauru had a remarkable 100% win record as a football nation – a 2-1 victory over the Solomon Islands in 1994. An impressive achievement, but a false one. It turns out the game was between Nauruans and some Solomon workers, by no means their national side. After many months of attempted email contact, Nauru's current football association stated that there is a team who are training on an old golf course. They don't seem to play very often. The Marshall Islands have the odd boast of being the only sovereign nation never to have even entertained the idea of a football team. Upon mentioning a football team to an Olympic Committee representative, he looked genuinely mystified and said he wouldn't know where to start. More pertinently, there simply isn't any interest on the major hubs of Majuro or Kwajalein, which is pretty much off-limits to anyone but US military personnel. There are 1156 other islands to try, but it's safe to say you'd have trouble starting a successful kick-around on any of them.

**Up Pohnpei: Micronesia's football renaissance**

However, a fortnight after the 2014 World Cup final, a very different final was being contested on a small Pacific island on a pitch composed of sand, mud, puddles and a small amount of grass. This was the Micronesian Games gold medal match held on the island of Pohnpei – one of the islands of the Federated States of Micronesia – and it saw the hosts defeat Palau 3-1 in front of around 300 fans. In isolation the game more closely resembled a Sunday League match than an international fixture, but the competition which also included two of the other four islands that form part of the Federated States of Micronesia – Chuuk and Yap – was a massive step forward for football in the Pacific. Sleepy Kosrae is yet to welcome the sport.

I became personally invested in the footballing travails of the Federated States of Micronesia in 2009. My arrival on the island of Pohnpei was the result of passion and delusion in equal measure. While labouring away as a failed semi-professional footballer, my flatmate Matt and I came up with the idea of finding the world's lowest ranked national team, naturalising and playing for them.

When we scoured the Fifa Rankings we found that even the lowest nations had professionals and wouldn't be excited to see us, but we discovered another list of rankings for places not recognised by Fifa for geographical, political or logistical reasons. At the bottom of that list we found Pohnpei, whose results included a heart-breaking penalty shootout defeat by Yap and a 16-1 thrashing from Guam in 1998 at the Micro Games – a small Olympics for the islands of the region. When we emailed the Pohnpei Football Assocation's general contact address, we received a friendly response from president, Charles Musana, but he apologised that he had just moved to Chingford in East London a week earlier. Seizing on this quirk of fate we met Musana, who told us that Pohnpeian football had gone into decline, but there were still keen players if we wanted to coach them. After due consideration, we decided that we did and set off for the island via flights to Dubai, Manila, Guam and the neighbouring island of Chuuk.

Pohnpei is among the wettest places on earth. It rains heavily almost every day and the pitch, PICS Field, is almost always under a foot of water, especially on the edge of the boxes where marshes are home to a sizeable colony of toads. The rotten goal nets on PICS pointed to a loss of belief in the game, but the Olympic Committee chief Jim Tobin had always tried to stimulate football growth despite the lack of resources. As part of the American 'sphere of influence', which means the USA pays a large sum for the right to place troops on Micronesia's islands should they need to, the islanders mostly wrestle, play basketball, baseball and volleyball. However, it very quickly became clear that there were talented footballers on the island, but they had never been given a reason to keep on with the sport, instead often turning to the almost omnipresent stupefying substances that permeate daily life on the island – *sakau,* a potent drink with anaesthetic properties, and betel nut, an acrid chew that can cause oral cancer and is mixed with slaked lime.

The turning point in our football mission came when we set up Pohnpei's first organised league, which brought existing players out of the woodwork and created a new generation of football lovers. The number of players increased steadily and a Pohnpei state team was formed which trained four times a week, but they had nobody to play against except cobbled-together teams of expats, which often included me. The problem, as ever, was funding: just getting the team to an opponent would cost at least £10,000.

It became clear that the only way to continue football development was with assistance from the game's governing body. However, there was one major initial stumbling block: Pohnpei isn't a country. While the Micro Games allows islands to compete individually, in order to be seen as anything more than a club team in the eyes of Fifa, Pohnpei, Chuuk, Yap and Kosrae, would need to be united, even though they are separated by nearly a million square miles of ocean with flights between any two costing in excess of £500 per person each way.

The Federated States of Micronesia had fielded a united team before. In 2003, a Micronesian team based in Yap assembled to compete in the South Pacific Games. They were led by an Israeli coach, Shimon Shenhar, who had come to the islands as a 'gift' in return for Micronesia's political support for Israel. Players from Pohnpei, Chuuk and Yap were included in a squad that went to Fiji relishing the prospect of international competition. At the South Pacific Games, Micronesia came up against teams that were 15 or 20 years further ahead in their development. They were beaten mercilessly, losing 10-0 to Papua New Guinea, 7-0 to Tonga, 18-0 to New Caledonia and 17-0 to Tahiti. Shenhar left and the united FSM team went back to their islands. The score lines should have come as no surprise to a fledgling football nation – almost every small country has to take its share of thrashings to become competitive – but the legacy of the South Pacific Games humblings was to prove devastating.

In 2010, I contacted the other islands and found that football was still being played in Chuuk and Yap. In Yap, the US Olympic Committee man Paul Lane had fought hard to get football back up and running after years of neglect. The small, traditional and beautiful island had been the most active footballing island of the four for years, but interest in the sport fell away as basketball swept in. Lane had ushered in a new era of passion for football with school leagues and the pristine Yap Sports Complex was full of life on game days. On Chuuk, a veteran of the last united FSM team, Curtis Graham, was running the sport. He happily reminisced about the 2002 South Pacific Games and stressed that while the results hurt a little, the players had believed them to be a necessary part of their learning curve. The authorities had disagreed and couldn't see the point in investing in a game that requires 16 flights to compete abroad when they had a better shot at glory in individual sports.

Back on Pohnpei, the players were getting restless and the idea of a tour to Guam was mooted. Guam is seen as the big brother of Micronesia's islands. A US territory, Guam has shot up the Fifa Rankings in recent years, inspired by excellent coaching – currently from the highly rated English coach Gary White – good administration and millions of dollars of Fifa money. The Guam FA was encouraging when approached and agreed to host a Pohnpei team in October 2010, leaving just the small issue of the £10,000 worth of flights. The saviour came in the form of a London-based cargo airline, Coyne Airways, whose football-loving owner Larry Coyne offered to finance the tour as an act of philanthropy. As a result, a squad of 16 players, most of whom had never left the island, went to Guam and even managed to win a game, hammering a Guam Second Division side 7-1. It wasn't exactly revenge for the 16-1 of 1998, but it was Pohnpei's first ever victory in a competitive match.

Matt and I returned to lives in England but before we did we helped set up a new Federated States of Micronesia Football Association, run by representatives from each of the islands and led by president Steve Finnen, a US lawyer who has become an honorary Pohnpeian for his years helping the community. The new FA's first goal was obvious –become part of Fifa. The process of joining Fifa begins with being admitted to one of the regional confederations. After two years in a confederation, full Fifa membership becomes possible. Being in the middle of the Pacific Ocean, the Oceania Football Confederation was the obvious first port of call. The OFC lists 11 member nations, but since Australia left for the East Asia Football Federation (EAFF), it has struggled to maintain its relevance. Tai Nicholas, the secretary general, was encouraging, but he admitted that the FSM would be better served following the route that Guam took and going to the Asian Football Confederation via EAFF. This was slightly at odds with the OFC's public position that it has a 'long term plan to develop football on all Pacific islands', but the honesty was appreciated.

The Federated States of Micronesia FA sent a message to the EAFF beginning the application process for associate membership in early 2011. A number of documents were produced, painstaking protocol followed and then the FSM's football officials waited. Eventually a message arrived stating that the first stage of the process would be a site visit from an EAFF official to ascertain the state of the game and its facilities in Micronesia. A date was set and then cancelled, set again and then cancelled. It appeared at some stages that the visiting party wasn't too sure of the geography of Micronesia or which island to visit. In the meantime, football continued to grow throughout FSM and the Olympic Committee chief Jim Tobin put plans in place for football to be included in the Micro Games in Pohnpei in 2014. The hope was that an official would come and watch those games in place of the cancelled site visits, but the invitation was politely declined. Even with Finnen, an experienced lawyer, and the Olympic Committee fighting the cause, the process remains difficult, so what chance do islands without such skilled administrators have?

**Tuvalu, Palau and Kiribati: playing but stuck in limbo**

The problems Micronesia has faced are all too familiar to fellow island nations that have gone in search of Fifa recognition. The tiny island of Tuvalu has been trying to gain acceptance for 26 years with only moderate success. Space is at a premium on Tuvalu's main island, so much so that the football pitch is adjacent to the airport runway. Nonetheless, football championships are played with a passion and Tuvalu is an associate member of the OFC. Associate members are in a waiting room for full membership – they get some financial assistance, although this can vary, but they can't enter Fifa competitions. However, in 2007 Tuvalu played in the Pacific Games, which double up as World Cup qualifiers, making Tuvalu the first nation to take part in qualification for a competition they weren't eligible to enter. Tuvalu also played at the 2011 Pacific Games where they beat the Fifa members American Samoa 4-0 and even drew with Guam, but no change in status occurred. Since 2008, Tuvalu's bid for the promised land of Fifa has had an unexpected champion in the form of a Dutch group called the Dutch Support Tuvalu Foundation. Inspired by the Tuvalu football association president's visit to Fifa in 2008, the Dutchman Paul Driessen made it his mission to get Tuvalu into Fifa. The group managed to raise a phenomenal sum of around £150,000 and brought a Tuvalu team to the Netherlands for a three-month tour at the end of 2013. Tuvalu acquitted themselves well on the pitch, although some players struggled with the lengthy stay in Europe, and the hope was that Fifa would take notice.

However, Fifa rejected Tuvalu's latest advances. The nation didn't qualify in part because it wasn't equipped to host a home game – for one thing it didn't have the necessary five-star hotel. Besides, Fifa insisted, some of the paperwork wasn't filled out properly, so they'd have to start again. Aside from the bureaucracy, Tuvalu had a right to feel aggrieved, as American Samoa and East Timor received full Fifa membership and millions in funding before they ever hosted a match.

The remote 33-island chain of Kiribati also felt the goal posts were moved during their attempt to get accepted into Fifa. After two years of correspondence, the FA chief Ioteba Redfearn insists that Fifa told him Kiribati couldn't qualify until it had a national championship, which is no mean feat when dealing with so many atolls. It also seemed unfair given that several member nations don't have leagues, including Liechtenstein, which only has a Cup competition. An associate member of OFC, Kiribati spoke to the Scottish Uefa A-Licence coach Kevin McGreskin, who was willing to help coach the team for a friendly fixture, but Fifa rejected the request to fund his visit. Instead they sent 300 footballs. Kiribati entered the 2011 Pacific Games in a bid to prove their credentials, but despite some respectable performances their 17-1 drubbings by Papua New Guinea and Tahiti only served to undermine their campaign.

Football programmes in the region remain fragile and are often dependent on one or two passionate people who take the game with them when they leave. Almost nobody in the Pacific is paid to develop football and the process of jumping through hoops for suited men in Switzerland is a baffling one for many of the people entrusted with taking the game forward on their islands. The main theme is that countries in the region have received different feedback and everyone has their theory on what needs to be done to appease the Fifa god. Most nations are happy to wait years for replies rather than rattle cages and risk offending the powers that be.

Several years ago, the FA chairman Geoff Thompson persuaded Fifa to set up the Small Nations Working Group working with Urs Klusner, who was in charge of development for Fifa. The group's *raison d'être* was to help the little places around the world cut through the red tape and get assistance. Thompson and Klusner visited Tuvalu, the Caribbean island of Sint Maarten and Jersey. A report they compiled apparently identified Tuvalu and Kiribati as worthy of development but wrote off Micronesia as unfeasible. After that they disbanded. The Committee was never replaced and it is currently not obvious whose role it is to help nations who want to climb the first rung on the ladder of development.

Fifa is understandably wary of pumping money into small islands of which it has no knowledge. Palau was an associate member of OFC in 2002 but that appears to have expired through a lack of activity, even though football continues to be played regularly, led by the passionate Charles Mitchell, who fought hard to raise money to take a team to Pohnpei this summer. Fifa appears so worried it will finance a non-existent football programme that a bizarre Catch 22 has emerged whereby development money is suspended for not being able to use it. Niue on the other hand remains an associate member of OFC although reports suggest there is almost no organised football on the island. The French territory of Wallis and Futuna played 20 matches at South Pacific Games between 1966 and 1995 and were sometimes listed as an associate of the OFC, but the organisation didn't even have a working phone number for the island's FA for years.

The simple fact is that the region is a minefield for Fifa. Many of the nations are groups of remote islands, like Micronesia, where costs of travelling between them are exorbitant. Paperwork slips through the net in these communities and emails go unanswered. However, football is not only being played but it is thriving in a region of the world where obesity is a massive problem and athletic opportunities are scarce. At present it seems that Fifa's plan is simply to stall and hope that island football programmes go away, but Tuvalu keeps plugging away, Kiribati sporadically pipes up and Palau and the Federated States of Micronesia are more active than ever. Development in the Pacific is a challenging, expensive and possibly thankless task that cannot be justified economically but Fifa, at least in principle, isn't a business, it's an NGO. And after all, Fifa develops football everywhere.

Blizzard Books
Johnny Cook: The Impossible Job
Iain Macintosh

# 106

## Theory

In this world, an honest man is one who is exactly where he is supposed to be.

# The Roundhead's Paradox

*Tony Pulis and the strangely conflicted character of British Puritanism*

**By Nicholas Blincoe**

**It is a Monday morning in late November 2013. Tony Pulis is being asked why he chose to become the new manager of Crystal Palace. He shrugs: "Why not?" It is not the most elegant answer. He blinks and begins to put together a less confrontational response. Crystal Palace is a Premier League side. They have achieved a great deal in getting this far. He believes the club has a future. Pulis is a poor speaker who grabs hold of clichés as someone else might "hum" or "ah", but everyone at the press conference knows why Pulis is being prickly. It is a month since his oldest and closest friend, Ian Holloway, resigned as manager. Why did it take so long to reach a deal? Pulis sits next to Steve Parish, the chief executive of Crystal Palace. Pulis is compact and bullet-headed, combative yet awkward. Parish can seem hesitant, but he has a languid, unassuming confidence. The two men barely seem to belong on the same planet, let alone the same stage. Nine months later, when Pulis walks out on Palace without any real explanation, this first press conference contains all the clues to the mystery. It is in the body language, the clothes, the haircuts. Parish is a cavalier, Pulis a roundhead; together they represent the two halves of British football – and all of the other, lesser aspects of national life.**

Pulis performed a miracle at Palace, overseeing a run of results that might be the greatest managerial achievement of all time. He inherited a side with only seven points from twelve matches and ended the season mid-table on forty-five points. Some even credit him with winning the three points against Hull on the weekend before he was officially appointed. Pulis was in the stands at Selhurst Park speaking to acting manager, Keith Millen, by telephone. In another inelegant moment at that first press conference, Pulis cannot resist drawing attention to the mid-game phone call.

Pulis resigned fewer than forty-eight hours before the opening weekend of the 2014-15 season, when Palace met Arsenal. Whenever Parish and Pulis are questioned in the weeks that follow, both men appear shell-shocked. In a *Match of the Day* interview, Gary Lineker leads Parish to speculate whether Pulis was approached by a bigger club. A clearly hurt Pulis quickly pops up to deny the suggestion. As the weeks pass, it becomes clear he is telling the truth: no one was waiting in the wings. Neither Pulis nor Parish are entirely impossible men. They are widely respected for their honesty, their work rate and intelligence. No doubt both find it difficult to give quarter, yet they wanted to make their relationship work. They failed. In the words of *1066 and All That*, the Cavalier is 'Wrong but Wromantic', the Roundhead is 'Right but Repulsive'.

Pulis is a strange kind of English Puritan. For a start, he is not English at all. He is Welsh, born in Pill, the old dockland area of Newport. The family name is Maltese. Pulis's grandfather was born in Zabbar, famous for the half dozen churches in the city devoted to the Virgin, who is revered, among other reasons, for being the patron saint of cyclists. An annual pilgrimage in Zabbar takes place on bicycles, a fact which may have played a role in Pulis's life-long love of the sport. He inherited his passion for football from his father, Angelo, a man he describes as "a football nut". Angelo had six children, four boys, two girls. Pulis and his brothers would play on the filled-in dock at the edge of the terraced streets, he says, "We would put our coats down and have a game of football for a few hours... We would smash the ball over the wood yard, climb in there and get chased out. We only had one ball."

Pill has been a noisy, often vibrant, multicultural town-within-a-town for over a century, and at the heart of Newport's sporting life for even longer, thanks to a piece of drained swamp known as Medalgief where locals played baseball (Newport has an established baseball tradition), football and rugby. In the 1960s and 70s, Pulis would watch Newport FC or travel the twelve miles to see Cardiff City. Neither was in the first division. Pulis has said that good football was something you only saw on TV. The local YMCA had a team, though. Angelo was a steel worker and Whiteheads, the local foundry, sponsored the Pill YMCA. Pulis says, "When I was a player at Bristol Rovers, at 16 or 17 years old, if there was a game called off at Bristol, I would get on the train and try to get down the YMCA for 1pm to pay my subs and play. I couldn't get in the first team though... they kept telling me I wasn't good enough... The YMCA thought it had the best football team in Wales."

Pulis remained at Bristol Rovers for almost 10 years, 1975-1984, with a season-long interlude in Hong Kong. He soon began taking his coaching badges, making him among the youngest professional football players to pursue a coaching career. His interest in teaching may reflect the fact that he has younger brothers (his brother Ray was a professional football player), but also that his experience in football came through a social club, where it was the responsibility of members to run their own affairs and bring out the talent of the younger players.

Pulis was a defender. He played 326 professional games in a career that lasted 17 years and he scored nine goals. Pulis is a slight and lean figure – not the kind of player who might occasionally pick out the goal from set pieces. But the lack of goals also speaks of a particular mentality, an understanding of defending as a relentless and never-ending business. You hold the line, you are never out of position. His training sessions at Stoke City were once described as "a thing of beauty" by a visiting sports journalist, though some young players found them stifling. One apprentice recalls running with the ball and being frozen out afterwards without any explanation as to what he had done that was so wrong. The entire point of the training sessions is the drill: you do not improvise, you do not try to show you have flair. You repeat, until the repetition hardens into habit. The Stoke defender, Danny Higginbotham, captured the ethos: "Nobody hid on the pitch because you couldn't in the system that he believed in; it required honest players." An embarrassed player could never claim that he was unlucky when a moment of inspiration didn't come off. Inspiration is never the point, maintaining shape is everything. In this world, an honest man is one who is exactly where he is supposed to be: where his teammates expect him to be. He refuses to indulge in wishful thinking or speculative runs. In some ways, it sounds like a solid working-class philosophy. You don't get ideas above your station. You keep a clean front step. However, one could easily argue for a working-class pull in the other direction, towards exuberance and generosity. A Pulis team is not only a marvel of organised defence, it speaks of a defensive mentality – a mentality often derided as 'negative' by football players and professionals alike. It is the philosophy of the puritanical roundhead who fears judgment, rather than the carefree cavalier who looks forward to goodwill and cheers.

There is a puritanical streak running through Wales, forming the spine of a culture based on non-conformist Protestantism, trade-unionism and the tightly-knit communities of the valleys where geography conspires to keep everyone in small villages. The Pulis family was never part of this narrow Protestant world, however. They lived in a sprawling city, part of a Maltese Catholic community within a larger and diverse immigrant society. Tony Pulis's defensiveness is the reaction of an ostracised outsider, a man determined to show he is as good as the people who look down on him. Higginbotham says, "Pulis was unbelievable at uniting the players and supporters as one... [He] created a siege mentality. He'd say: 'Look at this lot, they don't want us in the league.' I remember when we used to play against Arsenal, you could almost sense them thinking, 'What the hell are you doing on the same pitch as me?' That was the impression you got." At Stoke, Pulis did not simply build a defensive team, he encouraged a painfully thin-skinned, defensive world view.

Malta is a small Mediterranean island with a history of blockades and sieges. Their language, although it now has many Italian loan words, is descended from Siculo-Arabic, a fact Anthony Burgess makes great play of in his novel *Earthly Powers*: Malta is the only self-styled Christian nation that prays to Allah. The Maltese are conservative in the sense that they are staunchly Roman Catholic, but also because they are opposed to the idea of revolution, which they associate with atheism and French revolutionary imperialism. Zabbar unites these two strands: it is a city devoted to the Madonna and a bastion of resistance to the French occupation of 1798-1800. The Maltese are world-wise, independent and tough, however, like Sardinians, Corsicans and Sicilians. In the 20th century, Maltese immigrants to Wales gained a reputation as pimps because the dockland shebeens and brothels were often run by Maltese families. In 1936, when Angelo was a child, the sociologist Kenneth Little made a study of a shebeen owned by a Maltese man named Louis Fenech in the nearby port of Cardiff's Tiger Bay. Fenech's place was on Bute

Street, one of many operations that posed as cafés in order to stay open later than the pubs. At this time, according to Little's figures, Tiger Bay held 10,000 people of whom 6,000 were classified as 'non-white', including Somalians, West Africans and West Indians, with the majority being Arab. The remaining population was also predominantly immigrant, including Maltese, Irish and Sicilian. Alcohol was served in back rooms to visiting sailors and locals, with piano music and local Welsh 'café girls' who could be taken to the rooms above. Little's study is quoted in a biography of Shirley Bassey by the Welsh writer, John Williams, and Williams says that Pill was a very similar kind of place. Tiger Bay has long since been demolished, but the geography and culture of Pill remains intact, though the area may be more deprived today than in Pulis's childhood. Recent police raids have discovered amphetamine factories and wholesale quantities of heroin and cocaine as well as firearms.

The siege mentality that Higginbotham talks about may reflect a Maltese islander's world view or the experience of being the child of second generation immigrants at a time when Maltese immigrants would be pre-judged by 'respectable' society. For Pulis, the essence of team spirit lies in working together to put one over on the snobs from better addresses. The team is a place of selflessness, loyalty and, above all, a family spirit. Family is a prime virtue for Pulis, but it is coloured by pain and sacrifice. Pulis famously left his mother's deathbed to drive to Stoke, reaching the grounds at half-time to rally the side to a hard-won victory and receiving an ovation from the home fans. His last days at Stoke were overshadowed by the death of an infant grandchild and, after leaving Palace, he has said that unemployment has offered the chance to play an active role in the care of another grandchild. Pulis draws his friends into his family. Ian Holloway, a fellow apprentice at Bristol Rovers, is godfather to Pulis's son. Pulis bought a home in Poole to be close to Harry Redknapp, who encouraged Pulis's coaching ambitions at Bournemouth. When Redknapp left Bournemouth in 1990, Pulis stepped up to manager from his role as player/coach.

Pulis joined Stoke in 2002 where, he says, he came to see Peter Coates, a board member and one-time owner of Stoke, as a surrogate father. Angelo died in the late nineties, at a time when Pulis was specialising in bad career choices. He became embroiled in a court case with Gillingham and endured rocky times at Bristol City and Portsmouth before spending two years out of work. His task at Stoke was to avoid relegation from the second flight. Pulis turned the club into a solid second-tier side but left after falling out with the club's Icelandic owners. When the Icelandic financial crisis gave Peter Coates an opportunity to take back control of Stoke, Pulis was asked to return. It proved a successful partnership. Stoke were promoted, rebuilt and turned into a Premier League side that came close to winning the FA Cup and had a respectable run in Europe in 2011-12. It is odd for a man in his forties to talk of surrogate fathers, but Pulis and Coates were extremely close. It was painful when Coates asked Pulis to move on in May 2013, although Pulis refuses to voice any criticism. When asked about the breakdown of the relationship, Pulis would only say, characteristically, that Coates was invited to his daughter's wedding. To Pulis, that said everything.

In retrospect, the season in Europe was Pulis's downfall. He needed a larger squad, but created one filled with more or less similar players, intended to double up positions rather than introduce flexibility and variety. These factors became critical almost immediately. The 2012-13 season was a time of failed bids and tight budgets as older players could not easily be moved on. Stoke skirted relegation and divisions opened in the boardroom as Pulis clashed with the CEO, Tony Scholes, over transfer budgets. Pulis tried to regain the initiative by producing a report on how European clubs built effective youth academies. The sight of Pulis at Athletic of Bilbao and Bayer Leverkusen led to rumours that he intended to work abroad. The report came too late: Peter Coates and his son John sacked Pulis before he finished writing his study. His account of how he delivered the final copies reveals much about Pulis's connection to the Coates family. He said, "I've done my report, Peter Coates will look at it, and I'm sure John Coates will look at it, too." Pulis may have seen Coates as a father-figure, but he had a more distant relation with the Coates children. By this point, the ear of the father was no longer enough. The wealth of the Coates family did not flow downwards from the catering company owned by Peter, but upwards from the online betting site, Bet365, created by his daughter, Denise Coates. The Coates family wealth is now underwritten by the business genius of Denise, who owns a large majority of Bet365 stock. It is Bet365 that owns Stoke and although Denise does not sit on the board, John (her closest business associate) and her husband, Richard Smith, do.

The Stoke board felt that Pulis was not the man to see through the restructuring of the club and the bloated, bottle-necked squad that had emerged through the run in Europe. Perhaps, too, a family business saw no need for a prickly and thin-skinned adoptive son. However, the perception outside of the club was that Pulis had been sacked because Stoke wanted to play a new kind of football. Pulis was negative and ugly; perhaps it was time for romance and beauty.

Pulis left Stoke on 21 May 2013. When Holloway resigned from Palace on October 23, Pulis was the natural choice. Yet the perception that Pulis was 'negative' unsettled the Palace supporters. Palace is a relatively new club, but the fans feel strongly that it has a 'south London' identity. A little cheeky, youthful and bright – perhaps as far from a dour northern English club as one could imagine. The fact that Pulis is neither northern nor English was not relevant. He had managed Stoke for so long, the sense was that he and Stoke were indivisible and the supposed shortcomings of his game came under renewed scrutiny. It is easy enough to find videos of Pulis screaming, 'Get it up!' from the touchline, a reminder that Stoke favoured a long-ball game. He was criticised by the Fulham midfielder Danny Murphy for fostering a brutal spirit in his team talks, which Murphy argued led directly to reckless and savage tackles. In response, Pulis released a six-minute scripted defence that began, as Pulis statements often do, with a combative and facetious cliché about 'not letting the facts get in the way of a good story'.

He produced a few cherry-picked facts of his own that, he felt, showed Stoke were no more responsible for bad tackles than other teams. The bottom line for Pulis, however, was that football is a contact sport. This is debatable. It is impossible to imagine a football match without physical contact, but no one believes that football is essentlally a contact sport: the point is to play the ball. Pulis ended his statement with an *ad hominem* attack on Murphy, claiming that he was too aware of his career to attack the big clubs and preferred to lash out at easy targets like Stoke. It was a reprise of the Pulis team talk: they look down on us, they think we shouldn't be here.

If Stoke City was a family, it could be an unhappy one. The striker James Beattie forced an internal inquiry after Pulis burst out of a shower to remonstrate with him: a naked Pulis is said to have head-butted Beattie. When Pulis came into conflict with his players, he would plant his version of events in local papers while insisting the secrecy of the dressing-room remained inviolable, or so one-time Stoke player Dave Kitson claimed. However, the key charge against Pulis was always his style of play: a determination never to lose rather than a desire to win. Higginbotham gives a succinct account of Pulis's strategy at Stoke. The four defenders are extremely narrow, 'holding hands' in Higginbotham's words. This unit is augmented by two sitting midfield players, which leaves the wingers to cover the space vacated by the narrow defence: "They had to be the fittest people in the team," Higginbotham says. Pulis drilled his narrow six-man defence in passing to the side if they had one-touch, and crossing diagonally if they had two.

Steve Parish was a fan of Crystal Palace long before he became one of its owners, which makes him unusually sensitive to the club's sense of identity. Born in 1965, he saw the club achieve highs and lows under the inspirational managers Terry Venables and Steve Coppell. He took control of the club in 2010 by taking them out of administration, the third time Palace had faced oblivion in 20 years. In many ways, the south London-born businessman embodies the Palace ethos: he is direct, open and more than a little flash. His company, Tag, became a market leader in high-end printing at a time at a time when technology was changing the industry in unpredictable ways. Parish kept ahead of the innovations and, more crucially, built up trust with his clients. Tag works across London's advertising agencies, which means anything that happens in the industry passes through Tag's offices: every new pitch and every new campaign. Parish made sure the agencies trusted him by making himself as transparent and as available as they needed him to be.

Parish and his three fellow directors took control of Palace by buying the ground from one set of administrators and the club from another. Like Parish, Steve Browett of Farr Vintners bought out a company that he had joined at low-level position: Browett was once a van driver. Martin Long is the founder of both Direct Line and Churchill insurance brands. Jeremy Hosking is a financier, owner of the investment fund Marathon. His main hobby is running steam trains. It is unusual, today, for an owner to double up as CEO, but Parish's inexperienced partners have placed their trust in him. Parish sold Tag around the time he took over Palace and so had time to devote to football. In an interview with the stock market tipster Nick Batsford he spoke about wanting the fans to have high expectations, because that would challenge him to do better. It is a philosophy based on the power of positive thinking.

At his first meeting with his new Palace players, the *Telegraph* reported that Pulis said he was proud of never being relegated. Yet at the press conference, just a few hours later, Pulis is trying to put a different spin on his career. It is others who speak of him as a fire fighter, he claims. They say he is the man who has never been relegated, but he has also been promoted from every league he has worked in: "I've been pretty successful, given the opportunity and given the chance." A journalist points out that, true as that may be, the job at Palace is not to get relegated. Pulis accepts this, and begins talking about getting past Christmas in order to "wheel and deal" in the transfer window. To many Palace fans, it appeared the club had already traded in their ideals. They hoped the team would stay up, but anticipated a year of tetchy defensive football, punctuated by long balls from both crosses and throw-ins.

Then the miracle happened.

Crystal Palace won three of the next six matches. The position began to stabilise. Pulis endeared himself to fans through simple measures like introducing modern diets, yoga and a longer day that included an afternoon training session run by Pulis. When he was required to give interviews, he began to schedule them over breakfast at the club, as early as six and seven in the morning. He had learnt to play to his strengths, as he already did in training. It was all about show not tell. Why get snarled up with language? It was enough to show he worked harder, longer and stayed fitter than any other Premier League manager. Palace fans noted the way he gave press conferences standing up. It implied energy and direction.

In a season in which so many teams were facing relegation troubles, Crystal Palace began to look like they might edge to safety. They reached 31 points in style, beating Chelsea at the end of March 2014. A week before, it had seemed likely that Chelsea's José Mourinho would sneak the Premier League title but that day, the so-called Special One was undone by the Other One, the dark horse, Tony Pulis. It is worth noting that Mourinho and Pulis share a staunchly Catholic, conservative background and a commitment to a counter-attacking game. Crystal Palace was built around defence and, like his old Stoke side, there was a strong tall target man in Marouane Chamakh. But the goalkeeper Julian Speroni was in the form of his life, Mile Jedinak, the midfielder and captain, was emerging as a great leader and Palace had a truly fit and fast winger in Jason Puncheon. The other players grew in confidence as the season went on, which allowed Pulis to play a more mobile game. It is a very similar set-up to Mourinho's Chelsea and, with weaker players, Pulis could claim to be the real master of the style. Happily, the Palace fans saw it as a quintessentially English way of playing the game, rather than conservative and Mediterranean. Moreover, they saw it as a south London style, a sturdy back four with great wingers who could carry out 'smash-and-grab' raids on the 'mugs' they came up against. As the victories began to pile up, the Palace fans rejoiced in criminal slang. In their way, of course, Palace were just as honest as the Stoke side described by Higginbotham. But now they were honestly larcenous. At times they were winning matches with only 26% of possession. They passed the traditional safety mark of 40 points on April 16 when they beat Everton at Goodison Park but their greatest game was the draw against Liverpool on 5 May 2014. Crystal Palace spent the last 10 minutes repeatedly mugging Liverpool, overturning the three-goal lead that Liverpool had painfully built. Palace fans were not celebrating the goals as they went in – they were laughing.

Pulis seemed to have transcended his old negative ways and found a positive style that the fans believed represented the real Crystal Palace. Football lovers everywhere were talking about Palace as exciting and cutting-edge in a way they hadn't for more than 20 years. In football, the words 'positive' and 'negative' are used in the same way as self-help books or, for that matter, management guides. The aim of positive thinking is to create and build upon success. In the interview Steve Parish gave to Nick Batsford for the online channel Tip TV, Parish spoke about the importance of aspirations and said his golden rule was to find a business with potential to grow. If an industry puts limits on your ambitions, you can only stagnate once you hit them. On screen, Parish was as warm and straightforward as ever. He knew the names of everyone at Palace, staff and players alike, and spoke with the excitement of a fan. He and Batsford gushed, reminisced and swapped stats, by which they meant favourite results and unusual facts. As the name Tip TV implied, it was an interview addressed to punters, which served as a reminder that Pulis had flourished on the other side of the counter, among bookmakers. Denise Coates turned around a small local Potteries' bookmakers chain owned by her father, doubled it in size, then mortgaged it to build Bet365. She is a trained mathematician. In her world, stats means data: not stand-alone facts but reams of figures that can be crunched, compared and analysed. To a bookmaker, taking a positive approach means hard-headed analysis, not dreaming about the future, crossing one's fingers or rubbing a lucky rabbit's foot.

The paradox is that what we call positive and negative thinking in everyday conversation is the opposite to the way these terms are used in the philosophy of science. *Positivism* is a strategy focused upon whatever can be known and controlled, while reducing the risks in areas that are opaque or speculative. In this sense, the defensive, counter-attacking football that Pulis brought to Palace *is* positive. A team can always prepare a defence and plan strategies that are likely to harry or upset an opponent, forcing players to make mistakes. In contrast, a strategy based upon free-flowing attack will always depend upon a measure of wishful thinking. A romantic game deals with hopes and aspirations; in philosophy, this is the *work of the negative,* which is to say, of things that do not yet exist. The cavalier, like the punter, is a day-dreamer. Roundheads, like bookmakers, have the edge because they have minimised risk. Pulis is tense, uncomfortable in his own skin, inarticulate, combative. No one would say that he doesn't have baggage. Sitting beside Steve Parish, who supplied an upbeat and open response to every question, Pulis looked his worst: thin-skinned, dour, prickly. A roundhead. But as the idiom goes, the roundheads are the ones who are right.

# Wengerball

## *Arsène Wenger, the Invincibles and the transformation of Arsenal's philosophy*

**By Amy Lawrence**

***You didn't need to be a comedian to poke fun at what had become of Arsenal's style at the dog end of the George Graham era. The team had evolved a strategy based on super-resilience and mostly hoicking the ball up to Ian Wright, their explosive, maverick striker, as quickly as possible. It was perfect for cup runs, and Arsenal won three different cups in 1993 and 1994, but it wasn't always pretty. Alan Davies and his friends used to dream up silly diversions to deal with some of the tedium at Highbury. "There was a real lull," he says, chuckling to himself. "We used to have a little wall in front of us in the West Lower – we were in the front row – and we'd put a coin on top of the wall and move it along until there was a corner or a throw in, just to amuse ourselves because the football was so unbearable. That period when George signed John Jensen and Stefan Schwarz and Eddie McGoldrick. We used to sit there and shout 'Hayes ... Groves ... Papin!' The idea that someone like Papin would turn up and be in that team was laughable. In the seventies or eighties Ruud Krol was supposed to be coming and he never came."***

The rebirth of Arsenal, from a stylistic point of view, began with Dennis Bergkamp. He played the orchestra's first note. He was the oboist, whose clear, pitch-perfect A tunes every other musician around him. He starts, the rest respond. In terms of creating a new identity, he arrived, he elevated the standard, he embodied a nod to the Dutch ideal of total football – technical, inventive, collective – and he was a joy to watch. Within a year of his arrival, everything began to flourish as strong personalities came who could take this idea and effectively turn the solo into a symphony.

Wright credits Bergkamp as the most important signing in Arsenal's history. "Dennis changed the DNA of what our game was about," he reckons. "The player he was, our game had to change because you couldn't bypass him. Then Arsène Wenger coming in with his total football, it was brilliant. I could only wish I was four years younger. I knew the great times were coming." That's quite a statement from a man who had won medals, would break goal-scoring records and had fallen in love with the club even before the great sea change.

As a supporter, Nick Hornby watched it evolve, quite unexpectedly, right in front of his eyes. He was intrigued to observe how Wenger completely redefined what Arsenal meant to people. "I can't think of many football clubs that have a brand, actually," he says. "An actual brand as opposed to they're famous. Probably the only two are Barcelona and Arsenal, and Arsenal have done it through one man. At Barça they have to play football a certain way, but they also have the resources to achieve that. So it's quite remarkable that one man has taken something that meant one thing and turned it into something that meant the opposite. Within six or seven years everyone had forgotten the old Arsenal. And now when foreign people talk about Arsenal, or they play Arsenal football, everybody knows what that means and that's a relatively recent invention."

Bergkamp's arrival was serendipitous in that he was such a natural fit to instigate the change in advance of Wenger. The philosophy he absorbed at Ajax, the way he inherently thought about football, blended well with the incoming coach. The Ajax Academy, a football school renowned for the way it educates its youngsters, teaches according to what they now call the TIPS model. It stands for "technique, insight, personality and speed". All these things resonate totally with Wenger's footballing dogma.

Reflecting on the evolution of Arsenal's style, Bergkamp sees these components, which were so prevalent in the squad, as keys to the way they formed their game. The interplay that became a hallmark with, say, a burst of seemingly instinctive exchanges between Bergkamp, Henry and Pirès, was based as much on insight as pure technique. "I always try to copy the words that Arsène once told me: the ball always goes through the intelligent players in the team,"Bergkamp explains. "When you name those names, they're all very intelligent players, they saw the game, they saw the openings.

"The understanding was right. Why? Because we played to each other's strengths. So I knew exactly what the strength of Thierry was, or Patrick or Robert. That was the power in that team, we knew exactly where you could connect on the pitch. You also knew what the weaknesses were of the players. So you're always looking, as Arsène says, to make the right pass and put a player in his strength. With Thierry, I knew exactly what he wanted to do, he knew exactly from me what I could do for him. On the pitch we had all those connections happening. Maybe there were two or three players who weren't on the same level as we were, but they gave something else, they gave power to the team, or defending. They had the intelligence as well – when we get the ball we give it to Patrick or Thierry or Dennis. They don't want to do silly things. That's what Arsène wanted."

When a new player arrives, can you see that intelligence in them immediately?

"Yeah. You know that they always try to overachieve in the beginning, try to show themselves. But within those moves on the pitch or the way they control the ball, you would always know this is a good player, this is a player I can play with. Robert was a player who wanted to play one or two touches. Patrick the same. Thierry is different. You have to play him in or you have to put him in a position where he can play one against one. It could be behind the defenders or it could be in between them. It didn't take long, but after a few training sessions you knew exactly what a player's strength was, what his weakness was and how you as a team could grow."

The speed of the team – speed of thinking as well as movement – seemed sharper than anyone else in that era. "We were on a different level, I felt," says Bergkamp. "As an athlete or as a football player going out somewhere doing your thing but knowing already that you will be successful on that day is amazing. You're so confident and so full of quality and talent that you know you can make a difference. We had the same feeling as a team. I remember some goals, the timing, how quick it was from one side to the other side. It was not like we were a counter-attack team. In those moments, for the front four or five players, we knew exactly what was going to happen in the next 10 to 12 seconds and that's a fantastic feeling. And then it's all at the highest pace, with the highest quality. Let's go."

Fredrik Ljungberg felt that collective speed of thought evolved from the fact the group spent a lot of time analysing the game. "We all liked to think football," he says. "That I agree with. When people ask me about how we played, step-overs take a lot of technique, for example, but the speed of the pass, how it got smashed around to each other, that was the hard thing. Top teams do it, when the field is really wet and it gets smashed around, one touch. Before you get the ball, you need to think, where's the ball going after this? Because the ball is coming at real speed. With the speed of the ball we could still control it. It's not that we ran faster than everyone else, but the ball moved faster. Everybody thought how to get it faster to catch the opponents out."

Jens Lehmann agrees that the speed was critical. "What is the fastest thing on a football pitch?" he asks. It feels like a trick question. "It's not the ball," he says, grinning knowingly. "Nobody is faster on the pitch than a thought. And then the ball comes. And then the players come. So quick thinking was vital. I'm still convinced that we played a much faster football than the team today. We were playing one-touch, two-touch. When you look at the team today, it's three or four touches. Normally you say football is progressing so fast now. But I can honestly say between 2003 and 2006 we played such a fast football. Everything was faster. The opening, the finishing."

There were times during the Invincible season when the goalkeeper was in a very privileged position as Arsenal were zooming forward at full throttle, slicing through opponents, in his direct eyeline. "Plenty of games I was standing at the back just watching, because we had so much possession, we were playing so fast, we were playing tic-tak-tic-tak-tic. One touch. It was amazing to see. I said to myself, 'What an amazing group.'"

It was universally understood that work at London Colney translated directly into performances come match day. The message comes across loud and clear. "You play how you train. If you train well, generally you're good in a match," says Pirès. "If you think training is training and game is game, you lose the game,' adds Gilberto. 'We had to be careful not to injure each other but we had to train seriously. This for Arsène was really important."

Ray Parlour recalls being uncertain about what to expect when he first started training under Wenger. "But I remember David Dein said, 'This man will take us forward.' From day one, the training regime was great," he says. "The lads started to put the ball down. I loved George Graham, I thought he was great, but there was a lot of focus on defending, win 1–0, not great football. Suddenly we had freedom."

Was training fun?

"Oh yeah. I loved it. You had to concentrate, but it was always very enjoyable. No disrespect to other managers, but it was a little bit same old thing, forty-five minutes of that. And you think, Oh, I've had enough now. Your concentration goes after probably about 15, 20 minutes working on one thing. Wenger knew that, so then he goes on to something else, totally different. Then your mind is still working. That's why everything was always on the clock. He always knew the time span of people's top concentration."

For Pat Rice, the most striking aspect was how precise everything was. "The actual training system and the way that we trained was completely different to how we'd done it before," he says. "Whenever I used to referee the games – and we would play a game for fifteen minutes at the end of the session – I can remember Arsène shouting out to me, 'Pat, look at your watch, seven and a half minutes.' He would come up to me and say, 'When I say it's fifteen minutes, that means seven and a half minutes each way, that doesn't mean seven minutes or eight minutes, it means seven and a half minutes.' And everything was done to the clock." At first Rice was slightly bemused. He felt it wasn't necessarily enough to allow players to get into the flow. But he was soon convinced it had great merit, encouraging players to focus on something specific to work on during the mini-game. Sometimes Wenger would stop the game and send the players on sprints, then straight back into the second half. "It was just to see if you could switch on and off," explains Rice.

Sometimes Wenger would move the goals into the corner of the pitch, to create a situation where angled, cross-field passes were the focus. Other times if you completed 10 passes in the opposition half you would be awarded a goal to drum home the beauty of possession and attacking the ball. There were drills where the ball could not leave the floor. Lots of tricks, lots of detail, lots of precision. It all came together to produce this swifter, slicker approach. "You would have sessions like that, then all of a sudden you would bring that into the games that you actually play on a Saturday," says Rice. "They would be dragging the opponents all over the place."

For Bergkamp, the essence of training was in the enhancement of patterns. "Keep practising the patterns," he says. "Keep practising the passing. We did the sprints, we did tactical games, positional games. But when you've got a team who already know all the patterns, who already know the strength of each other, and you are doing that at the highest pace, then you make other teams look silly, to be fair. It's like you're on a different level."

*This is an edited extract from* Invincible: Inside Arsenal's Unbeaten 2003-2004 Season, *which is published by Viking, Penguin and is available now in hardback priced £16.99 or in ebook*

Blizzard Books

# Erbstein: The triumph and tragedy of football's forgotten pioneer

Dominic Bliss

# The Archduke and the Offside Law

*Did the First World War lead to the most significant ever change to the Laws of the Game?*

**By Jonny Singer**

**On 28 June 1914, Archduke Franz Ferdinand was shot by Gavrilo Princip. It was an assassination that plunged the world into panic – international tension that had been building up for years erupted into violence as one of the bloodiest wars that humanity has ever fought began. A century later, on 28 June 2014, thousands of miles away from the streets of Sarajevo, Brazil and Colombia recorded victories over Chile and Uruguay to reach the quarter-finals of the World Cup.**

These two events seem, on the face of it, totally unconnected, except that they happened to be the most prominent events occurring on the same day, a century apart. But in actual fact the assassination of the Austrian Archduke had a profound effect on how football is played today. So much has changed in a century of football that it would be wrong to identify any one moment as shaping the game more than any other – but if one were so inclined, the start of the First World War would be up there as one of the key moments.

In 1925 the International Football Association Board made a slight alteration to the offside law, intended to have a small effect on defensive play. The unforeseen results of the change actually served to revolutionise the entire sport. In the run-up to the change and in the years since this alteration has mostly been attributed to one man – Billy McCracken. In fact, it owes much more to the conflict that swept across Europe.

McCracken was, and to an extent still is, a somewhat mythical figure; a powerful full-back who defied the Ireland national team by refusing to play for them because the match fee was only half of that which the English players received, although he was later accepted back into the fold. Domestically he was a player with Newcastle United for over a decade during the club's most successful era, at a time when they were famed for their defending. Add in the image of him as "the man who forced the rule change"and the legend grows still further.

During McCracken's time at Newcastle he and Frank Hudspeth, it is claimed, became so good at the 'one-back game' that matches practically ground to a halt with stoppages[1].

Indeed, the Irishman has become almost synonymous with the one-back game, such was his prowess. And thus, the story has it, the FA were forced into changing the offside law. It's not hard to see why this is a tempting myth to maintain. McCracken was a legend of the game –a *Daily Express* poll in 1921 ranked him as the best full-back in the game. Even five years after he left Newcastle, the *Express* described him as a "professor of offside tactics".

How enticing then, both in the press at the time and for later commentators to single him out as the single significant actor in a move that would change the history of the game. Football fans, and perhaps football journalists even more so, love to do this. The cult of the personality lies beneath much of our sports writing but it rarely reflects reality.

McCracken was merely one of many players exploiting the laws as they stood. Before the First World War, not only were other players doing it, but offside tactics weren't seen as a problem, at least in England. When the Scottish FA proposed changing the offside law, as early as 1913, the English rejection was, according to the *Scotsman* "practically unanimous against the change, which would merely assist forwards not brainy enough to overcome the one-back game".

However, in the years between 1913 and 1925, something changed and it is here that the war played its part. In reports on matches after 1919, a pattern emerges – the standard of attacking play appears to have plummeted. This is not surprising. With very little real football for four years and a distinct lack of training the tricky art of scoring goals suffered, even for those who never went to war.

But the war's impact was far deeper than that. Players were urged to sign up to fight and professional footballers were used to encourage their club's supporters to enlist. The Scottish league leaders Hearts sent at least eleven of their players, seven of whom were killed over the following four years, to the Edinburgh City Pals Battalion, which raised 1300 men in just six days with help from players from Falkirk, Hibernian and Raith Rovers. The idea that fans could serve alongside their footballing heroes was clearly attractive.

In England the response was less striking. The so-called Football Battalion, the 17th Middlesex, was established to encourage professionals to join up, but only 35 did so immediately out of a possible 5000. However, by March 1915, 122 professional footballers had joined the Battalion and the number of players who took part in some way or other would grow significantly once conscription came in a year later.

Over the course of the war, the Football Battalion saw around 600 professional footballers pass through its ranks, while others of course served elsewhere – the *Times* reported as early as November 1918 that "not less than 2000 [footballers] are serving in various branches of his Majesty's forces."

[1] *The offside law in those days meant that rather than two defenders (usually the goalkeeper and the rear-most defender) needed to play an opponent onside as it is now, three were required. The one-back game was a way of defending in which the two full-backs were staggered, one staying forward to play forwards offside and the other covering in case he got it wrong.*

Major Frank Buckley, the commander of the Battalion and a footballer himself, whose career was more or less ended by poison gas in 1917, suggested that five of every six players had their careers ended, through injury or death, by the war. Buckley, who would go on to manage Norwich, Blackpool and Wolves, probably overestimated, but the number was not insignificant.

The likelihood is simply that shortly after a war in which a huge number of men between the ages of 16 and 40 had died the quality of player would have been diminished when football returned in peacetime. As with any skill-based pursuit, taking four years of training, development and performance out of a career is likely to reduce seriously the future level of performance.

Even if players did keep up with the game during the four years, and returned home alive and uninjured, a lack of match practice meant that everything from fitness to technique, and with some even appetite for the game, had lessened.

Those who had reached the peak of their game had lost the best years of performance, while those who were coming to what should have been of their careers in football had missed out on the key part of their development, the years which normally turn a player from a raw talent into an experienced professional.

A decline in skill levels was to be expected then.Lack of skill affected forwards far more than backs in the 1920s. Backs, usually uncompromising and unconcerned with tricky play, were, according to all contemporaries, simply less skilled. A drop in quality would affect them, but not nearly as much as forwards.

But there was a still more significant change that the war brought about – the introduction of organisation. As Herbert Chapman, perhaps the greatest manager of the age, put it, "In my playing days no attempt was made, shall we say, to organise victory. The most that I remember was an occasional chat between, say, two men playing together on a wing...The day of haphazard football, when men went out to do their bit according to their own ideas, has gone. All teams now are highly organised."

Everything had changed and, as Chapman himself recognised, it was the war that changed it. "You have talented, mostly young players – they need a general to lead them," he told the Huddersfield Town board in 1921. Chapman, who had co-ordinated a munitions factory during the war with great success, implemented the lessons of specialisation, organisation and division of labour into his football teams.

He was not alone. Charlie Buchan, who helped Chapman tactically with the W-M formation at Arsenal, rose through the ranks during the war, took part in officer training and by the end held the rank of second lieutenant.

Most strikingly, Major Buckley took his war-time experiences back to the training pitch. The England defender Stan Cullis, who played under Buckley at Wolves, explained that "his style of management in football was very similar to his attitude in the army. Major Buckley implanted into my mind the direct method of playing which did away with close inter-passing and square-ball play."

Chapman, Buchan and Buckley (and there are many more) show clearly that those involved in the war came back with a changed outlook on football. A generation of men used to military organisation could be differently, and more effectively, organised on the pitch.

Thus, rather than harming defensive play, the war actually led to the increased efficiency of defending while also draining the pool of attacking talent. With increased organisation and greater planning between players the one-back game, among other defensive ploys, became more successful. The number of stoppages rocketed and the media grew restless.

In February 1925 the *Times* had bemoaned "the general slowing up of the game through incessant, but necessary, whistle blowing, and the consequent exasperation both of players and spectators", while the *Manchester Guardian* commented in the week the new rule passed that "there is nothing in professional football, except perhaps the applications of the rule about foul play, which checks the free run of the game so much as 'offside', and it is probably this, rather than the deliberate use of the device as a piece of tactics, that has led the authorities to make a change."

Their complaints were not unreasonable – an FA Cup tie between Arsenal and West Ham in 1925 had contained 30 offside calls – one every three minutes. This was higher than the average, but not by much. This represents a marked rise, yet newspaper reports from the early 1920s make it clear that it was not the number of teams using the offside tactics but rather the efficiency of those teams that had changed. In other words, there is not much of an indication that the one-back game, a significant but minority tactic pre-war, became a majority tactic after it. What did change was how well that minority carried it out.

Thus football arrived at a rule change that would alter it forever. Following in its wake came the realisation that defending with only two backs was no longer possible and the result was the W-M formation. This innovation, which saw the introduction of a third back, paved the way for world football to become more defensively minded. A short-term spike in the number of goals ensued, but the long-term trend was downward.

A game in which everyone played with two defensive players and five forwards has developed into one in which having no forwards at all is seen as a viable option, with four defenders the normal state of affairs. And the 1925 law change, it has been convincingly argued, is the starting point for that change.

100 years later, the game is unrecognisable – as any sport that survives a century must be. But so much of that change has grown out of the geopolitical events of 1914-1918. And that gunshot in Sarajevo. 

# Pep Talk

*How Guardiola inspired Bayern Munich before the Super Cup shoot-out against Chelsea*

**By Marti Pararnu**

**Prague, 30 August 2013.**

**It's a feverish, tense, agonising final. Bayern equalise 51 seconds after the 120 minutes have been played. The Swedish referee Jonas Eriksson has added one minute for stoppages and there are nine seconds to go before Pep Guardiola's team lose their second final in a month when a player who only three days previously was booked in for surgery scores for Bayern.**

Once again, they're going head-to-head with Chelsea in a penalty shoot-out, and everyone's thoughts turn to the Allianz Arena one year earlier. That day the English team beat Bayern in the Champions League final, in a penalty shoot-out. This could be payback time but, given the option, Guardiola wouldn't have wished for penalties. In the previous four weeks the men from Munich have scored only three of the five penalties they have taken.

On the way back from Freiburg, Guardiola realises that Bastian Schweinsteiger will miss the European Super Cup. His ankle is terribly swollen and they're going to have to postpone Javi Martínez's groin surgery. Thiago Alcantera had surgery the day before and the combination of injuries and the fact that Mario Götze has had very little training means that Pep will be forced to put Thomas Müller in the centre of the field as an attacking midfielder again. Given the results of this experiment so far, he had promised himself never to repeat this strategy, but there is nobody else he can use. He decides that Toni Kroos will be the organising midfielder, with the captain Philipp Lahm on hand to protect him as a No.8.

Pep draws up his final line-up with great reluctance. Having Kroos as *pivote* is a real problem, particularly against Mourinho, the expert in making his teams get in behind a *pivote* via speedy counter-attacks. Bayern's line-up reads like this: Neuer; Rafinha, Boateng, Dante, Alaba; Kroos, Lahm, Müller; Robben, Mandžukić and Ribéry.

This final will be the 16th time Guardiola and Mourinho have met and the balance of victories up till now is in Pep's favour. He has won seven of the games against Mourinho's three, with five draws. They know each other inside out. When Guardiola was captain at Barça, Mourinho was assistant coach. They shared a dressing-room, training sessions, knowledge and confidences. Years later they would fight it out in unforgettable tactical battles. There are no secrets between these two men. Mourinho knows that Pep wants his team to get the ball and come out attacking. Guardiola knows that Mourinho will start with his team in banks of defence, just waiting to pounce on a lost or loose ball and inflict deadly damage.

In this latest tussle between a team that likes to dominate the ball and one that wants to control the space, Chelsea come out on top. All it takes is a threat in the shape of Fernando Torres for Kroos to lose his position. Then Eden Hazard gets away from Rafinha and Bayern's defensive organisation crumbles. Chelsea attack aggressively and score the first goal while the Munich defenders look on passively.

Thirty minutes into the match something happens that will affect Bayern's entire season. Kroos continues to suffer every time Chelsea play the ball behind him, because turning quickly and then defending isn't his greatest attribute. The assistant coach Domènec Torrent turns to Pep and says: 'Why don't we try Lahm as a *pivote?*'

Guardiola hesitates for the time it takes him to take a sip of water, then he leaps to his feet and, almost running on to the pitch, shouts at Kroos: "Toni! You, No.8. You, No.8 and Philipp, No.6!" This moment, switching the two, marks the start of Philipp Lahm's metamorphosis into a midfielder.

Lahm started playing for Bayern aged 11, having come from FT Gern, and during his time in the youth categories trained under Hermann Gerland, who was assistant coach under Jupp Heynckes and stayed on to work for Guardiola. He had used Lahm in a variety of positions: from right-back to winger and even occasionally in midfield, where he was coached by Roman Grill, who is now his agent. When Ottmar Hitzfeld promoted Lahm into the first team at 19, the full-back positions were filled by the likes of Willy Sagnol and Bixente Lizarazu, so Gerland took it upon himself to persuade Felix Magath, then Stuttgart's coach, to take Lahm on loan. Once there, he shone at left-back. Ten years later, Guardiola started to use him as a midfielder and now, in the middle of the European Super Cup final, while losing, puts him into the intricate position of *pivote* – the linchpin of the team.

Months later, towards the end of November, Guardiola will recall this moment: "It was Domè's suggestion that made all the difference. If we win something this season, that will be the reason. I'm completely serious. If we win anything this season it will be thanks to that decision to move Lahm. All the other pieces fell into place the minute we put him in central midfield."

Very slowly, Bayern begin to dominate. Pep not only puts Lahm in midfield, but moves Rafinha higher up the pitch and the team starts to attack using a 3-3-1-3 formation. Rafinha helps tighten things up in midfield, aiding Lahm, which frees Kroos to play creatively and Müller to play off the strikers. After half-time Ribéry scores with a fierce shot – a chance created by Kroos's excellent build-up work.

A euphoric Ribéry runs straight to his coach to celebrate. Guardiola grabs him by the neck and the two bump heads. Ribéry raises his left fist as if dedicating his second goal in six days to his boss. Having been voted the best

European player of 2013, he was in Monaco the previous night and unable to train with the team. Pep insisted that he be there to receive his well-deserved award. He has set himself the task of convincing Ribéry that he has huge potential as a goal-scorer and the player is responding magnificently.

After the equaliser Bayern control the rhythm of the match. Guardiola decides that a few more adjustments might just win them the game. The day before, he and Javi Martínez had decided that the player should have an anti-inflammatory injection so that he would be fit to play. 10 minutes after the break, Pep takes Rafinha off and brings on Martínez in an attempt to stretch the game – more attacking depth. He hopes Javi can change things by getting up and down the middle. At first Bayern suffer because, with Lahm giving over the *pivote* position to Javi, the German must do a double-shift at right-back and on the right of midfield. And the manager makes another change – Götze for Müller. But Chelsea go up a gear, making three good chances. Neuer needs to excel and Chelsea hit the bar.

Kroos and Ribéry both have scoring chances but what scars the closing moments is Ramires's violent foul on Götze, which sees him sent off with five minutes of normal time left.

Götze is left with a serious ankle injury and will end up in plaster. In the break before extra-time Guardiola tells his players he wants aggression, particularly when they are defending. He doesn't want Chelsea getting another goal and wants to see his men maintaining the pressure.

The complete opposite happens. Ninety seconds into extra time David Luiz frees the fabulous Eden Hazard who is wide on the left. He runs at the penalty area, easily passing Lahm and then Boateng, who barely tries to tackle, meekly allowing him past. He shoots and Neuer fumbles badly. With 10 men, Mourinho's team are back in front and the clock is in their favour.

The Bayern supporters react with greater speed than the players themselves and their impassioned chanting echoes around the stadium. They are losing with just a few minutes to go but the fans of the European champions are holding out for the equaliser. They unfurl their flags, roar their lungs out and spur their players on to an epic comeback. Inspired by the fervour and excitement in the stands, Guardiola's men produce an avalanche of shots on Petr Čech's goal. Kroos is back at *pivote,* Lahm is running the whole of the right touchline. Javi Martínez is alternating between second striker and centre-forward. Time and again Bayern make scoring chances, time and again they are thwarted by the formidable Czech goalkeeper. Xherdan Shaqiri, Mario Mandžukić and Javi all fail to score. Shaqiri misses for a second time, as do Götze and Ribéry and then, at the end of 120 minutes of play, Mandžukić fails to hit the mark once again. Bayern have had 38 shots, have taken 19 corners and hit three times as many accurate passes as Chelsea but, with 60 seconds left, they are losing the final.

German teams have a reputation for fighting until the last second. They will only accept defeat once they're in the shower. And in this final Pep's men more than live up to this reputation. With nine seconds left, Alaba crosses, Mandžukić lays it off, the ball bounces off Dante and drops to the left leg of the injured Javi Martínez – who scores. The combined efforts of an Austrian, a Croatian, a Brazilian and a Spaniard have the German supporters leaping to their feet in an explosion of joy that thunders across the Prague night.

Mourinho turns to Guardiola's bench and clasps his hands in a gesture that says, "Pure dumb luck!" And he's right. There are four principal elements in football: the ball, space, time and luck. Of these, Chelsea have certainly been the master of space, but Pep's team have had the ball, the right timing and, at last, luck has intervened on their behalf. Of course, there's still the penalty shoot-out.

In the middle of all the euphoria Pep steps up to the plate, emotional but icily calm. He calls his people together in one big huddle. Everyone is there: doctors, physios, assistant coaches, players, substitutes and even the injured men, like Schweinsteiger. This is Pep at his brilliant best. The guy who rises to the big occasions and dazzles his men.

Relaxed and smiling, he pays no heed to the thousands of frenzied supporters around them. Apparently unaffected by the tension, he issues no battle cry, opting instead for an anecdote. About water polo. "Lads, I don't know how to take penalties myself," he said. "I've never taken one in my life. But here's the best penalty taker in the whole world."

And he points to a figure half hidden, right at the back of the huddle. "I'm talking about Manel [Estiarte]. He was the best water polo player in the world. He took penalties better than anyone. Hundreds of them. Water polo is like football. Only four out of every five penalty kicks hit the target, but Manel put them all away! He is the world expert on penalties."

Pep hasn't just managed to get the player's attention. He has completely changed the expressions on their faces. They had been waiting for motivational oratory, an adrenalin boost. What they receive, standing here in the midst of the clamouring, heaving mass of humanity that rocks the stadium, is a simple tale.

Van Buyten and Starke stand just behind Pep in their tracksuits, hugging each other; Doctor Müller-Wohlfart is beside them. Kroos, Lahm and Ribéry are right at the front. Alaba is leaning his elbow on Müller, also wearing a tracksuit, like Robben. Then there's a second circle: Javi Martínez, Shaqiri, Dante, Boateng and Mandžukić; the assistant coaches, Domènec Torrent and Hermann Gerland; Kirchhoff, the substitute; the physio Gianni Bianchi; the fitness coaches Lorenzo Buenaventura and Andreas Kornmayer; Götze; Claudio Pizarro; Rafinha and Contento. Matthias Sammer and Bastian Schweinsteiger are slightly separated from the main group and Manuel Neuer isn't here. He's off getting Toni Tapalović's advice about the Chelsea penalty takers. Estiarte, too, has stepped back a few metres.

The players are smiling. Silent but relaxed. They're enjoying the tone of this team talk. "I've learned two things from Manel and his penalties, so listen up. These are the only two things you need to do now. Firstly, make up your mind immediately as to where you're going to put the ball and stick with that decision. I'll say it again. Decide now, and don't change your mind no matter what happens. Secondly, keep telling yourselves that you're going to score. Repeat it a thousand times and don't stop until after you've taken the penalty. Don't worry and don't change your minds."

"What a team talk. Incredible!" Matthias Sammer says later.

But Pep hasn't finished. He gives them his advice and then says, "Lads, there's no list. You can choose whether or not to take one. You choose. You're all going to score anyway, so you decide who's taking them. Who's up for it?"

Alaba is the first to step forward, Kroos lifts his left hand next, followed quickly by Lahm. Pep gives his captain one of his little taps on the cheek. Next, Ribéry adds his name to the list and the coach slaps him encouragingly on the chest. It's Shaqiri's turn after that and he's rewarded with "Bravo, Shaq!" The players have come up with the list themselves, but what about the order they'll take them in?

"You sort that out. Take them in any order you want. Whatever you're comfortable with. It doesn't matter anyway, because they're all going in."

They decide to take them in the same order they volunteered. The referee indicates that it's time and they all turn away. Pep grabs Ribéry and Lahm, stopping the whole group in their tracks.

"Just one last thing. Don't forget. You've decided where you're putting the ball. Go and do it. And from now until you shoot keep telling yourself, 'It's going in'. With every step you take, say it, 'Goal, goal, goal...'"

Of the seven players who had practised on Monday scoring 42 out of 42, only Kroos and Shaqiri take penalties. Müller and Robben have both been substituted. Pizarro started on the substitutes' bench and of course Schweinsteiger is injured. Of the players who had not taken part in the practice session, Alaba, Lahm and Ribéry have been happy to volunteer. All five score. Neuer saves Chelsea's fifth penalty, taken by Romelu Lukaku, and Bayern have won the title that has so far eluded them. Pep has his first trophy with Bayern and his third European Super Cup.

Voted man of the match, Franck Ribéry dedicates the honour to his boss. "I know how much this means to him, his first title. I also know about his old rivalry with Mourinho." The Portuguese coach has left the pitch without congratulating Guardiola, in contrast to the obvious warmth between the two teams.

An hour later, in a corner of the press room in Prague's Eden Stadion, Guardiola and Estiarte chat to a couple of Catalan journalists, Isaac Lluch, of *Ara* and Ramon Besa of *El País*. Pep is absolutely radiant. His eyes are shining with happiness, but above all there is a sense of enormous relief. "The team needed this win. If we hadn't won, I don't know how we would have moved forward."

---

*This is an edited extract from Marti Perarnau's book* Pep Confidential, *published by BackPage Press.*

# 131

## The Sense of an Ending

"'It didn't look like the body of a man dragged for 50 metres under such a heavy truck."

# Fallen Eagle

*The death of the former Nigeria striker Rashidi Yekini remains shrouded in mystery*

**By Ewan MacKenna**

**Yemisi Yekini has a couple of overwhelming memories of her father. The first she makes sure to hold close every day. She wasn't yet a teenager but it's the simplicity of a stroll in the dense heat of a west Nigerian night, just her and him as they went to buy some spicy meat and sugar cane from a nearby market in Ibadan and shot the breeze along the way. "Everyone was saying hello to him and he was joking with me about things and it was just so lovely. I felt so close to him and felt so much love for him and I'll have that with me forever," she recalled.**

The other recollection she can never shed no matter how hard she tries. It's from a week after his funeral in the tiny village of Irra as – after travelling from London where she was born, raised and still lives – for the first time she laid eyes on his resting place in front of her grandmother's house. "The spot they buried him, it's so horrible," she said. "I mean, it's really horrible. When I was there it was just cement poured on top of him. I try to forget that and remember how he loved African movies and crime films and CSI and I remember being in his house watching those with him. But how can I forget what happened then? How can I ever forget it?"

Twenty years ago Rashidi Yekini gave us one of the most iconic images of the 1994 World Cup. His goal in the rout of Bulgaria was his country's first ever in the tournament and the emotion of the moment poured out across television screens around the globe as he stood entangled in the back of the net screaming. But in May of 2012 some reports say he died screaming in a traditional healing home, tied to the floor. His family in Nigeria are adamant he was suffering from mental health problems and they tried to intervene, but his friends and local police say he had a restraining order against them and that his family kidnapped him shortly before his death.

It was a bizarre, mysterious and shocking end to a life of noisy and historical highs entangled with the echoes of lonely lows. But if his death was incomprehensible by any standards, his life was unlikely considering his boyhood standards. He had little chance to be a somebody but he fought ferociously against nature and nurture as his close friend and barrister Jibril Mohammed recalled. "He lost his father when he was six or seven so he grew up with an uncle who was very, very mean to him. That left him with no one to look up to and he was bullied by that uncle and that shaped his personality a lot. His uncle chained him up, beat him and because of that he had problems trusting people. The only thing he had from his Dad was a portable radio which he used to listen to football matches on. But his uncle broke that radio so he got up at that moment and ran away from home."

Yekini was only 10 when he fled. He got by on the few coins he earned by washing boots and doing odd jobs for footballers at a nearby club. But other players weren't as accommodating once he started out on his own journey within the sport. As a striker with Africa Sports in Côte d'Ivoire in the 1980s, his trust issues continued to stalk him after he let a friend stay in his house only to discover afterwards the cash he was saving in his room had vanished while the friend had coincidentally just bought a new car. "He was a very shy person because of his background and throughout his life he grew very suspicious of people because of the way he grew up," said Mohammed. "That's why he kept to himself and people wrongly saw him as reclusive."

His brief marriage collapsed as he and his wife returned home apart from their honeymoon and separated. "What I gathered was when they got there he discovered that she had an ex-boyfriend and he was really not happy and had to break up with her," said Mohammed. But if his life off the field was turbulent, his life on it was tumultuous. Having scored 45 goals in 53 outings for Shooting Stars, he was just as astounding in Europe. Between 1990 and 1994 he hit 90 goals in 108 games for Vitória Setúbal before setting the World Cup ablaze.

"He was a very gentle and a very jovial person, he would make you laugh a lot at training and during matches," said his international teammate Mutiu Adepoju. "We all remember that goal but prior to the World Cup he won the African Nations Cup. The way he scored goals was fantastic and he is our record goalscorer which sums up his efforts. But you saw the emotion when he got that goal against Bulgaria, what it meant to him and of course he's always been proud to represent Nigeria. That celebration just showed what his country meant to him. He knew his country loved football and everyone in his country knew he loved them."

By the end, though, you got the sense that same country had abandoned him after the final whistle had sounded.

Yemisi Yekini had always suspected her real father lived elsewhere and it was on a trip to Nigeria a decade ago that her mother told the then 19 year old she was going to introduce her to her birth father. Asked about her emotions, she smiled. "Spending a couple of days with a man I'd never met and didn't know – well, I was terrified and didn't know what it would be like." She didn't know anything about Rashidi either and the name didn't set bells ringing as it would have with most football fans. However, the trophies dotted around the shelves and cabinets of his house prompted questions and pretty soon she was watching YouTube clips of him open-mouthed.

"I was so proud," she continued. "We sat down and he told me everything. About the break-up, about his time in Portugal, about his goals, about the World Cup. But I didn't see him as this superstar because he was so humble. OK, his house was big but there was nothing fancy about it. And not many people would come to visit him. There was one Muslim priest that he'd talk to but not much more than that. Everyone knew him there so it didn't seem like he was a big deal because everyone would say hello on the street and that's just how it was. They were used to seeing him walking around and he just quietly fitted in there."

On that trip she met her paternal grandmother as well: "She nearly died. They were like, 'Come here, is it really you?'" But after she'd returned to London, the situation in Nigeria slowly changed. "He was close with his family," said Mohammed. "In fact, he spent half of his fortune on his family. He opened a supermarket for his sister, for his younger brother he bought so many things, he bought his mother a two-storey building, for another one of his brothers he sponsored a trip to Côte d'Ivoire because he was a fine footballer. But Rashidi told me his change in attitude towards his siblings and mother was because they were concerned about his wealth and nothing more.

"That main problem started back as far as 2009. Plus, he was mad with his mother when she harboured a lady who claimed to have a baby for him. He was furious about that. Matters deteriorated from there. That hurt him a lot. He was seeking traditional solutions to those problems and met one or two people who were telling him to make sacrifices and that would appease God, like buy a ham and give it to a blind man and this kind of thing. But a lot of people misunderstood his personality. He was a very generous person and he was sponsoring people for education and was feeding homeless people. He never told anyone about it but word would get out about his charity and people thought that was strange and that there must be something odd about him."

Others have since suggested that he wasn't merely different but sick. Neighbours were quoted in Nigerian newspapers stating that he would wander aimlessly in the town, that his cars were in a state of disrepair to the point of being useless, that he was seen going to the toilet in a ditch, that he sacked his security guard and lived alone with a flock of peacocks and that his only company was the Champions League matches he'd watch on his own after firing up a generator outside his house. Another noted, "There was a time one of his younger brothers came from Kaduna or somewhere in the north, but because he was not expected, he was not allowed in. The guy slept outside and went back the following morning." Such tales led to claims ranging from depression to bipolar disorder and everything in between.

"No, no, he was fine," his daughter insisted. "Really, he was fine. When he called me he was perfect, usually every Sunday. He'd even talk to my Mum and tell her to get him some football gear because she'd travel from London quite a lot. He'd tell her, 'You know my favourite colour already so get me this and that.'" This is a view backed up by others. "Rashidi was very, very well towards the end of his life," said Mohammed. "He had a physician attend to his health and there was nothing wrong. But the money thing, everyone knows his family were greedy and it was a major problem.

"When his family were coming too much he felt he needed protection from the police to keep them away. I assisted him and we went to the commissioner of the police for the state and they asked what he was going through and why he needed protection. After that, the police called his family and they received a caution. The commissioner said they must respect his privacy as those were his wishes. But they couldn't control their greed. When he was giving them money, they didn't stop him. When he gave his money to people they thought didn't merit it, they couldn't handle that."

Yekini's mother, Alhaja Sikiratu, rejects the accusation. "We have been on the problem since 2010 and we tried our best but my son refused to be taken care of," she said. "When he came back, we asked him why he had done what he did but he replied by burning all his belongings. I lost my husband in 1978 and Rashidi has been with me since then."

Whatever the precise cause, turmoil in the family marked the beginning of his end.

The screensaver on the mobile phone of Mutiu Adepoju is a shot of Yekini from a time when the world was theirs. He says he'll keep it there forever because the past is all that can soothe the present. "I heard his family kidnapped him, that he had restraining orders against him," he said. "They came and took him because he was having mental problems but no one has ever confirmed that, it was just said a lot. And of course it's a mystery how he died, because nobody knew where they took him or what they did and nobody has put together a picture of what really happened."

Some facts that are known. When returning to his house from the regular training he did in the local stadium to stay in shape after his playing days were over, he got out of his car and went to unlock the gates of his compound. It was then that family members surprised him, placing him in shackles and dragging him into a nearby van. "When they came he was shouting that he wanted to be protected but nobody cared," said Mohammed.

A few days later, the phones of those closest to Rashidi Yekini began to ring. In London, Yemisi Yekini got a call from her aunt and was asked to come to the house. "I couldn't believe it," she said. "It just wasn't right, there were no answers, nothing. He didn't call as much as he used to and I was thinking about that afterwards. I should have known. But maybe I didn't talk to him as much as I should. Why didn't I call him? I blame myself for that every day. I was thinking he's my dad, he's a hero, he'll live forever. But I should have known something was wrong and made a call and helped him."

Back in Ibadan, Jibril Mohammed picked up the phone to news he refused to believe. "I said that could not be true, because I'd be one of the first to hear. I was asking where, when, how? I was told the burial would commence before dawn and he was buried without any inquiry, without any inquest, without any answers. He died of cardiac shock, the report said, but he had no history of any problem. It makes you wonder how that came about. When someone dies in mysterious circumstances there must be an inquest. That didn't happen because nobody cared. I did everything in my power but no one wanted to ask questions. He did so much for this country and it forgot him then.

"Who handled him when he was dying, who treated him, what did they treat him for, what drugs were they administering? And the real question is where did he die? He was taken to a home and was chained to the ground, he was chained to the floor. This man was chained to the floor in a traditional healing home. He died and his family took him straight to his home town and by the following morning he was buried by 10. I requested it be postponed so any inquest could be made into his death but nobody cared. His family came to take him away and he died in their hands."

Nearby, Mutiu Adepoju broke down when he heard of the death of the man he shared his greatest moments with two decades before: "Just complete shock when the words were said to me. I couldn't sleep. And unfortunately for some months before he died we were not able to talk with him, he was not able to be contacted. He seemed to withdraw further and further, even when you call him he would never pick up calls. You are left with this empty feeling. It's horrible."

At the burial Mohammed was furious with the family and told Yekini's mother she should be remorseful and not give interviews to media while showing so little regret. "I thought there was something fishy because of her reaction," he said. "She refused to tell me about the traditional home, she refused to tell anyone that. She just kept saying he died and that's all."

But when Yemisi made it to the ceremony to mark a week after the burial, she dared not even raise the issue. "When I went, there was this massive meal and his family were all claiming money," she said. "They can have it, I don't care about that, but it was so awkward to be in the middle of them. He's just buried and they are fighting over his money. Who does that? And I felt scared, kids in Africa, they can't say anything. Especially in Nigeria, you have to be so careful. I had a security guard at the anniversary. I had to have a security guard with me for my protection – to see my dad's grave. They say he was sick, but where are the records? There's no proof, no death certificate, did he even see a doctor?

"Did anyone even see the body? He was buried under concrete so quickly, and his family there didn't even call me and there are so many ways to call from Nigeria. But they didn't even do that. I never even saw his body. All I kept thinking was my Dad is dead, my Dad is dead, my Dad is dead. And now the biggest thing is the lack of closure. None of it makes any sense. It's all so wrong. He's supposed to be this Nigerian superstar, he's supposed to be this hero to people there, they are supposed to love him. I know it's corrupt there but what happened is so disgusting. And what if..."

She paused for a moment before finishing the sentence. "What if it was his own family," she cried. "It makes it so inhumane and makes my stomach feel sick. And honestly, I think that every day because it all comes back to money and I saw that after the funeral. And of course I look online and read reports in African papers saying he was tied and chained up and dragged from his house. And a week later he was dead. It hurts so much to read all of that. That pain won't go away."

# On the Road

*25 years ago the Cosenza midfielder Denis Bergamini was run over by a truck. Was it murder?*

**By Alessandro Mastrolucca**

**A dead body on a wet road in front of a truck, a Hitchcockian girl and a mysterious car. These elements form a puzzle still missing vital pieces after 25 years. Why was the Cosenza midfielder Denis Bergamini, real name Donato, who had been born in Boccaleone d'Argenta, near Ferrara, found dead on Saturday 18 November 1989? A sloppy enquiry concluded he had committed suicide because he was sick of Italy and the world of football. Too many pieces of evidence, however, weren't considered and the case has since been reinvestigated as a murder.**

That Saturday, Cosenza, then playing in the Italian second division, completed their final training session before the following day's derby against Messina. A couple of seasons before, the *Rossoblu* were denied a dreamlike promotion to Serie A by an unfavourable goal difference. But then, the club's financial conditions worsened and they were almost forced to declare bankruptcy. The 1989-90 season started disappointingly and Cosenza had collected just nine points in the twelve matches before the derby.

The morning of Bergamini's last day began with a bad omen. During training, he found a dead owl on the pitch. In an interview with the local paper *Gazzetta del Sud,* he had encouraged his teammates, as he always did on the pitch. On the same pages, that same day, there was an article detailing the dangerousness of the Statale Jonica, the coast road from Reggio Calabria to Taranto, accompanied by an image of the castle at Roseto Capo Spulico. Bergamini would be found dead just there.

Bergamini's body lies prone, the head pointing towards the centre of the road, in front of a red truck. His hair was brushed, his gilet impeccably pressed, his shoes clean even though it had been raining for hours, his wristwatch still working. At 19:30, Brigadiere Francesco Barbuscio of the *carabinieri* arrived. Two hours earlier, Barbuscio had stopped Bergamini's car, a white Maserati, at Roseto Marina just few miles away. At the crime scene, *carabinieri* found only Raffaele Pisano, the truck driver, who was carrying 138 tons of tangerines from Rosarno to Milan. He explained that Bergamini had thrown himself under his truck and that he'd kept going for 50 metres before managing to stop the vehicle. He then moved briefly in reverse to check if Bergamini was still alive. But it didn't look like the body of a man dragged for 50 metres under such a heavy truck.

When he stopped, Pisano added, a young woman came from the Maserati that she had manoeuvred towards the road and said, "He was my boyfriend, he wanted to kill himself." She was Isabella Internò, Bergamini's sometime girlfriend. They had been engaged from 1985 to the end of 1988, after which their relationship suffered a lot of ups and downs. She moved the car, according to the official version, from the edge of the road where it was parked: the photos taken by the *carabinieri* showed, in fact, the Maserati behind Pisano's truck at the scene. Internò, however, wasn't there. Pisano told Barbuscio she had stopped a man passing by in his car and that he had taken her to Roseto Marina. In his report, Barbuscio wrote he found Isabella outside a bar-restaurant in the Maserati, the same he had seen and reported on the crime scene few minutes earlier. No matter how confusing it may sound, he wrote in his report that he had seen the same Maserati in two different places almost at the same time. Consequently, it became much harder to answer to the most relevant question in this story: how did Isabella arrive there? That's the key issue, the main mystery in this shadowy story.

Internò said, and has maintained, that Denis Bergamini committed suicide. She said that her former boyfriend called her at about 16:00, picked her up in his white Maserati and set off towards Taranto because he was sick of football and wanted to go to Greece or to the Azores to change his life. She believed him even though he hadn't brought any luggage or money, except the cheque with which he was paid his salary. They talked for a long time, she said, in an unpaved area by the side of the road, then Bergamini asked her to go back before getting out of the car and throwing himself under the wheels of the truck like a diver plunging into a swimming pool.

The image, though, doesn't fit with the results of the autopsy produced on 4 January 1990, two months after Bergamini's death. Initially, Cosenza's president had persuaded his family to forgo the autopsy so they could take his body back home sooner. Dr Avato found a single wound, located to the front and on the right side of his trunk. If he had really dived with his head towards the centre of the road with the truck coming from his left, the wound should have been located exactly on the opposite side. The doctor concluded that the truck was going very slowly while a single wheel only partially ran over his body – not at all like a body dragged for 50 metres.

Bergamini's family didn't believe the story from the start. Bergamini was a model of professionalism and had never abandoned a training camp or session before a match: to them, this account of his behaviour had always sounded strange. Football was his dream, his priority, and the previous summer Parma and Fiorentina, two leading clubs in Serie A at the time, approached him and Cosenza agreed to triple his wages to persuade him not to leave. Could a man in his position, starting to realise his ambition, a man considered a true icon by his fans, who named an end of the stadium after him, have suddenly become sick of football?

When his family arrived from Ferrara, driving all night to identify Bergamini's body, Barbuscio repeated to Domizio, Denis's father, the story Isabella had told him and reluctantly agreed to take them to the spot where he had found the body. However, the family didn't see any evidence, any trace of blood and it was only some days later, watching television, that they realised Barbuscio had taken them somewhere else. In the morgue, meanwhile, a nurse had prevented Bergamini's mother from giving her son a final kiss because, she had said, his body was destroyed. Lifting up the sheet, though, his mother saw Denis's face almost intact. They asked to have at least his clothes back and they were told they had already been burned. Yet his teammates remembered that the clothes officials described were on the team bus after the funeral. Bergamini's family has never recovered them. They obtained just the watch, his gold chain and the shoes he was wearing when he died, which were surrounded by a further mystery. It was a club handyman, Domenico Corrente, who grabbed the shoes and gave them to Domizio Bergamini, promising he would have something important to tell him at the end of the season. But after the final match, he died in a car accident near Roseto Capo Spulico with another warehouse worker, Alfredo Rende. Strangely, Corrente's family strongly denies this story and denies that Domenico had anything to do with the shoes. Why are they so sensitive, given Domenico is not being accused of anything but is being praised for having done the right thing?

The day after the body was discovered, the coroner examined it and established that Bergamini died on Saturday afternoon between 13:50 and 18:50. Less than 24 hours after his death, *carabinieri* had in front of them a self-evident inconsistency about the time of death, but nobody checked Internò or Pisano's story to see why they had put the time of death at around 19:30. Besides, the tachograph card of Pisano's truck showed he made a stop between 17:55 and 18:05 without turning off the engine. Could that be the true time of death? And, if so, what happened in following hour and a half, before the Cosenza coach Gigi Simoni received the dramatic call announcing Bergamini's death?

Despite all the contradictions, the *carabinieri* were immediately persuaded that Bergamini committed suicide. They didn't look back. They were so committed to this version that they gave the Maserati back to Bergamini's family the same night and allowed Pisano to leave their headquarters in his truck, without completing any kind of analysis. Even the expert witness appointed to reconstruct what could have happened was forced to base his conclusions exclusively on the photographs taken by the *carabinieri*. And yet, there were plenty of reasons to believe things weren't so simple.

The previous Sunday, 12 November 1989, after his last match in Monza, Bergamini remained in Milan, sleeping with a friend, Giuliana, at the Hilton Hotel. The following Monday he went back home and spontaneously declared he hadn't had sex with her. He was normally shy, so why did he decide to confess such a detail? Bergamini seemed happy, recalls his sister Donata, and eager to celebrate her daughter's fifth birthday. At around 19:30 he got a short phone call. He said almost nothing, but his mood dramatically changed. He started to sweat and looked shocked for a while, before calming down. He offered no detail about the call. Then, on Thursday 17, according to *Gazzetta dello Sport*, two men threatened Bergamini while he was having dinner in a restaurant near Cosenza. Michele Padovano, the former Juventus striker who was at the time playing at Cosenza and living in the same house as Bergamini, denied this. He said they shared almost every meal in the same restaurant and that nothing like that had occurred. Nobody has ever checked what really happened, but the next day Bergamini called his girlfriend, Roberta, and told her that someone in Cosenza had something against him. When she tried to find out more, Denis said the only thing he had done wrong was to break with Isabella. Why did he believe that decision could have been perceived as a fault?

On the morning of his last day, Bergamini finished training at 11:45 before going to the Motel Agip in Rende, a tiny town nearby, as Cossenza's players did before all their home matches. He arrived at 12:30. During those 45 minutes Francesco Marino and his teammate Castagnini met Internò at Commenda di Rende. They met casually, he said, and had a brief chat, but she didn't tell Denis. After lunch, Denis went to the room that he shared with Padovano, who testified that Denis received a phone call at around 14:45 that changed his mood. As ever, he didn't share his feelings. According to the usual routine before home matches, at 16:30 players and staff went to a cinema, the Garden, in Rende. Unusually, on this occasion Bergamini decided to make the short journey in his car with the masseur, Giuseppe Maltese, one of his closest friends in the squad. He had rarely gone to the cinema with the players, but that day he made an exception. So it seemed odd when Bergamini asked him, knowing he wasn't used to going there, where the bathrooms were. The movie hadn't started but the lights had already been turned off when Denis left the room and the cinema. That was the last time his teammates saw Denis alive. One of the players, Sergio Galeazzi, testified he saw two figures, two shadows near Bergamini while he was going down the stairs: however, they could have been simply two late customers searching for their seats.

In 2010, the man who worked as a car park attendant at the Garden in 1989 said that Bergamini left the cinema in a black car with a beautiful girl. But he was suffering from Alzheimer's disease: can his memory be relied upon? There's another relevant witness, though, the former owner of the Garden: he remembered that Bergamini made two phone calls and then left the cinema alone. Did he call Internò from there at 16:00? Perhaps. Did someone chase him from the cinema car park? Nobody knows.

That is not even the most puzzling aspect of that dramatic afternoon. After the movie, Simoni realised that the most professional player in his squad had disappeared. He was surprised but, according to his statement to the *carabinieri,* he didn't ask his players to see if any of them knew what had happened. None of them did anything; they simply came back to the motel. Only Maltese, a little concerned, asked the receptionist if Bergamini was back. He hadn't seen him, he said, adding that the keys to his room hadn't been handed in. Maltese went upstairs and found them in the keyhole, on the outside of the door. The room was empty but the lights were on. What had happened? Did Denis forget to turn them off and inadvertently left the keys going out? Or had he come back from the cinema during the movie?

The only trial conducted so far didn't answer any of these questions. Pisano was charged with second-degree murder in 1991 and acquitted: the lower court and the appeal court believed Internò and were persuaded that Bergamini committed suicide, although they weren't able to identify a plausible reason.

It's impossible in this story to know the exact position and the movements of the main characters at the crucial minutes. We don't know what Bergamini did or where he went when he left the cinema. Above all, we don't know how Isabella Internò arrived from Roseto Capo Spulico, where she said her ex-boyfriend had just committed suicide, at Roseto Marina, 3km north of that point. In Roseto Marina, she and Denis had been stopped at a checkpoint at 17:30. After Denis's death, a driver passing by took Isabella to a bar-restaurant in Roseto Marina where she made some phone calls. It was outside there that the *carabinieri* found her, as Barbuscio wrote. But how did she get there?

Mario Infantino, the bar's owner, told the *carabinieri* that he had spoken with the unknown helper: "a man", he said, "who left his family in their car and drove Isabella in her Maserati." Did he bring the car back, too? Did Isabella trust him so much? A month later, however, he changed his version of events, saying Isabella had arrived in the helper's car around 19:30. Some years ago, the Bergaminis' lawyer, Eugenio Gallerani, managed to find the unknown driver, a man named Mario Panunzio, during his enquiry that led to the case being reopened.

The second, related, mystery remained just as unclear: whom did she call? Bergamini's mother and Cosenza's coach, Gigi Simoni, Isabella said in her first statements to the *carabinieri.* Infantino soon contradicted her, recalling she had made three calls, the last to Francesco Marino, the player she had met that morning in Commenda di Rende. Is that just a coincidence? Simoni, anyway, said he had spoken twice with Internò, who had briefly handed the phone to an unknown man: so, was the helper, Panunzio, with her or not? And why had Isabella never said this during the preliminary enquiries?

Finally, why did Isabella ask to speak to Marino, of all the players? According to Simoni, because they were good friends, but Marino denied this. Isabella asked him if Bergamini had confided something to him that day: a strange question to ask to a not-so-close friend, hours after a casual meeting: but was it really casual? Why did neither Internò nor Marino tell Denis about it? We'll never know. All Isabella said to the public prosecutor Ottavio Abate on July 1990 was that she had forgotten to tell *carabinieri* about that call to Marino because it didn't matter to her.

But there's a final *coup de théâtre.* In 2011, Infantino testified to the new prosecutor in Castrovillari, Franco Giacomantonio. In a television interview, he had already revealed a detail that contradicted his previous version and the whole reconstruction of events. Now he said that Isabella's helper remained outside the bar and that they must have arrived much before 19:30 because you could see the sun. So, when exactly did Bergamini die?

Denis's car, the white Maserati, plays a crucial role in the mystery surrounding his death, not only because in Cosenza at that time, it was almost unique and so immediately recognisable. Bergamini bought it from Santo Fiorentino, a Cosenza executive, cousin of a local criminal whose wife owned the car. Bergamini paid 35 million lire for the Maserati, but he and Fiorentino agreed to put on record a lower price, 25 million.

According to local journalists, the club insisted that Bergamini should buy that car, leading to much speculation. They talked about drug-trafficking, they said that someone unknown to him had carried drugs in a hidden compartment, benefiting from the substantial protection the Maserati's celebrity guaranteed, and concluded he was killed because he had discovered the trick. In 2011, however, Bergamini's family and their lawyer, Eugenio Gallerani, traced the car and found it in the garage of its latest owners, a couple of collectors living in Valle di Cadore in the north of Italy. They had bought the car in 1993 and almost never drove it, so they agreed to resell it to the Bergaminis for €1000. The *carabinieri* of the Special Investigations Unit (RIS) in Messina inspected the Maserati, found it had all the original parts and no false bottoms. Although traffickers could have transported drugs in another way, the theory presents more than a few problems. Why would hypothetical traffickers have left the Maserati, the proof of their crime, on the scene? And it's almost as implausible to believe the same hypothetical criminals didn't stage a more plausible accident.

The recent enquiry focused on the love story between Denis and Isabella Internò, believing the cause of his death is hidden in the context of their troublesome relationship. She was almost 16 when she met Bergamini, 23 at the time. She was in love and jealous, he was in love too but messed around with other women, according to his teammates. He was handsome, a footballer, an icon in Cosenza: it's easy to imagine how many women wanted to have sex with him, and apparently he seldom said no.

In the summer of 1987, Internò fell pregnant, but wanted an abortion. Denis asked his sister Donata for help and she took Isabella to her gynaecologist. He confirmed Internò was five months pregnant, meaning an abortion was illegal. Denis assured his girlfriend he was ready to take responsibility for the child, but Internò insisted. Her aunt found a private clinic in London where Denis accompanied her to have the abortion. In his wallet, after his death, *carabinieri* found a handwritten note with the address and the phone number of that clinic, together with some banknotes and a post-dated cheque from the club. Why did he take that note with him on that day, more than two years after the abortion? Nobody knows.

Isabella and Denis broke up in September 1988, but she continued to call him, to search for him, even though he had a new girlfriend. In the summer of 1988, Bergamini discovered Isabella had had an affair with a former

Cosenza player, Gabriele Baldassarri, although they never had sex. Bergamini was angry, knowing how word gets around in the world of football. From then on, Denis seemed changed, worried. Initially his family thought it was due to a serious injury he had suffered in November 1988 but matters didn't improve after he came back to play football.

In the same period, Isabella had a second abortion in Cosenza, according to the *carabinieri* inspecting the register of a clinic dating back to the winter of 1988 and the beginning of 1989. Was Bergamini the father? Did her family know the whole truth about it? After a quarter of a century, finding the answers to these questions might finally lead to close the case.

# 146

## Fiction

"Tea's got lazy. Tea's stood still."

# Quantum of Bobby

*Spinning through time and space, Bobby Manager finds himself at Roy Keane's Sunderland*

**By Iain Macintosh**

***Theorising that radio-controlled clouds could help Qatar manufacture a climate suitable for football, the authorities experimented...and nearly killed their national coach Bobby Manager with one. Manager awoke to find himself trapped in the past, facing challenges that were not his own, driven to change history for the better. His only guide on this journey is Karren Brady, or at least a subconscious manifestation of Karren Brady, who speaks to him in a voice that only Bobby can hear. And so Bobby Manager finds himself leaping from life to life, striving to put right what once went wrong and hoping each time that his next leap will be the leap home.***

Thump. You always land with a thump. I don't know why, I don't really understand the process, but when you're ripped through space and time and deposited somewhere new, it's definitely with a thump, like you've been unceremoniously dropped from the jaws of a mechanical digger. And then there's the pain.

Oh God, the pain. Drunks might learn how to drink, sailors may become accustomed to the sea, but I will never get used to leaping. A searing internal pain, as if your spine has been ripped out and hurled through a plate glass window, mixed with swirling nausea and a headache that could...

"I'm not even sorry!" roared a furious Irish voice.

"What?" I whimpered, face down on wet grass. I rolled over, opened my eyes and was horrified to see a dark-haired, bearded man with eyes like the fires of hell itself leaning over me, his finger jabbing just inches from my face. First impressions can often be deceiving, but he really seemed upset about something.

"Take that, you cunt!" he shouted. "I remember what you did! I remember how you acted! I've waited a long time for this!"

"What did I do?" I shrieked, looking around. A couple of dozen footballers, clad in black and red, simply stared at their shoes.

"You read my newspaper, you bastard. I can always tell, you know. I can always tell. The fold is all out of kilter, you shitbag!"

Well, I did the only thing a man can do when he's at the mercy of a maniac. I let my eyes roll back in my head and went as limp as a warm salad.

"Don't pretend you're unconscious!" he bellowed. "Don't be a liar as well as a thief!" He shook me like a crumpled duvet. I gave up playing dead.

"This isn't how you deal with a head injury!" I wailed, eyes still tightly closed against his rain of spittle.

"Boss!" shouted one of the players. "Come on, boss, leave him alone!"

He stopped shaking me and dropped me back on the turf. Then he turned around to the source of the sound.

"Nyron fucking Nosworthy," he sneered. "I never knew you had the balls. As for the rest of you, you sicken me. I'm assaulting your assistant manager right in front of you and all you can do is stand there quietly and watch. What kind of a team do I have here? What kind of men are you? No wonder everyone keeps beating us."

And with that, he stood up and stormed off the training pitch, delivering a full payload of inventively assembled swearwords as he went.

Some of the players helped me to my feet. One of them examined my forehead.

"Are you all right, Bobby?" asked Nyron kindly. "That was a pretty heavy hit you took."

"Where am I?" I wibbled.

"Aye, let's get you back in the dressing-room, Bobby," said a large, middle-aged Scotsman. "You've had a bang on the head. We'll get you a cup of tea, that'll set you right. Come on lads, back to work. Let's have two laps before I'm back and we'll split up into groups."

"Who are you?" I asked as he helped me off the pitch, wrapping my arm around his thick shoulders.

He chuckled.

"He hit you pretty hard, didn't he? I'm Ricky Sbragia, I'm the coach. You're Bobby Manager. And that force of nature who just shook you silly, that was Roy Keane."

"Oh boy," I said.

"Don't worry," said Ricky. "It's not like you're the first person he's lost his rag with this year. You remember how he threatened to break all of Pascal Chimbonda's fingers after the 5-0 at Stamford Bridge? And poor Andy Reid after we lost at home to Portsmouth? How he said he'd feed him to the pigs, but we didn't have enough pigs to even make a dent in his big, fat arse? Aye, he's having a tough time of it, is the boss."

"And this is how he motivates people to do better?"

"Yep," smiled Ricky. "Welcome to Sunderland. I think you'll find..."

There were panicked shouts from behind us. Ricky spun around.

"What's going on?" I asked.

"Aw, crap. El-Hadji Diouf's gone broken arrow again. It's hard to tell from here, but it looks like he's sitting on Michael Chopra and he's trying to spit in his mouth. God's teeth, I really thought we'd sorted this out. Bobby, are you all right to get to the dressing-room on your own? Just have a shower and a bit of a rest, aye? I'm sure the boss will be along to talk it out with you soon. He never stays mad for long. Mind you, he never stays happy for long either. What a life, eh? DIOUF! STOP GOBBING IN CHOPS' MOUTH, MAN!"

Ricky thundered off to break up the scuffle and I was left to stagger into the dressing-room alone. Just once, it would be nice if I didn't arrive in a new point in space and time with a traumatic head injury. Maybe one day I could just wake up in a nice, soft bed, surrounded by cushions with a nice cup of tea on the bedside table. Would that be too much to ask? I stripped off my muddy training kit and stepped into the shower, letting the hot water do its work.

"Ah, Bobby, we meet again," said a firm female voice in my head.

"Karren Brady, I presume?" I said, as I began to wash the mud out of my hair.

"But, of course!"

"So, come on then, give me the spiel."

"Spiel, Bobby? Spiel? I'm not pitching for a movie, you know. This is serious stuff. A series of intellectual challenges, each more difficult than the last, designed and engineered to test every facet of your ability as a manager. Bobby, everything we do together here is interwoven, dozens of stories combining to one end only: to bring you out of this coma. This is the only way, Bobby. All else is darkness."

"But Sunderland? Seriously?"

"Sunderland indeed. November 2008. The last days of Roy Keane's reign at the Stadium of Light. After dragging this football club straight back into the Premier League and just about holding them there in their first season back, it's all started to fall apart. A summer spending spree has made little difference to results. Morale in the dressing-room is rock bottom. The players are terrified of their manager but, as I gather you've just discovered, they have good reason. A win over Blackburn Rovers at the weekend has provided some respite, but Keane does not have long."

"So I have to save Keane's job?" I said, reaching out to turn off the water.

"Perhaps not even that," said Karren enigmatically.

"You never make it easy, do you?"

"Why would I make it easy?" she hissed. "The whole point is to make you work. You're flat out in a hospital bed in Qatar, Bobby. Your muscles are atrophying, your brain is wasting away. But if you die, I die. And I do not wish to die today. So, yes, Bobby, I do make it hard. I do strive to find ever more testing circumstances for you. But with good reason."

"I know, Karren. And I do appreciate it, but just sometimes, I don't know, maybe sometimes you could make it seem like you're having less fun?"

"Who's Karren?" came a voice from outside the shower, low and even, as calm as a circling shark.

I wrapped a towel around myself hurriedly and stepped out into the dressing-room. Roy was sat on one of the benches, straight-backed and alert, staring at me in a way that made me feel like a main course.

"You hear them too, do you Bobby?"

"Hear what, sorry?" I asked uncertainly. "The voices in the shower," he said, looking around nervously. "They come to me as well."

I wasn't sure what to say.

"Sometimes they tell me to do things, Bobby. The voices. They tell me to do things that I don't want to do."

I offered a trembling smile.

"Okay. Well...erm..."

"Bobby?"

"Yes?" I squeaked.

"I'm fucking with you."

"Okay!" I blurted.

"Come on, man? Where's your sense of humour?" He stood up, strode over and gave me a slap on the shoulder. "I'm sorry about earlier, Bobby. I've been having a bit of a time of it and I lost my temper. Come on, get your clothes on and we'll have a cup of tea."

He walked out and left me alone in the dressing-room, trembling in my towel. I had never needed a poo more.

Roy could not have been more charming when I arrived in his office, ten minutes later. He welcomed me in to his domain warmly, offered me a seat in front of his desk and then buzzed his secretary for refreshments.

"Time to talk West Ham, Bobby," he said. "The players enjoyed the Blackburn win, and right enough too. They did well. But we couldn't ask for a better opportunity to get back-to-back wins than this. They're seven games without a win and it's a long journey for them. Their heads will be low and they'll be tired and out of sorts. It's three points waiting to happen, so I don't want any mistakes here. Win this and I think we can start to turn this season around."

The door opened and his secretary slipped in with a tray of tea.

"I'll be Mam, shall I?" smiled Roy as he poured from the pot. "I'm so sorry, Bobby. I can't remember if you take sugar or not."

"I don't, thanks," I said.

"Neither do I," he twinkled. "I think we're both sweet enough already, eh? Ha!"

"Roy," I said. "What happened this morning?"

"We've spoken about this morning," he said, still smiling. "Don't give it another moment's thought. This is a Premier League football club. If we stopped to analyse every bit of friction, we'd never get anything done. We both want to win, that's a good thing, a positive thing. We'll leave it at that."

I nodded and took a long sip of tea.

"Mmmm," I said approvingly. "That is a lovely cup of tea,"

A shadow seemed to pass across the room.

"Is it?" he said coldly.

"Well...yes, I think so," I said quietly.

"Do you want to know what I think?" he said, not even pausing for an answer. "I think to myself, sure, tea's been good in the past, tea's been great, tea's been the perfect antidote to anything from a bad day in the office to a slight case of the snuffles, but you know what? Tea's got lazy. Tea's stood still. Tea's spent too much time patting itself on the back and showing off its medals. And it hasn't even noticed that coffee is getting better all the time."

"Okay..."

"No, Bobby, it's not okay. This is exactly the kind of thing I was talking about. We've all got complacent here. We're all, la lala, we got promoted. We're all, la lala, we stayed up. We're so busy celebrating the last thing that happened that we never think about the next step. What the fuck have we got to celebrate, eh? We're a bog standard Premier League club. The biggest team we beat last season was Aston Villa. The biggest team we've beaten this season is Newcastle, and that doesn't count because Joe Kinnear is their manager."

"But Roy..."

"No, don't you 'But Roy' me, Bobby. Don't you dare," he said, jabbing his finger again. "We win against West Ham, or so help me God, I will go to town on this squad with a pick-axe."

"I just said that it was a nice cup of tea, Roy."

He sat back in his chair and shook his head. The room seemed to brighten slightly.

"Well, let's just agree to differ, shall we? Now, tell me what you know about West Ham."

It didn't take me long to realise that this was just a part of life with Roy. That you had to cope with these extraordinary mood swings, that when the storm broke, you simply had to tape up the windows and hide under the table until it passed. It was the same for the whole squad. The next day, I was walking to the canteen with Djibril Cissé and we heard Roy's voice coming around the corner. Djibril squealed in fear, ripped a ventilation cover off the wall and spent the afternoon hiding in the air conditioning ducts. All because he knew that Roy thought he should have scored two against Blackburn, not just one.

It didn't seem like a very healthy way to run a football team. I thought that Roy would do better to moderate his moods a little, but every time I suggested anything of the sort, he just turned those eyes on me and my legs went to jelly.

But my suspicions were confirmed when West Ham came to the Stadium of Light. One goal down at half-time thanks to our failure to clear our lines at a set-piece, I'd watched from the bench as Roy had run the full gamut of emotions from angry to angrier. His fists clenched and unclenched as we struggled to get to grips with Gianfranco Zola's side. When Djibril headed wide when unmarked in the box, Roy made a low, ominous rumbling noise that seemed to last for many minutes. Movement up above me caught my eye and I saw hundreds of birds, all sorts of breeds, flapping in a panic, desperate to clear our airspace. It was all a little disconcerting. Roy left the technical area just before the half-time whistle blew.

"Chin up, Djibril," I said, patting our striker on the back as we walked down the tunnel. "You're getting in the right positions, that's what counts. And besides..." I leaned into him and whispered, "...If the boss is going to have a pop at anyone, it's going to be El-Hadji Diouf, isn't it?"

We both turned and saw Diouf spitting in the face of Delilah, the Black Cat mascot who'd tried to shake his hand as he walked down the tunnel. We laughed. Yep, Diouf would clearly be the whipping boy today. We were wrong.

We knew something was amiss as soon as we walked into the dressing-room because the tactics board was on fire. We stood and stared as the smoke coiled around the room, too stunned to know what to do.

"Out of the way, ya daft bastards! Let me put it out!" shouted Ricky and he bundled in with a large fire extinguisher.

"Leave that fire alone!" roared Roy's voice from a toilet cubicle.

"Are you crazy, Roy?" Ricky bellowed back. "We'll all die of smoke inhalation here!"

There was a long pause and then a crash as the door to the cubicle was booted off its hinges. Calmly, Roy strode out, picked up the door and used it to smash the blazing tactics board across the room, guiding it straight into the shower with a perfectly executed square cut that would not have looked out of place down the road at Chester-le-Street, were it not for the fact that it was executed with a toilet door. Roy then threw the door down, reached into the showers and turned them on, condemning what remained of his plans to a watery grave. He turned around and looked his squad up and down.

"El-Hadji," he said with a sepulchral rasp. "If I hear of you violating Delilah again, I will remove your saliva glands with a ice cream scoop."

El-Hadji fainted.

"Reidy," he said, addressing our tubby winger. "If you don't start tackling back, I'll make you eat them."

Andy looked thoughtful for a moment and then conflicted. Then he shuddered and turned away. Then licked his lips. Then he started to sob.

"Roy?" I asked quietly.

"Shut it, Bobby."

"Okay!" I said brightly.

Roy reached behind him and pulled a claw hammer out of his back pocket. The whole squad took a step backwards as one.

"You will get back out there and win this game," he growled. "Or I will start popping kneecaps. Do you understand me?

They didn't win. They lost. And a number of players jumped the advertising hoardings and sneaked out with the fans.

"What are you going to do?" whispered Karren as I watched Kenwyne Jones try to squeeze himself into the hood of an old lady's anorak. "Keane won't last long if he carries on like this."

"I don't know," I mumbled. "But I'm going to have to try something, aren't I? If we don't beat Bolton next weekend, we're in serious trouble."

The following afternoon, I took Roy to a quiet little cafe in Roker. It was a bracing autumnal day, overcast and moody. The sea was crashing against Roker Pier, sending white spray all over the small lighthouse at the end. It was the perfect sort of day to hide away with a nice cup of tea. Having spent the last few weeks in a German prisoner-of-war camp in 1944 and a week before that at Italia 90 with Bobby Robson, I suddenly realised how much I'd missed home.

But any thought of relaxation vanished when Roy told the old lady behind the counter that, "Did you want a mug or a cup?" was, "a stupid question, the kind of pointless, stupid, ridiculous question that no-one really cares about. Have you really not got anything better to ask me than, 'Did you want a mug or a cup?' Stick it up your bollix."

It was so awkward, the poor woman had a bit of a funny turn and the owner had to call her husband to pick her up.

We sat down as discreetly as we could at a small table by a vast window that looked out to sea. Behind me, a noticeboard carried a cheerful advert for Christmas shopping with cartoon penguins all over it.

"Penguins," he snarled at me, shaking his head in dismay. "Absolute gobshite wankers."

I shook my head.

"Roy, this isn't working." I said firmly.

"Well, that's your fault, Bobby, you chose this place."

"No, not the cafe, Roy," I said. "This. This job. Sunderland. You're not happy and the players are not happy and the club is going to get relegated. You've got to change. You can't keep treating people like this. It doesn't matter who it is, it could be your top goalscorer, your assistant manager or even that poor woman who was only doing her job by asking you if you wanted a mug or a cup. You've got everyone running scared and no-one works well when they're scared."

"Pah!" snorted Roy. "You want to know what it's like working scared, you should have worked with Brian Clough. He once removed one of Darren Wassall's kidneys in his sleep and sold it to Malaysian organ traders, just to teach him not to be late for training. But I'll tell you what, it worked. That's discipline, Bobby."

"That's not discipline, Roy," I said in horror. "That's awful. And illegal on a number of levels."

"And what about Ferguson, eh?" smiled Keane grimly. "I mean, I wasn't scared of him and you can forget about that hairdryer nonsense, but I still remember him threatening to nail Nani to the wall as a warning to others. And look at all the things Ferguson won."

"But you're missing the point, Roy. The game has changed. We don't respond to that level of discipline anymore. Football's changed, there isn't the risk in the dressing-room now. In your day, the manager could fine you two weeks wages and you might struggle to make your mortgage payment that month. Nowadays, the players might not even notice. In the old days, if you were shipped out of a big club because you'd upset the manager, your reputation would be poisoned and you might never get back at that level. Christ, Roy, a modern-day player could gun down a litter of puppies on live television and the supporters would hit Twitter in their droves, posting grainy pictures to 'prove' that the puppies fired first. Even if the club did sack him or sell him, there would be five other clubs tripping over themselves to offer him enormous wages. You can't frighten these people into following instructions. It's a false economy. What you need to do is care."

"Why Bobby? You tell me one reason why I should care," he snarled.

"Because if you don't," I said, "you'll be out of this job in no time. They'll stop playing for you, they'll resent you and they'll cost you your best chance at replicating your success as a player in the dugout. And, yeah, you might get another job, but it won't be at this level and if you don't change your ways, the same things will happen. You've got to change. "

"I'm not changing," he said coldly. "They can change."

"You've got to change, Roy," I said quietly. "Because if you're not in football, you'll be outside football looking in. You'll be an angry pundit, losing his temper with everything. You'll be a columnist, railing against the dying of the light and telling everyone how much better it used to be in your day. You'll be writing autobiography after autobiography, every one a bleak and nasty exercise in score settling. Roy, if you don't change...you'll be Eamon Dunphy."

Roy stared at me.

"You say that again...If you've got the balls."

"You. Will. Be. Eamon. Dunphy."

"I should kill you where you stand," Roy growled.

"Search your heart, Roy. You know it to be true."

Outside, the rain lashed against the window, the trees bent almost double against the wind.

"Look at that out there," he said quietly. "Wet, windy, wild and nasty. And it's like that here almost every day from September to April. God, I love it here in the North-East. I don't want to leave."

"You don't have to leave, Roy. You can make this work. You just need to control your emotions."

Roy's head dropped.

"I just get so...angry, Bobby. It's like an explosion inside me and I just can't stop it from going off."

"I have some relaxation techniques. I can share them with you if you like?"

He stared at me.

"None of that hippy crap is it? Because you can stick that up your bollix."

"No, it's not...hang on, how would I stick it up my bollocks? How would I stick anything up my bollocks?"

"It's a figure of speech, Bobby."

"I've genuinely never heard anyone but you say that before."

"Are you sure?"

"Yes," I said. "I've heard of stick it up your arse. Everyone's heard of that. But physiologically speaking, it should be impossible to stick anything up your bollocks."

"Tell me about the relaxation technique, Bobby."

"Okay. Shut your eyes."

Roy's eyes widened.

"It's okay, Roy. Just shut your eyes and listen to what I say."

He stared at me for a few moments but then relented and did what I said.

"Okay, I want you to imagine the countryside, huge fields, long hedgerows, rolling hills, that sort of thing."

"Done."

"Right," I said. "Now keep in mind that countryside, but now imagine a small village in the middle of that countryside."

"Is it an evil village?"

I sighed.

"No, it's not an evil village. It's a nice village. There are cottages, there's a grocery shop, there's a post office, there's a pub. That sort of thing."

"Okay, Bobby. I've got your village. Now, what do you want me to do with it? Do you want me to set on fire?"

"No! No, just keep it in mind. Your village, in the countryside, but now it's evening. It's dusk. And it's starting to snow."

"Ok, it's snowing."

"See the snow, Roy. See it falling on the village. Watch it gently piling up on the rooftops."

"I can see it."

"Tell me about it."

"It's white."

I shook my head sadly.

"Tell me more."

Roy took a deep breath and then it all came out.

"Ok. I can see it piling up. I can see it on the top of the branches in the trees. I can see it covering the gardens. I can see it piling up on the old post box there. And on the walls. And...Bobby! There's a cat out on the wall, a big ginger tabby cat and he's out in the snow!"

"Ok, that's great, Roy. Why don't you have someone open a window, let the light of the house spill out on the snow and have the cat climb through the window and into the warm."

"Yeah," said Roy. "There he goes, look at that. He's in now. He's in the window. He's so warm and toasty, the little scamp. I'm going to find some milk for... hang on."

He shook himself back into the now, looking baffled.

"That was extraordinary, Bobby. I've not felt that calm since before Triggs passed away. How do you do that?"

I shrugged.

"It's nothing, just a basic bit of visualisation. It comes in handy when your boss is a malevolent six-inch heeled monster who rules with a rod of steel and you need to be able to sleep at night."

"I'm taking that as a compliment, Bobby," whispered Karren.

"It's not a compliment!" I said.

"What?" asked Roy.

"Nothing," I blustered.

"Whatever," said Roy. "So when do I have to do this? When I go to sleep? When I wake up?"

"No," I said. "Just do it when you need to. Make it your calm place. Make sure that you go there whenever you feel the fires burning. And then see what happens. We can still turn this around, you know."

I said it with the greatest confidence, but I must admit that I didn't feel so bold at half-time with Bolton beating us 3-1 in front of our own fans. It had all started so brightly. Djibril had opened the scoring and it looked as if we might be on the way to three crucial points. But then Matty Taylor equalised with a header, another set-piece cost us two minutes later thanks to Gary Cahill and then Johan Elmander rounded Craig Gordon to make it three. Never mind the players, I feared for my own safety back in the dressing-room.

Once again, Roy had made his way down there early and he was waiting for us. The lads were a bit unsure and I physically had to push a sobbing Chimbonda into the room. At the first sight of the hapless French full-back, I saw Roy's jawbone jut out and I watched in trepidation as his fists started to flex as if they were kneading invisible dough. The room was silent.

"Look at it now," he whispered audibly, "...piling up on those rooftops...so crisp, so firm."

The players exchanged worried looks.

"Lads, sit down. Take a drink. And listen to me. You're holding on too tight, you're frightened of your own shadow. And a lot of that is my fault. Look, you've got to believe in yourselves. I brought you to this club because I know good players. I played with good players my entire career. Except for that weird bit with Kléberson and Eric Djemba-Djemba. But the rest of the time they were really, really good. And you're good too. You just need to calm down and let it show."

I couldn't believe what I was seeing. Roy went round the room, stopping with every player and telling them what he thought was their greatest attribute. Then, like every decent football-themed after-dinner speaker, he finished off with a Cloughie anecdote.

"Lads, let me tell you what Brian Clough said to my team once when we'd lost our way. He said, 'Just get the ball and give it to someone else in a red shirt. That's all. Don't worry about the rest. Everything else will follow. That's what I want you to do now.' Would you do that for me now, lads?"

They would. And they did. First Kenwyne Jones bundled past Cahill and lashed a shot into the top corner. Then, with 10 minutes left, Reid's swirling cross found Djibril at the far post and he levelled from close range. We almost got a winner too, but Jussi Jaaskelainen made an incredible save to prevent Djibril from sealing his hat-trick. It didn't matter though. We'd reacted. We'd grabbed a game back having let it slip. And we'd done it because Roy had kept his temper and remembered that there are two sides to man-management.

I looked at him out there, disappointed with himself that two points had been dropped, but not ashamed of himself because of the performance that had saved one. He knew what had happened here. He turned and gave me a smile.

I tried to lean forward to give him a hug, but I couldn't shift my weight forward. He looked at me strangely as I hung on my heels for a moment and then slowly tipped over onto my back.

"Sxghhhlrbvrmatc," I burbled, slowing down as I approached the ground and then passing gently through it, past the grass, and then the soil and then some complicated pipework and away into a swirling vortex of everything and nothing.

I was leaping. I was leaping through time and space. I hoped against hope that this leap would be my leap home. Oh boy, was I wrong.

GOALS
ARE OVERRATED
THE
BEAUTY IS IN
THE STRUGGLE
BLZ
ZRD

GOALS
ARE OVERRATED
THE
BEAUTY IS IN
THE STRUGGLE
BLZ
ZRD

THE
Blizzard
THE FOOTBALL QUARTERLY

goalsoul

# 160

## Greatest Games

"He wiped his fringe slowly across his forehead in a mixture of embarrassment and shame, as though he was attempting to draw a curtain over his entire face and blot out his surroundings."

# Liverpool 3 Newcastle United 0

*FA Cup final, Wembley Stadium, London, 4 May 1974*

**By Scott Murray**

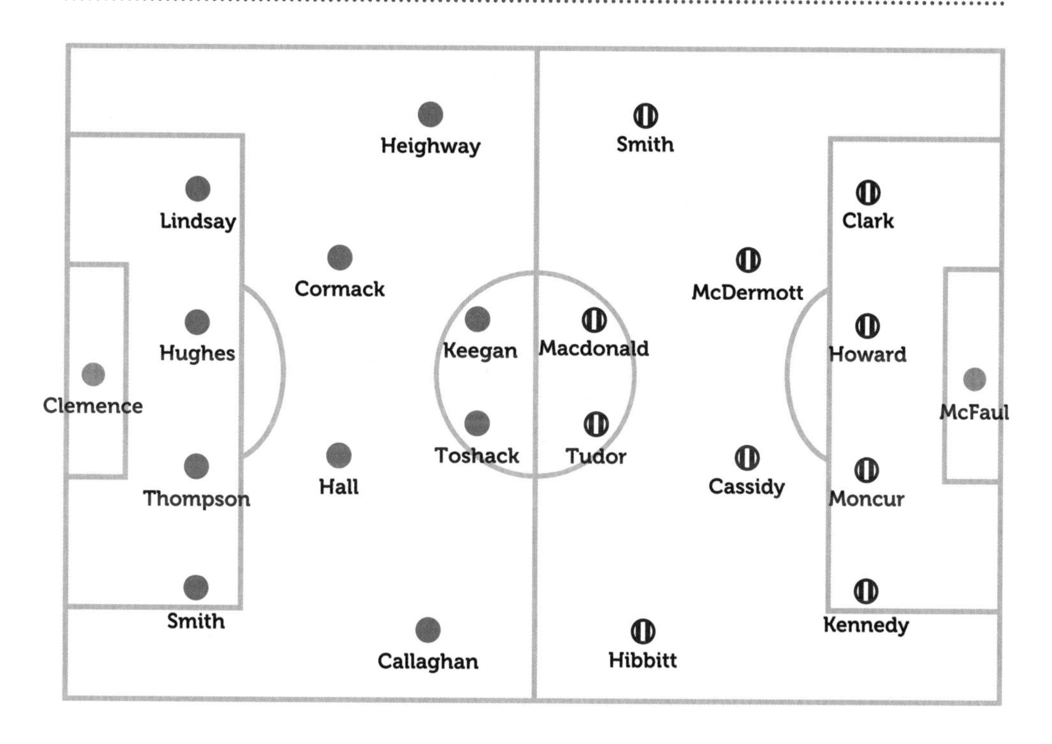


Bill Shankly. Unquestionably one of the greats, some would say the greatest. Either way, try to settle on a signature match – a single piece of action, *some actual football* – best to sum up the man's career. It's not quite as easy as you'd think. The 5-0 win over Arsenal in 1964 that brought Liverpool their first title of the modern era, perhaps? That's more memorable for the *Panorama* presenter John Morgan swooning in front of the Kop as they belted out some Bert Bacharach or Ron Yeats embarking on a lap of honour waving a papier-mâché version of the championship trophy above his head. The 1965 FA Cup final? A dull match; the fact that Liverpool ended their 73-year wait for the game's oldest prize proving more important than the actual manner of their doing it. (And in any case, Billy Bremner's slow-motion precision volley was the highlight of the day.) That perfect training-ground free-kick routine against Internazionale in the European Cup semi? Emlyn Hughes's screamer against Everton? Kevin Keegan's diving header in the 1973 Uefa Cup final? Shanks himself skittering aroundan Amsterdam pitch

**in late '66, bollocking his own players for succumbing to Ajax, under cover of thick fog?**

All majestic moments, with plenty of titles and cups to show for them too, and yet none quite nail the reason for his exalted position in football's managerial canon. Because in fairness to Shankly, his act was primarily a mood piece. Despite his heartfelt belief that first was first and second was nothing, trophies are very much a secondary consideration when assessing the man's importance in the grand scheme of things. He's all about the pithy aphorisms, the messianic gestures, the corralling of a red army that would shame Chairman Mao, acts which burrowed down to Liverpool's emotional core and gave the club its unique (sometimes mocked, but unique) heart-on-sleeve identity. Some people think football management is a matter of results; Shankly proved some things are much, much more important than that.

But a showman's a showman's a showman – ain't that the truth? – and Bill Shankly had perfect showman's timing. And there it is, at the very end of the man's 15-year Anfield reign: the 1974 FA Cup final. Shankly's *pièce de résistance,* arguably the most complete performance in Liverpool's long history. A near-perfect realisation of the Boot Room's possession-based pass-and-move doctrine, three wonder strikes plus one of the best disallowed goals of all time, in a show of such pomp and panache that Newcastle United – a club which had never lost a cup final – found themselves blown away. Bill the showman saved the best till last. Out at the very top. His signature indelibly scribbled with a flourish at the end.

---

Neither Liverpool nor Newcastle United started their campaigns for the 1974 FA Cup particularly well. Not well at all. In the third round, Joe Harvey's Newcastle hosted Hendon Town, champions of the Isthmian League and a San Marino-style melange of salesmen, accountants, draughtsmen and office clerks. Hendon came away from St James' Park with a 1-1 draw, another humiliating experience for the Toon, who had famously been sent packing from the same competition two years earlier by non-league Hereford United, Ronnie Radford and all that.

On the same day, the self-same Hereford, newly promoted members of Division Three, came within five minutes of knocking out West Ham United on their own turf, while non-league Boston United held Derby County, champions two seasons previously, at the Baseball Ground. At Anfield, Bill Shankly, ever the romantic, hopelessly in thrall to the old-school unpredictability of the third round, leant back in his chair and cooed: "Hendon, Boston and Hereford, eh? Marvellous!" Someone then asked whether Doncaster Rovers should be added to his list. Doncaster, bottom of the entire Football League, had just earned a 2-2 draw at Anfield, home of the reigning league champions who were second in the First Division, unquestionably the biggest upset of the day. Unsurprisingly, Shanks demurred. "Naw, we gave them two goals," he shot back, before delivering, with perfect comic timing, a cymbal-crash pay-off which distanced his response from accusations of sour grapes: "Gifts from the gods!"

It was true that Doncaster's goals had been parcelled up and wrapped with pretty bows by a generously slapdash Liverpool: Kevin Keegan had opened the scoring early, but Ray Clemence let a weak shot slip under his body, then Hughes failed to deal with a simple cross and within 19 minutes the hosts were losing. Doncaster held their 2-1 lead for the best part of 40 minutes until Keegan headed a second and would have won the tie had Peter Kitchen's lob over a stranded Clemence on 90 minutes not cruelly hit the crossbar. Liverpool won a fuss-free replay 2-0. Meanwhile Newcastle also saw off their lower-league irritants second time around, beating Hendon 4-0.

There was more of the same in the fourth round, with Liverpool held to a goalless draw at Anfield by promotion-chasing Carlisle United of the Second Division, while Newcastle again drew at St James' Park, this time against Scunthorpe United of the Fourth. ("After their initial draw with Hendon, Newcastle are showing the sort of erratic form that leads to Wembley," quipped the *Observer* with some prescience.) Both of the big boys again made it through after replays, whereupon Liverpool marched on to the final via less traumatic encounters with Ipswich Town, Bristol City and, comprehensively after a semi-final replay, Leicester City.

Newcastle United being Newcastle United, the rest of their route to Wembley would be rather more scenic. Their quarter-final tie with second-division Nottingham Forest proved to be one of the most famous and infamous of all FA Cup encounters. The Toon were again making a meal of lower-league opposition at home, 2-1 down early in the second half, when Pat Howard battered Duncan McKenzie to the floor in the area. The referee Gordon Kew pointed to the spot, booked Howard, and then after a full and frank exchange of views, sent the player off. George Lyall smacked the penalty home. Newcastle were 3-1 down, with only 10 men on the pitch. The jig was surely up.

But play restarted and at this point ... well, the man from the *Observer* tells it best. "Suddenly a fat gentleman in civvies appeared in the Forest area, waving and shouting. His chubby strivings set off a riot. The crowd came on, the teams came off, the Force brought the dogs in. It was eight minutes before a version of football could resume."

Chubby strivings! Five bobbies were required to pin the paunchy pugilist to the floor and perhaps inspired by the impressive (if misguided) levels of passion shown by this bare-chested warrior, Newcastle rallied spectacularly after the restart. Malcolm Macdonald was bundled over by the Forest keeper Jim Barron for a penalty of Newcastle's own, which Terry McDermott dispatched. John Tudor's diving header levelled the scores. And with 40 seconds left on the clock, Bobby Moncur latched onto a Macdonald knockdown to volley home a scarcely believable winner. Scarcely believable not least because, in the opinion of one Forest player, "It was yards offside, but with the crowd in that mood, the linesman dare not have put his flag up. He would have been lynched!"

Newcastle's 4-3 win was soon declared void by the FA and the two teams ordered to replay at Goodison Park. Officials from both clubs seemed happy enough with the decision – Forest were back in the Cup, while Newcastle had been fearful of disqualification – although the Toon vice-captain Frank Clark bemoaned, "We produced one of the greatest recoveries in FA Cup history over that last half-hour, and it is surely cruel that we should not have the reward. No one was happier to resume the game than the Forest players. When play restarted they played their best football of the match for several minutes. Nobody who was there could dispute that. So how could they be judged to have been adversely affected by the hold-up? They just collapsed after their goalkeeper had given away the penalty kick which enabled us to make it 3-2." Justice, in Clark's eyes, would eventually be done: after a 0-0 draw, a second replay at Goodison was decided by a single Macdonald goal.

That quarter-final encounter was sandwiched between confident wins against two decent sides, West Bromwich Albion in the fifth round and Burnley in the semis. Given the absurd nature of their run to Wembley, it was hard to shake off the feeling that Newcastle's name was on the Cup. It was the first time in 13 years that they'd got past the fourth round. They'd reached the semis, and subsequently the final, for the first time since their previous win in 1955. They'd never lost an FA Cup final in five visits to Wembley and – while things like this should never matter, they so often do – no side wearing stripes had lost an FA Cup final since the war. Not even Sunderland against Leeds United the year before. No wonder Macdonald was supremely confident in the run-up to the final: "I guarantee a goal at Wembley," trumpeted the brazen striker, whom the *Times* described as "agreeably arrogant ... the Muhammad Ali of English football".

Oh Supermac.

Newcastle's return to the final for the first time since their Fifties heyday, soundtracked by the noises coming out of Macdonald's fast mouth, might have ensured their tale was the more compelling. But Liverpool were favourites going into the match. They had become used to winning trophies again after six barren seasons, having landed a league and Uefa Cup double the year before. They were in the process of finishing second in the league this time round, tasting defeat only twice in the 27 games since Boxing Day. Newcastle, meanwhile, had won only three times since the turn of the year and had flirted with relegation.

But in truth neither team was in form. Since their triumphs in the semi-finals, Liverpool had won two of eight games, Newcastle just the one. Liverpool's Achilles heel appeared to be a lack of firepower: they'd only scored 51 times in 41 league matches that season. Newcastle's main problem was a leaky defence, which had only held out 15 times in 61 matches. A narrow win for Shankly's side was the pick of most newspaper and television pundits. Of the nine experts asked in the *Times*, only the respected ITV presenter and commentator Brian Moore offered Newcastle any hope. He plumped for a

2-1 Newcastle win, "based on the belief that Liverpool will not be able to contain Macdonald's burning ambition and blistering finish for a full afternoon."

This wasn't, however, the party line of Independent Television. The astrologer from the channel's listings magazine, *TV Times,* offered the following analysis: "Jupiter is going into Pisces so I can assure you that Malcolm McDonald will be terribly depressed and will be overwhelmed afterwards with a desire to recount his troubles. Joe Harvey is in for emotional upsets, but Bill Shankly's Jupiter aspects look marvellous and Keegan's restless creative activity is just bursting to get loose." Not a bad call at all, as things would turn out, although not quite as close as the one made by the *Times* writer Tom Freeman, who predicted a 2-0 Liverpool win. "The goals will be scored in the second half," he predicted, in a piece so eerily prescient it should have been accompanied by a free flexidisc of jazz solos played on Theremin, "probably by Heighway and Keegan."

ITV having had their say, a man from the BBC took centre stage just before kick off. "Ladies and gentlemen, Mr Bruce Forsyth will now lead you in the singing of the traditional Cup final hymn." And with that, the star of Saturday night staple *The Generation Game* romped onto the pitch to a predictable cacophony of abuse from all four corners of the ground. Equally predictably, within 20 seconds, Brucie had the very same abusers eating from the palm of his hand. The band of the Royal Marines belted out the theme tune to *The Generation Game,* Brucie showed decent technique and touch for a big man to skelp a ball from distance into an empty net, and soon enough, after a chorus of "Nice One Brucie, Nice One Son," both Newcastle and Liverpool fans were joining in with *that* call-and-response catchphrase. Nice to hear it, to hear it nice, especially as the opening couplet to "Abide With Me" shares a not dissimilar grammatical construction with Brucie's calling card: Abide with me ... lord with me abide! (And tonight's the night when the darkness deepens.)

The darkness would eventually envelop Newcastle all right, but not quite in the manner the received wisdom has it. The 1974 FA Cup final has gone down as a lop-sided rout – and the game did eventually end up like that – but the first half was closer than is now remembered. During a studio discussion before a rerun of the game on LFC TV, Alan Kennedy – who played for Newcastle that day as a wet-behind-the-ears 19-year-old left-back – said that his team had been "lucky to get nil" in the first half, though he also admitted he had never sat down to watch the game since, suggesting what subsequently occurred in the second period had warped and curdled a few memories.

While it's true that Liverpool were the better side in the first half, just, they didn't have it all their own way. They had the first big chance of the game: on seven minutes, Ian Callaghan swept a gorgeous Gerrardesque cross-field ball from right to left for the dependable and occasionally spectacular left-back Alec Lindsay, who crossed into the area where the presence of John Toshack and Keegan caused enough panic to require

Kennedy to clear off his own line.
But Newcastle came just as close in the opening exchanges, not once but twice. A couple of minutes after Kennedy's clearance, Terry Hibbitt reached the by-line down the Newcastle left and lifted a cross over Clemence's head. Only a last-ditch eyebrow from Hughes stopped Tudor following the ball in. On 18 minutes, Macdonald flicked on a long pass from his captain Bobby Moncur, instigating a rare old stramash in the Liverpool box as Hughes and Tommy Smith both miskicked, the ball sitting up, inviting either Tudor or Jim Smith to lash home from six yards. Fortunately for Liverpool, the Newcastle pair took clean fresh-air swipes as well and Clemence flopped over the loose ball.

Liverpool were dominating possession but doing very little with it. On 20 minutes, Heighway skinned Clark – already a winner at Wembley having lifted the FA Amateur Cup with Crook Town in 1962 – down the left. His cross from the by-line was a fraction behind Toshack, who arced his back in a futile attempt to connect with his head. Tommy Smith, bombing in from the other wing, met the cross but shanked woefully wide. Keegan had a snapshot from a tight angle just after the half hour, but it was easily gathered by Willie McFaul.

Newcastle, on the other hand, were threatening to unlock Liverpool. McDermott – like Kennedy, destined to become a Liverpool legend but playing for Newcastle that day – was the best player on the park in the first half, a bundle of creative energy in the centre and on both flanks, invariably at the heart of the action. He and Smith combined crisply down the right but the final ball let them down. Hibbitt drew Liverpool's defence out with a meander down the inside-left channel, then flicked the ball inside to release Macdonald on goal. The flag went up for offside, but it was clear from the checked lines on the turf that Hughes was playing him on.

Liverpool could count themselves fortunate, with the possible exception of Brian Hall who took a full-force Kennedy clearance straight in his startled boat. Joe Fagan came on to cool Hall's fevered brow, dabbing him with the magic sponge. An incongruous sight to the modern eye, a future European Cup-winning manager rushing on in tracksuit and trainers, wielding a bucket and flannels various. But it's nothing Bob Paisley hadn't done years before, once famously carrying Hughes off the pitch on his shoulders. Managerial geniuses mucking in at the coal face is a big part of the Boot Room's retro charm.

Liverpool woke up with 10 minutes of the half to go, and did enough during the final stretch of the opening period to claim the upper hand. Moncur was forced to intercept a clever Toshack header across the face of the Newcastle goal with Keegan lurking. An adroit Keegan chest-down on the edge of the box set up Toshack for a low drive that was deflected wide. Keegan, beginning to impose himself in a relentless, busy and skilful style which had more than a little of the Luis Suárezes about it, buzzed down the inside-right and slipped a ball forward for Hall who flashed it straight through Newcastle's six-yard box. Finally Heighway tore off down the left and fizzed one in from the other side, forcing Howard to hack off the line.

On the bench, Shankly and Paisley sat together, kitted out in that early Seventies mix of the garish and grim. Paisley to the left, in a brown suit, impassive. Shanks in a dark brown mac and purple shirt, calm and unreadable. Immediately to Shankly's right – *immediately* to Shankly's right, the Wembley bench in those days one big love-in – the Newcastle manager Joe Harvey, sporting grey suit and kipper tie, nervously chugging on a cheroot. The juxtaposition of the managerial moods was a sign of Liverpool's increasing confidence in their game plan. Newcastle had easily matched Liverpool in terms of chances for 30-odd minutes, but Shankly's side had always enjoyed the lion's share of possession; towards the end of the half, it was beginning to reap a dividend.

This was one of the first signs that painful lessons had been learned from Liverpool's comprehensive defeat at the hands of Crvena Zvezda of Belgrade in that season's European Cup. Shankly had at the time publicly dismissed Zvezda's patient possession-based style, arguing that English crowds wanted to see something a bit more up-tempo. But behind the curtain, he and Paisley were drumming a new metronomic mantra into the Liverpool team, one that would serve them astonishingly well for the next 15 years.

The first green shoots had emerged towards the end of that first half; the second period would witness their full blossoming. Within 40 seconds of the restart, Hughes, Keegan, Toshack and the wily Peter Cormack triangulated on the edge of the Newcastle box; Keegan eventually slammed a no-backlift snapshot inches wide of the left-hand post. It was a statement of intent. Another 90 seconds had elapsed when Moncur clumsily clipped Toshack's ankles on the edge of the box. A penalty? Probably just outside the box, but the referee gave nothing at all. (And the identity of that ref? One Gordon Kew, the unfortunate whistler who found himself caught in the eye of the storm at St James' during that preposterous quarter-final between Newcastle and Forest. Poor Kew may, for a split second, in his mind's eye, have seen our old friend the Chubby Striver hoving into view from left-field, belly out and arms windmilling. You could hardly blame the put-upon official for erring on the side of caution.)

After six minutes of the second half came the greatest FA Cup final goal that never was. Lindsay robbed Smith down the left, played a storming one-two with Keegan, and from a tight angle skelped a full-cream rising shot past McFaul and into the roof of the net. He scampered off to celebrate only to have his gallop sickeningly halted by a linesman's flag. Offside by a hair's breadth, which would have been fair enough, except the one-two had actually rebounded off Kennedy and not Keegan, playing Lindsay on.

Three more minutes and there was Toshack threading a low shot just wide right of goal, only for Keegan's pullback from the by-line on the right to have been judged out of play. Another minute and Keegan released Toshack into the box with a clever scooped pass down the middle. The big Welsh striker tucked the chance away, but was flagged for offside. Newcastle's back line was battered out of shape to such an extent that the decision was at the very least questionable.

"Ee-ay-addio, we're going to win the Cup," trilled the travelling Kop, a throwback to the more innocent terrace sounds of the Sixties. There was a sense that something simply had to happen soon. Newcastle's body language began to betray their concerns: Smith shook his head, Macdonald frowned, Clark stood with his arms stretched out, pleading to nobody in particular. The BBC commentator David Coleman, with exquisite timing, announced that "Shanks's army, this Liverpool side, are swarming forward now." A split-second later, Smith, out on the right, lofted a cross into the centre towards Hall, who ducked under it. The ball made its way to Keegan, who tickled the ball before caressing a shot into the top right. Coleman had just displayed immaculate judgement by calling Liverpool's supremacy; now it was time to showcase a little lyricism. "Goals pay the rent, Keegan does his share!" A line for the ages and just the right side of gibberish; eccentric, whimsical, witty. David Coleman versus modern commentators? One-nil.

On the bench, Shankly chipped in with one of the images that's been replayed a million times, that left-to-right-and-back-again hand shuffle which, it's often claimed, meant nothing, even if the meaning could hardly be clearer: pass and move. Shankly kept shuffling; Liverpool kept passing and moving. Newcastle had no answer. Hughes – who in the build-up to the game played it for laughs by boasting of his "100%" shots-to-goal ratio for the season, two taken, two scored – buggered up his perfect stat by whistling a superlative rising shot from the left of the D towards the top right, the ball drifting inches over the bar. Clark was penalised for obstruction on Heighway and emitted one of the great sporting whines – "Aaaaaaaawwwwwwwwfuckinell!" – as incredulity gave way to impotent frustration. On Shankly's left shoulder, poor Joe Harvey had started chain smoking, each and every drag set to 'Industrial Hoover'.

The Kop, out on manoeuvres and in full voice, belted out "You'll Never Walk Alone". The Leazes End, also displaced for the day, did their bit with the "Blaydon Races", admirably so given what was unfolding in front of them. It was an astonishing atmosphere; Bruce Forsyth one hell of a warm-up man. Keegan had a shot blocked from the edge of the box. Kennedy was fortunate to get away with handling the ball on his own penalty spot as Keegan tried to flick it round him on the turn, another moment of Suárezesque cheek. The referee saw no intention, though a modern interpretation might consider why the player's left arm was dangling out unnecessarily. McDermott won a free-kick for Newcastle in a dangerous area down the right, but even that ended in a quick Liverpool break, Cormack feeding Callaghan down the left wing, Heighway not quite managing to bend his run to receive a pass through the middle in an onside position. Had he managed to stay a couple of feet back up the field, the winger would have had a clear run on goal from the halfway line.

Seven of Liverpool's outfield players – Hughes, the 20-year-old newcomer Phil Thompson, Smith, Toshack, Hall,

Callaghan and Keegan – put together an 11-pass move which started on the left but ended on the right, Keegan eventually smearing a shot inches left of the target. "That was almost a dozen passes," ran David Coleman's perfectly judged commentary, a sharp-eyed feat in the days before commentators were propped up by ranks of statisticians and banks of computers. Keegan-Suárez then flicked a header on the turn to scuttle round a flat-footed Pat Howard down the left, the ball then shuttled inside via Cormack to Hall, coming in from the right. Hall's shot flew wildly over.

Liverpool were relentless. McFaul launched a long drop kick upfield, Smith stepped out from the back and met the dropping ball with a first-time flick wide right to Callaghan. Liverpool were immediately back on the attack. The pattern was finally broken when, with 17 minutes left, Newcastle won their first corner of the match, McDermott having busied himself down the right. Hibbitt floated a decent ball into the six-yard box, but Clemence, on the case despite having had so little to do, gently shouldered Macdonald out of the way and claimed the dropping cross: wonderfully efficient keeping, though already the striker looked a broken man, perplexed and utterly defeated.

Two minutes later, Liverpool scored a simple second, Toshack flicking the ball on for Heighway to break into the area and lash a shot into the left-hand side of McFaul's goal. On the bench, Shankly again launched into his pass-and-move hand shuffle, but it was a rhythmic dance now, arms flicking to and fro in time to the chants of the crowd.

Macdonald had a chance to respond almost instantly, Tudor rolling the ball to him on the left-hand edge of the Liverpool box, the culmination of a rare Newcastle attack, their opponents momentarily giddy after taking a two-goal lead. But the striker squirted an incompetent shot miles left. He wiped his fringe slowly across his forehead in a mixture of embarrassment and shame, as though he was attempting to draw a curtain over his entire face and blot out his surroundings.

As the last 10 minutes ticked on, Toshack would miss two more chances, flicking a Keegan right-wing cross wide left and failing to extend a leg to poke home Lindsay's fine left-wing fizzer. And Macdonald would suffer an even more egregious humiliation, sent clear down the left by Tommy Cassidy's long pass, only to chest down and launch some filthy nonsense miles high and wide to the left. An abject capitulation from the man who had spent the previous week guaranteeing goals. The Muhammad Ali of English football was flat out on the canvas.

But the conclusion of this Cup final was all about Shankly. The travelling Kop broke into "Amazing Grace", reworked as a paean to their manager, sung softly, with feeling, at proper hymnal tempo. Real love. In retrospect, the knowledge that Shankly would retire a couple of months after the match makes this scene almost too bittersweet to bear. But even at the time, it was enough to crack the hardest heart and would certainly have melted the sentimental Shankly to the core.

Time for one last crescendo, and the apotheosis of Shankly's time at

Liverpool. Hall to Toshack down the right. Back to Smith, who sprays wide left to Lindsay. A flick down the wing finds Keegan, who bustles, turns, cuts back up the flank and inside, launching a cross-field pass towards Smith. The defender flicks the dropping ball along the right wing for Hall. Smith under-laps, then takes up possession again before swiftly exchanging passes with Heighway. Having reached the by-line, Smith rolls the ball through the Newcastle six-yard box for Keegan, falling backwards, to guide home. Pass and move, pass and move. Shankly's gestures made flesh. What a way to end the match. What a way to end Shankly's reign.

"Newcastle were undressed!" screamed the BBC's Coleman. "Absolutely stripped naked." Coleman then added a final flourish as rhythmical as Liverpool's metronomic brilliance, art imitating art: "Keegan two, Heighway one; Liverpool three, Newcastle none." On the bench, before the final whistle had sounded, Liverpool having lit a metaphorical cigar, Bob Paisley sparked a real one and puffed away with great contentment. Nearby, Joe Harvey was smoking too, still, but now looked as drained as the 40 stubs scattered about his feet, a cadaver pallor washing over him. It was all over. Shankly stood and, arms aloft in his trademark preacher's style, saluted the crowd. "We want Shankly," the Kop insisted. They eventually got their way, as the manager walked onto the pitch and embraced each player one by one, reserving special embraces for the veteran Callaghan and the prodigy Keegan, plus a bear hug for Hughes, his captain, his favourite.

Shankly quietly, shyly, contentedly watched Hughes climb the 39 steps to the Royal Box and nearly get decapitated en route by the over-zealous embraces of joyous revellers. Hughes lifted the cup. The rest of the team trooped past to collect their medals, Thompson bedecked in a swapped Newcastle jersey and black-and-white bowler hat. Then the vanquished. Young Kennedy trudged past. "His time will surely come again," predicted Coleman, of a player who would later transfer to Liverpool for whom he'd score two European Cup-winning goals. Finally, the man with whom Thompson had swapped his red shirt: the Liverpool-mad Terry McDermott, Newcastle's man of the match and a player destined for Anfield six months later. McDermott would put together an astonishing portfolio of goals for Liverpool: a lob in an FA Cup semi against Everton, the opener in the 1977 European Cup final against Borussia Mönchengladbach, that header against Tottenham, a glorious chip against Alex Ferguson's Aberdeen.

In Kennedy and McDermott, Liverpool would be assured a glorious future. Nobody knew that yet, of course. And nobody knew that for Shanks, the die was also cast. He would resign in early July, an abdication which has never been fully explained and was soon regretted by the man himself. And yet the old showman must have subconsciously twigged that the leaving of Liverpool was the right thing to do, with reference to those hoary old showbiz maxims: leave them wanting more, go out at the very top.

Which is undoubtedly what this was, in an era when the FA Cup still meant everything. Shankly bequeathed Liverpool a precious blueprint for a decade of red domination in Europe. But more importantly, he took his leave of the stage clutching silverware, and saving his very best till last, and according to his beloved socialist beliefs too. His men had delivered the greatest team performance of any FA Cup final, one which culminated in one of the great team goals, while his people sang hymns which rang down Wembley Way. Shankly's signature, right there, right at the very end.

# 172

## Eight Bells

"Don't let Gazza in the ambulance."

# Dethronings

*A selection of champions who surrendered their titles in decisive fashion*

**By Rob Smyth**

### 1 Aston Villa 1-0 Internazionale (aggregate 1-1; 4-3 on pens), Uefa Cup first round second leg, Villa Park, 29 September 1994

Ron Atkinson was one of the great cup managers. To describe him as such can be misleading, in that it suggests he failed as a league manager. Yet even though he never won a league title, he significantly improved the league position of almost every club he managed. Even so, it was the instant glory of cup football that stimulated Atkinson the most. He dealt in famous days and particularly in glory glory nights, and not just at Manchester United. His underrated three-year spell at Aston Villa included victory in the League Cup, which ultimately denied Manchester United a domestic treble, and a Uefa Cup victory over Internazionale which Atkinson placed above United's legendary comeback against Diego Maradona's Barcelona in 1984.

In truth, this was not the greatest Inter side. They had finished 13th the previous season, only one point and two places off relegation, but they were the Uefa Cup holders and their team included Dennis Bergkamp, Gianluca Pagliuca, Nicola Berti, Darko Pančev, Ruben Sosa and Giuseppe Bergomi. It's also worth remembering that, back then, all European football and particularly Serie A had an enormous aura and mystique.

British teams had, with the exception of Manchester United and Arsenal in the relatively weak Cup-Winners' Cup, been callow and beatable since readmission in 1990. Because of that there was a sense, the obvious rivalries excepted, of everyone being it in together and of wanting other English teams to do well. And Villa, particularly because of Atkinson's likeability, invited more goodwill than most. When Phil King scored the penalty that knocked out the holders Internazionale, the ITV commentators Alan Parry and Kevin Keegan shouted "YES!" in unison, followed by a heartfelt "You beauty!" from Parry.

The first leg had also been shown on ITV – but only the second half, with those in charge deciding it was not an option to reschedule *The Bill* and *The Big Story,* in which Dermot Murnaghan went in search of the authentic British yob. Talk of an authentic British yob has absolutely nothing to do with the football style of John Fashanu, whose short spell at Villa has been largely forgotten. He was identified by both Villa and Inter as a key man before the tie. "From my conversations with several of the Inter players, I know they are worried for two reasons – and the main one is called John Fashanu," said David Platt, who was at Sampdoria. (The other reason was that they had lost 2-0 at Villa Park in 1990-91 before winning the second leg 3-0.) Not everyone was afraid of Big Fash, however. When his name was mentioned, Bergkamp sniffed imperiously, "Where does he play?"

Fashanu had moved from Wimbledon in the summer and was looking forward to his European debut at the age of 31. "I personally know what to expect from the Italians, the petulant kicking of ankles, spitting and all the rest," said the paragon of fair play. There was little of that, though sadly Fashanu's performance on his European debut was sufficiently anonymous for some Villa fans to joke he still hadn't played in Europe. Inter won 1-0, thanks to a penalty from Bergkamp that was earned dubiously by Sosa. "There was no physical contact between myself and the gentleman who fell over me," said the keeper Nigel Spink, temporarily speaking like the Harry Enfield character Mr Cholmondley Warner. "I made my feelings known to him after the game."

Often defeats are described as costly but this was the opposite. ITV said they would only show the second leg – and thus give Villa big wads of cash – if the tie was still alive. The concept of Thursday-night football was sufficiently new that adjustments to the fixture list were beyond the wit of man and Villa had to play at the leaders Newcastle just 36 hours later. Thursday night, channel three – but nobody was looking down their nose at the Uefa Cup. Back then it was a huge tournament, and the 1994-95 version included Blackburn, Juventus, Real Madrid, Borussia Dortmund and Nantes – the teams who would win Europe's big five leagues that season.

ITV certainly got their money's worth. Those who went to the game got even more bang for their buck – this was one of the great Villa Park nights, with a wonderful, heightened atmosphere that makes you tingle even when you watch it on YouTube 20 years later. This despite the fact part of the Holte End was closed. It was not a great match, but every minute crackled with tension and it was unquestionably a great occasion.

Although Berti smacked the angle of post and bar early on, with Pančev launching the rebound into orbit, Villa created the clearer chances. Houghton, who had famously scored past Pagliuca at the World Cup three months earlier, rammed in the only goal from a few yards just before half-time. Pagliuca was a Villa fan, having fallen in love with their title-winning side – and particularly their kit – of 1980-81. His favourite player was Tony Morley and he described himself as "a true Villan" earlier this year.

"The second leg in that beautiful stadium was emotional," he said of his first visit in 1994. Villa should really have won the tie in 90 or at least 120 minutes. Guy Whittingham's marvellous chip hit the bar, with a weary Houghton fluffing the rebound. Instead it went to penalties. The first six were scored, the next three missed by Davide Fontolan, Whittingham and Sosa. King sauntered forward from the centre circle with the happy demeanour of a postman nearing the end of his round. He had mild cramp, so decided to take three steps and blast it down the middle. Pagliuca dived out the way, and King's hands were raised in celebration almost before the ball hit the net. You beauty indeed. As fans invaded the pitch Atkinson punched the air, with a young fan called Lee Hendrie unwittingly photobombing Atkinson's moment of triumph.

The Inter game was not part of a grand cup run. Villa were beaten by Trabzonspor in the next round, Atkinson was sacked six weeks later and King, not fancied by the new manager Brian Little, only played 20 games in three years at Villa Park. Frankly, who cares? Both Atkinson and King are indelibly associated with Villa's greatest European night of the last 32 years. With some cup victories you feel like you have to win the trophy to make it all mean something. That wasn't the case with Villa and Internazionale. A night this like lasts forever.

### 2 Spain 1-5 Netherlands, World Cup Group B, Salvador, 13 June 2014

As the dust settles, it becomes clear that Brazil 2014 was a decent World Cup but no more, the persuasive mood of innocence and positivity not remotely matched by the football once things got series in the knockout stage. To call it the greatest of all time, as some did after about two games, was infantile and desperate. Yet there was one aspect in which it was surely the greatest of all time: the seismic shocks, with two so severe that they almost broke football's Richter scale.

In football, shocks generally refer to acts of giant-killing. Yet what's even more shocking than seeing David kill Goliath is seeing Goliath beat another Goliath to a gruesome pulp. Brazil 2014 was topped and tailed by two of the very best: Brazil 1-7 Germany, which a few months later still feels like the most amazing sporting result ever, and Spain 1-5 Netherlands.

It takes years to build an aura and just over half an hour to shatter it. When Daley Blind launched a ball towards Robin van Persie just before half-time in Salvador, Spain, with their unique brand of *tiki-takanaccio,* had conceded three goals in the previous 1622 minutes at the World Cup and European Championship. Van Persie's astonishing flying header was the first of five they conceded in the following 36 minutes.

There was a slight sense that Spain were relatively fragile coming into the tournament, yet it was no stronger than that. They still had the best squad in the competition, especially as Diego Costa had filled the one gap in their team. For much of the first half against the Netherlands, in which Spain were excellent, it looked like Costa might be turning them into Spain 2.0. With Spain winning 1-0 and looking comfortable, David Silva missed an excellent chance when his chip was clawed away by Jasper Cillessen. Eighty-one seconds later Van Persie scored and Friday 13 began to unfold like a horror film.

Spain lost the match, lost their next game against Chile and were out of the tournament within the first week. Yet sport's capacity to perpetuate itself is such that, had Silva scored, Spain might well have gone to win the tournament. The aura would have been refreshed by victory over the

Netherlands, Chile would have been a completely different game, and if Spain had won the group – as they surely would if they had beaten the Dutch – their path to the final would have been Mexico, Costa Rica and an Argentina side without Ángel di Maria. Not much to worry about there, at least not when you're playing well. Nor would a fine but not great German side in the final have concerned them unduly, even after the 7-1.

Spain were obviously over the hill, as much because of Xavi's decline as anything, but in they could easily have postponed their decline for just one more month. It's not as if grinding out results while not playing well – albeit in their unique way – was alien to them after the events of 2010 and 2012. In a parallel universe, Spain are still world and European champions. The line between extreme success and extreme failure is mind-blowingly fine.

### 3 Marseille 1-0 Milan (aggregate: 2-1), European Cup quarter-final second leg, Stade Vélodrome, 20 March 1991

Retaining the Champions League has become football's holiest grail. AC Milan were the last side to do so, back when it was still called the European Cup. Yet were it not for Marseille, they might conceivably have won the competition six times in a row. They were champions in 1989, 1990 and 1994, lost to Marseille in the 1991 quarter-final and 1993 final, and were banned in 1992 – when they were arguably at their peak and went the entire Serie A season unbeaten.

They were banned for their risible antics in that 1991 defeat to Marseille. There is a proud tradition of champions surrendering their trophy about as willingly as Tony Montana surrendered his life in *Scarface*. Think of Argentina picking a fight with the entire world at Italia 90 or Diego Maradona high-kicking all-comers when his Barcelona side had their Copa del Rey taken from them by Athletic in 1984. Milan did things a little differently, walking off the field and refusing to restart the match after an insignificant floodlight failure towards the end of a game they were obviously going to lose anyway.

Marseille were a thrilling side built around a front three of Abedi Pelé, Jean-Pierre Papin and Chris Waddle – good enough that the coach Raymond Goethals temporarily ostracised Eric Cantona purely for football reasons. Goethals was Marseille's third coach of the season, after Gérard Gili and Franz Beckenbauer – whose short, sour spell at the club is often forgotten – and they were bang in form by the time of their meeting with Milan in the quarter-finals. Milan, by contrast, were without Marco van Basten for both legs; he was sent off in the previous round against Club Brugge for elbowing the defender Pascal Plovie, breaking his cheekbone and knocking out two of his teeth.

Marseille deservedly drew the first leg 1-1 in the San Siro, with Pelé's storming run and Waddle's clever pass creating Papin's equaliser. The second leg was largely cagey, with Marseille knowing a 0-0 draw would take them through and Milan prepared to play the long game and nick the tie near the end. Waddle's preparation for the biggest club match of his life had not exactly been a spa retreat – he had a recuperating Paul Gascoigne staying with him, along with Gazza's father and Jimmy Five Bellies. Gascoigne had his first meeting with an army of Lazio representatives at Waddle's villa. He also spent his time teaching Waddle's young daughter Brooke to tell her parents what she wanted to be when she grew up: Gazza's wife.

Waddle had far less to worry about on the field. After all, he was only facing Paolo Maldini. He had given Maldini a fearful chasing at Wembley in November 1989, a game he regards as his best for England, and a couple of extremely vigorous challenges confirmed that Maldini remembered the game too. There were also suggestions that Maldini rabbit-punched Waddle off the ball. (Waddle's published recollection – "he done us again in the second half" – is pretty ambiguous.) Either way, Waddle was dizzy throughout that second half and only really recalls one incident: his beautifully precise right-footed volley, which shimmered across the turf like a bowling ball before fading inside the far post. That gave Marseille the lead in the 72nd minute. As things stood they would have gone through on away goals anyway, but it was confirmation of their slight but vital superiority in the tie.

Waddle was a great advert for concussion: in the second half he was comfortably the best player on the pitch, a constant spark of creativity in an otherwise scruffy game. In the last minute, with Marseille hanging on relatively comfortably, Waddle almost scored the goal of his life. As he broke from deep inside his own half, one of the floodlights went out, though the light was still good enough for him to run 70 yards, snake insidiously between two defenders on the edge of the area and go round the keeper Sebastiano Rossi only inadvertently to run the ball out of play rather than into the net.

That was when the fun really started. The referee stopped the game to allow for floodlight repairs, though in truth it was playable anyway. Some players and fans thought the match was over, which led to a small pitch invasion. Milan, spotting the only chance they'd had all night, ran with a burgeoning mood of faux outrage. They said it was too dark to resume, even though the floodlights had been partially repaired – and even though they were working sufficiently to highlight the bald dome of the chief rabble-rouser, Milan director Adriano Galliani.

The Milan players declined to return to the field, summoning righteousness as only the guilty can. They looked for any excuse they could find, stopping just short of complaining that the pre-match Evian in the their dressing-room was not at the requested temperature. After the match, Galliani released a preposterous statement: "I didn't think there was enough light, and the players told me they didn't feel in the right spirit to continue playing again." He had scandalously besmirched the proud reputation of a country that produced Macchiavelli.

"It was a disgraceful exhibition by a Milan side from whom football has come to expect something better" wrote David Lacey in the *Guardian*. "For more than two seasons they had restored European football to something approaching its former excellence. Last night they were just another Italian team trying it on." Uefa didn't fall for it: they awarded Marseille a 3-0 win and banned Milan from European football for a year. Milan's behaviour was disgraceful but, far worse, it was utterly pathetic. "The sad part," said Glenn Hoddle, "is that this Milan side will now be remembered for the way they lost the European Cup rather than the way they won it."

Hoddle, along with Gascoigne, was among the party who went for dinner with Waddle after the game. After a while Waddle stepped outside because he felt unwell. Dr Gascoigne, thinking Waddle was flagging in the unmanly style, innocently prescribed a couple of pints as the cure to all his ills. In fact Waddle's lights were in danger of going out; he started to vomit on the kerb and an ambulance was called. Waddle, fearing another questionable prognosis, uttered one solemn plea to anyone who would listen: "Don't let Gazza in the ambulance."

It turned out he had concussion because of his clash with Maldini, an injury that kiboshed a likely recall to the England's squad to play Ireland a week later. It was a huge blow at a time when he was playing as well as anyone in Europe. Before the European Cup final two months later. Waddle was told by a number of French journalists that, if Marseille won, he would win the Ballon d'Or. That may not have been the case – it went to Papin, even though Marseille lost the final to Crvena Zvezda – but the fact it was discussed is a reflection of Waddle's status at the time.

He might conceivably have had three or four more years with England; instead he only earned one more cap, against Turkey in October 1991. It's not entirely Graham Taylor's fault – the timing of Waddle's injuries before both Ireland games in qualification for Euro 92 was particularly unfortunate – but it will always be a peculiar paradox: Waddle was not good enough for one of the worst England teams in recent memory, yet he was good enough to end the last European Cup dynasty.

### 4 Kickers Offenbach 6-0 Bayern Munich, Bundesliga, Waldstadion, Frankfurt, 24 August 1974

The great Bayern Munich side of the mid-1970s celebrated their third consecutive Bundesliga, and their first European Cup, by losing their next two league games 5-0 and 6-0. Heroically rock and roll, you might think, from a team who obviously couldn't wait until October for their own Munich Beer Festival. Except that the two matches were three months apart.

The first, a 5-0 thrashing away to their great rivals Borussia Mönchengladbach, didn't matter. Bayern had won their first European Cup in Brussels only 17 hours earlier, with nine of that starting XI also playing against Mönchengladbach. Many of them were still drunk; none of them cared about the defeat. That was not the case with the second, which came when they were spectacularly ransacked by Otto Rehhagel's Kickers Offenbach on the opening day of the 1974-75 season.

Rehhagel, in Britain at least, will always be associated with the 1-0 victory. That was the preferred weapon of his Greece side that inexplicably yet emphatically won Euro 2004, including their defeat of the champions France in the quarter-finals. Yet Rehhagel was also in charge for two of the most startling thrashings of a champion in the history of the game. In 1989-90, Werder Bremen slaughtered the Uefa Cup holders, Diego Maradona's Napoli, 8-3 on aggregate. Fifteen years earlier, Rehhagel's side hammered both the world champions and the European champions in the same game.

To explain. Bayern were the European champions and the side that took on Rehhagel's Kickers Offenbach contained five players who, six weeks earlier, had won the World Cup for West Germany against Holland: Sepp Maier, Hans-Georg Schwarzenbeck, Franz Beckenbauer, Uli Hoeneß and Gerd Müller. There would have been six but Paul Breitner, who originally planned to quit football at the age of 22 to devote his life to teaching handicapped children, moved unexpectedly to Real Madrid.

Bayern were part of some astonishing Bundesliga games in the 1970s. There was an 11-1 win over Dortmund and a 7-0 defeat at home to Schalke. They won and lost games 7-4, 6-5 and 7-1. They drew 5-5. There was also the comically spiteful 8-0 win over Ajax in Johan Cruyff's testimonial. Yet their 6-0 defeat to Offenbach surely tops the lot. It's one of those scorelines – like Wiener Sports Club 7-0 Juventus in the European Cup in 1958-59 – which will always look bizarre to modern eyes, especially now that Offenbach play in the fourth tier of German football.

Offenbach had returned to the Bundesliga after the match-fixing scandal of 1971 and had some fine players, most notably Siggi Held, who was part of the West Germany team at the 1966 and 1970 World Cups, and Erwin Kostedde, who later became Germany's first black international. Even so, they had no place beating Bayern 6-0. Nobody did; this was Bayern's biggest Bundesliga defeat. The teenage substitute Egon Bihn, who scored the sixth goal, summed up Kickers' mood before the game, "We had no hope."

In fact it was Bayern who were hopeless. Once Offenbach took the lead, they simply destroyed Bayern with fast, direct running on the counter-attack. Bayern's defenders looked like they were running with weighted backpacks – and with good reason. Before the season, the club were so keen to maximise the commercial potential of their European and world champions that they played 19 friendlies in 26 days. 19 games in 26 days. In a World Cup year! In effect, Bayern's stars played the 1973-75 season without a break.

The second goal was a classic piece of unscripted human comedy. Norbert Janzon ran straight at Franz Beckenbauer, who had to get his knees dirty for the first time in years. His sliding tackle just about stopped the danger, even if he did do a thoroughly unbecoming cartwheel in his follow through. As Beckenbauer got his bearings he didn't know Maier was running up behind him, about to pick up the loose ball. Instead, with the instinctive reaction of a man who had just woken up and seen something right in front of his nose, Beckenbauer stabbed the ball out of harm's way, just outside the area. Except it went straight to Dieter

Schwemmle, and with Maier well out of his goal, he waved an insouciant lofted shot into the net.

Offenbach added four more in the second half to complete a perfect day. What's better than beating Bayern 6-0? Beating Bayern 6-0 at the home of your great rivals Eintracht Frankfurt. The match was played in the Waldstadion because of construction work at Offenbach's ground.

It was an appropriate start to a thoroughly weird season for Bayern. They won the second of three consecutive European Cups, yet the best team in Europe were only the 10th best in Germany. All sense of domestic invincibility was gone by September, when they lost their 74-match, four-year unbeaten run at home. *World Soccer* called them "the most erratic team in the Bundesliga", which, given the unpredictable nature of the league at the time, was quite a feat. It was also the first of five consecutive seasons without a title, which is worth about 60 seasons in normal club years, and easily Bayern's longest fallow period since they went big time in the late 1960s.

The World Cup win had gone to everyone's head, particularly the players and those in the commercial department. Bayern's stars became celebrities who played a bit of football on the side. When Hoeneß was injured, he decided to swan off on a personal publicity tour. That was to the irritation of his manager UdoLattek and Hoeneß's penance was to donate his December and January bonuses to an old people's home.

Maier was the only one to steer clear of the sort of mud-slinging that makes Kevin Pietersen's fallout with the England seem like a fleeting disagreement over who nicked the last bottle of Gatorade. Nor was this done in autobiographies a year after the event; these were real-time fallouts, although at least the Bayern players stabbed each other and their manager in the front.

Lattek eventually went to the chairman insisting that changes needed to be made. The chairman concurred and sacked him. Bayern couldn't even take revenge on Offenbach. In the return fixture they roared into a 2-0 lead, yet Offenbach came back to win 3-2, aided by an own goal from Beckenbauer. He also scored an own goal the following week and a month later endured a miserable time at Wembley – West Germany were beaten 2-0 in a friendly and Beckenbauer was reduced to crawling around on all fours like a confused dog, making a diving save with his left hand to stop Malcolm Macdonald running clear on goal.

The great Bayern and West Germany sides looked finished during the 1974-75 season. In truth they were, yet West Germany – who were already a little past their best during their World Cup win in 1974, having peaked so imperiously at Euro 72 – came within a penalty competition of winning Euro 76 and Bayern went on two win two more European Cups. They were staggering feats of mental strength, not least because of the tonkings they took along the way.

### 5 Cardiff 0-0 Sporting (aggregate 2-1), Cup-Winners' Cup second round second leg, Ninian Park, 22 December 1964

These days, the recent example of Swansea excepted, Welsh clubs play all their European games in June, July and – if they really go on a cup run – in August. In the past they used to play them from September onwards; sometimes even in March and April. Until 1995, clubs who took part in the English leagues were allowed to play in the Welsh Cup and potentially earn a place in the Cup-Winners' Cup. That led to a number of stories that dripped with romantic charm. Wrexham reached the quarter-finals in 1975-76 and put out Porto in 1984-85. Newport reached the quarter-finals in 1981. Cardiff reached the semis in 1967-68, where they lost 4-3 on aggregate to Hamburg, and beat Real Madrid 1-0 at home in the quarter-final of 1970-71 before losing the second leg 2-0. They also reached the quarters in their first European campaign, 1964-65, when they eliminated the holders Sporting.

On the way to winning the cup, Sporting overcame a 4-1 first-leg deficit to batter Manchester United 5-0. The United team included all the greats of Matt Busby's signature side, including Bobby Charlton, George Best and Denis Law. In an earlier round, Sporting demolished Apoel 16-1 at home. They also had five players who would be part of the brilliant Portugal squad at the 1966 World Cup. Cardiff, by contrast, had only qualified by beating Bangor City of the Cheshire League in a Welsh Cup final replay, and then struggled to beat the Danish side Esbjerg 1-0 on aggregate. When they drew Sporting, the prevailing mood was,"That'll be that then! Seeya!" Few people even bothered to patronise Cardiff by saying they had an outside chance. Kenneth Wolstenholme didn't think it was all over, he knew it was: he previewed the game on BBC Wales by saying he could not see how Cardiff could avoid defeat.

Their new Scottish manager Jimmy Scoular – "his language could honestly be described as industrial," said the forward Derek Tapscott in his autobiography – had other ideas, even if he had no idea who his opposite number was. Sporting, who were having a dismal domestic season, suspended their coach Jean Luciano on the eve of the game. Scoular also had no notion that all of his players were wearing women's knickers during the biggest game of their lives. The kitman Harry Parsons had forgotten the players' jockstraps and had to improvise on the afternoon of the game. Jockstrap culture wasn't exactly thriving in Lisbon at the time, so Parsons had to make do with 18 pairs of women's briefs, which he told the players to put on before Scoular came in the dressing-room. Parsons knew that Scoular's language would be more than industrial if he found out about his players' replacement kit.

Whether it was the effect of the soft lacy fibres against their skin or just because they happened to play better football on the night, Cardiff pulled off a staggering victory in Lisbon. They led at half-time through Greg Farrell's excellent first-time shot and went further ahead when Tapscott, on the right touchline, mishit a cross towards the near post that the keeper Joaquim Carvalho could only help into the net. "A goal I could not repeat if I tried it a hundred times," said Tapscott.

At the other end, Cardiff's stout defending was led by the great John

Charles, playing sweeper for the first time in his career at the age of 32. He needed stitches after being headbutted early on but, in the clichéd style of the old don whose legs are going but whose brain is sharper than ever, he was majestic. "I went into every challenge as though my very life depended on it." Three of those challenges saved certain goals. Despite an impatient late volley from Figueiredo, Cardiff pulled off the most improbable 2-1 victory, with Charles in tears of joy as he left the field. "We half hoped for a draw," said the chairman Fred Dewey, "but we never dreamed we could win."

The players celebrated in a Lisbon bar, where the staff tried to rip them off with the bill. Charles was called over, with the players hoping his fluent Italian might somehow help them communicate. Instead he settled matters in a universal language, by pinning a waiter to the wall by the neck until the bill became more agreeable.

Charles was again immense in the return leg, played two days before Christmas, with Cardiff holding for a 0-0 draw. The 20-year-old goalkeeper Dilwyn John made two excellent first-half saves, yet as the match went on he had increasingly little to do because of the performance of another 20 year old, Gareth Williams, and Charles in defence.

Sporting were a slick side, far more skilful than Cardiff. The *Times* said Cardiff "went to the last inch in speed and fibre". A goal for Sporting would have meant a replay in Madrid – there was no away-goals rule in those days – but if anything Cardiff looked the likelier scorers. Peter King had a shot cleared off the line and Carvalho made a couple of vital saves.

As the match wore on, Sporting became increasingly irritated by their inability to break down their apparent inferiors. When a Sporting player found something on the pitch, he launched it back into the crowd like a discus, with sinew-busting ferocity and a comically extravagant follow-through. Then the keeper Carvalho collided with the flying Tapscott as they went for a near-post cross. Tapscott had barely hit the floor when Carvalho, springing straight to his feet as all good keepers are trained to do, picked Tapscott up and threw him over the touchline, like an impatient motorist tossing a dead animal to the side of the road. It almost sparked a brawl, with players from both sides shoving each other and putting their dukes up. "He looks like he's had a row with Cassius Clay," said Wolstenholme as Tapscott staggered back onto the field.

There were people charging onto the field in disbelief when the final whistle went, with the most joyous of pitch invasions taking place. There were umpteen gentlemen wearing long, light-coloured coats that flapped in the night air as they made a beeline for their heroes, and the black-and-white TV pictures made it look like an invasion of the butchers. "This in a way was Dylan Thomas against Vasco da Gama," said the man from the *Times*. "One discovered a word. The other discovered a bit of the world." Fifty years later we still haven't clue what it means, but it's a suitably grandiose description for an endearing and enduring triumph of the human spirit.

## 6 Napoli 2-3 AC Milan, Serie A, Stadio San Paolo, 1 May 1988

It does not have to be a cup competition for the holders to be symbolically dethroned. If anything it can be even more powerful in a league match – victory over a whole season has greater gravitas and sometimes symbolises a changing of the guard or at the very least the emergence of a serious rival. That was the case in one of Serie A's most famous matches, an undeniable epic between the champions Napoli and the challengers Milan in May 1988.

Diego Maradona's Napoli had started their title defence in awesome style, winning 16 of their first 20 games as the Ma-Gi-Ca attacking trio of Maradona, Bruno Giordano and Careca rammed in goals all over the place. Milan plugged them 4-1 at the San Siro but that was Napoli's only defeat and they were cruising to the title. "Physically I was in tip-top form," said Maradona, "like I had never been before, like a bullet." With a third of the 30-game season remaining, Napoli's lead – in an era of two points for a win – was a huge five points. Then the goals and points dried up. Arrigo Sacchi's Milan, who had just about stayed within range, began to hunt them down and Napoli lost the plot. *World Soccer* said, "they collapsed in an orgy of internal back-stabbing."

By that stage Maradona was used to being stabbed. He was no longer in tip-top form physically and needed injections to get through games. "There was nowhere left around my lower back or my knee for the needle to go in," he said in his autobiography. Napoli went into their third-last game, at home to Milan, with their lead reduced to just one point. With everybody else a mile back this was an undeniable four-pointer.

"I really had no idea what a game between AC Milan and Napoli actually entailed," said Ruud Gullit. "I was intrigued when the club hired two planes instead of one to take us to Naples. It turned out one was for our food and drink." Milan were so paranoid that their food would be spiked that they brought Silvio Berlusconi's personal chef, with hotel staff and waiters allowed nowhere near their meals. The food even had its own bodyguards when it was brought to the players. Milan were staying at the inaptly named Jolly Hotel and thought a combination of a newly erected fence and being as high as the 25th floor would keep them away from the noise of Napoli supporters. Some chance. A few Napoli fans somehow got onto the 26th floor and made a racket the night before the game. The build-up, said Gullit, "was worthy of a film script."

The ride to the hotel would have made for a particularly compelling scene. Milan's team bus – and a police escort – were waiting for them on the runway when they arrived in Naples, and they took a different route to avoid the home fans. It was blissfully quiet – until they hit the welcoming committee near the hotel. Gullit, on the bus, was distracted by the sight of a sweet little old lady among the crowd, a little oasis of humanity amid the hostility. "As I watched her," said Gullit, "she turned to face us and made the most obscene gesture possible. Only the way Italians can do it." The coach was bombarded with spit, stones, tomatoes, oranges and plenty else besides. "You should," said Gullit, "have seen the state of it."

The match also had to be seen to be believed. The silver-haired sniffer Pietro

Virdis, one of Italy's great uncapped players, gave Milan the lead before Maradona equalised with a glorious free-kick just before half-time. He later said it was the best of his career. At the time, with Marco van Basten just coming back from injury and yet to have his life-changing Euro 88, Maradona's main rival for the title of best player in the world was Gullit, holder of the Ballon d'Or and Milan's inspiration. He lived up to his status with a masterful second-half performance.

Having sledged his marker – "I can't remember his name" – into a needless booking, Gullit goaded him further. "I now have you in my pocket." A run and cross led to a smartly taken second from Virdis, then Gullit charged more than half the length of the field to set up the substitute Van Basten. Careca pulled one back but Milan held on in a last 10 minutes of such tension as to make the partisan want to renounce football. Sacchi was on the pitch at one stage, screaming instructions. At the end of the game, that partisanship was put on hold in extraordinary circumstances. For all the hostility before and during the match, the Napoli fans applauded the Milan team from the field, a remarkable gesture which, Gullit says, "will live with me forever."

Napoli's collapse, seven points from the last 10 games, was one for the ages. They completed it by losing their last two games, allowing Milan to ease to the title with two draws. As Napoli's season unravelled, the players and the coach Ottavio Bianchi started flinging mud at each other. "Once I had a great team and a great Maradona," said Bianchi. "Now all I have is a great Maradona." The Napoli players released a statement saying nobody had got on with Bianchi and that he hadn't done his job properly. On the day they did so, Maradona sent his personal masseur to the club to tell them he wouldn't be attending training and then buggered off in his boat for a few days. His opinion of Bianchi was later expressed without ambiguity in his autobiography. "Bianchi, the wanker, had started experimenting and had left Giordano out," said Maradona. "Everything turned to shit."

For Milan, it was the opposite. Their victory in Naples was a classic story of a great team on the way up meeting a champion on the way down. Milan just knew, instinctively, that this was their day, their game, their time. "We were hurtling downhill through the championship, and at the bottom of the hill the *Scudetto* awaited us," said Carlo Ancelotti. "Napoli 2-3 AC Milan; we're the ones, we're the ones, we're the champions of Italy."

In the previous 19 years they had won a single *Scudetto* and no European Cups. In the next eight years there were five *Scudetti,* three European Cups, two Intercontinental Cups and two more European Cup finals. The Napoli match was Milan's shortcut to greatness.

### 7 Hamburg 3-2 Dinamo Bucharest (aggregate: 3-5), European Cup first round, second leg, Volksparkstadion, 2 November 1983

Arsenal reflect the good and bad of the Champions League. They have reached the last 16 for the last 14 seasons – it'll probably be 15 seasons by the time you read this – yet they have never won it and have only one final and one semi-final to show for their work. Theirs is a world of largely pointless equilibrium. Contrast that with the European Cup's all-or-nothing period, when teams either had a medal placed around their neck in spring or their throats slit in autumn. In the 15 seasons between 1969-70 and 1983-84, the champions either retained the cup or went out in the first round on 11 occasions. (Or, in the case of Ajax in 1973 and Hamburg in 1983, in their first tie after receiving a bye to the second round.) Of the five teams to fall at their first hurdle in that time – Feyenoord, Ajax, Liverpool, Nottingham Forest and Hamburg – Hamburg's defeat to Dinamo Bucharest was the most dramatic.

Steaua Bucharest won the European Cup in 1985-86, but two years before that Romanian club football had little pedigree. UTA Arad had put the holders Feyenoord out in 1970-71; that was about it for Romanian sides in the European Cup. The chance to change that was sufficient incentive for the players of Dinamo, whose win bonus of 14,000 lei was just about enough to buy a colour TV. They spent two weeks in the mountains preparing for the game, trying to get their physical level somewhere near that of Hamburg. They took other measures, too. Before the first leg in Bucharest, the president asked the Dinamo legend Cornel Dinu to give the referee Jan Keizer a gift. After informing the referee that Dinamo were playing the offside trap, he handed him a briefcase. At half-time in the match the referee even told Dinu to calm down Ionel Augustin, who had been flying into challenges.

Dinamo won the first leg 3-0 in front of more than 70,000 spectators. Ernst Happel, the Hamburg coach, was furious with the referee and with the number of bottles being thrown onto the pitch – so much so that he stopped the game for three minutes. Even with a 3-0 deficit, Hamburg fancied their chances going into the second leg. "Miracles happen in football," said Happel. Hamburg battered Dinamo and were 3-0 up just after the hour. The centre-back Ditmar Jakobs scored either side of half-time, with the substitute Thomas von Heesen levelling the aggregate score. "When we pulled back to 3-0 I couldn't see anything going wrong," said Happel. But his players could. For the first 62 minutes they just attacked. Then at 3-0 they started to think and were caught between pushing for a fourth and waiting for their superior fitness to tell in extra-time.

The classic European sting came five minutes from time, when Dinamo substitute Cornel Talnar knifed Hamburg on the counter-attack. They then needed to score twice and threw so many men forward in desperation and confusion that Gheorghe Multescu's wound-salting 90th-minute breakaway became inevitable. It was a remarkable double twist: Hamburg completed Mission Impossible only to have a coronary at the moment of triumph. "Miracles," said the Dinamo coach Dimitru Nicolae, "can happen in football."

"We have defeated ourselves," thundered the Hamburg captain Felix Magath afterwards, knowing full well these were not the kind of wounds that could be healed by cheese. In a sense they still haven't healed. Few people expected Hamburg to establish a European dynasty, but they were supposed to do a lot better than this – especially as they were unquestionably the best team in West Germany at the time, having won the title in three of the previous five seasons. But Horst Hrubesch, sold in the summer of 1983, was never adequately replaced and Hamburg have not won the Bundesliga or a European trophy in the 31 years since.

### 8 Manchester United 2-0 Arsenal, Premier League, Old Trafford, 24 October 2004

Society loves a moan, but it can't stand a moaner. Given our propensity for self-pity, we can be remarkably unsympathetic towards the complaints of others. Just let it go, mate. Yet some wrongs are bigger than others and sometimes the injustice is so profound that it's almost impossible to sit still. It's over a decade since Arsenal's 49-match unbeaten run ended at Old Trafford, yet the resentment lingers. In Amy Lawrence's superb new book *Invincible,* Kolo Touré was asked about that game. "I still have that here," he replied, banging a fist against his chest.

Arsenal's 2-0 defeat was one of the biggest injustices imaginable. Ruud van Nistelrooy should have been sent off in the first half for a studs-up challenge on Ashley Cole that brought a three-match ban after the game; Rio Ferdinand should also probably have gone before half-time for a last-man foul on Freddie Ljungberg. United's opening goal came from a penalty awarded for a dive by Wayne Rooney. To compound Arsenal's misery, it was scored by the man they detested, Van Nistelrooy, whose cathartic groans – he had missed a penalty in the same fixture a year earlier, after which he was manhandled by a number of players – were described by Rooney as "the most genuine emotion I've ever seen in a footballer after scoring."

United should have had a penalty after that, for a foul by Cole on Cristiano Ronaldo, but Arsenal will argue that this – and Rooney's injury-time goal – would not have happened had the referee Mike Riley done his job earlier in the game.

It's worth recalling the context of the game. Arsenal went unbeaten in the League throughout the previous season – and then they got even better. They were like the Invincibles Plus, with their first nine games of the 2004-05 season bringing 25 points and 29 goals. United's first nine games yielded 14 points and nine goals.

Arsenal's aura wasn't gone with one lost game – but it was a month later. Few sides have ever had such an extreme reaction to a defeat. There were only two over-30s in that starting XI at Old Trafford, yet the team died instantly. They dropped 12 points in just over a month and never fully recovered. "The game did us more damage than we realised at the time," said Patrick Vieira. "We were cheated out of our record. It sticks in the throat. The game was a joke."

Apart from his early struggles, the years between 2003 and 2006 were by far the hardest of Ferguson's reign at Old Trafford: no league titles, constant failure in Europe, consecutive third-placed finishes. But he achieved something far more remarkable than many of his trophies at Old Trafford. He got so far under Arsenal's skin that he ruined them, setting in motion a sequence of events in which Arsenal went from being unbeatable in October 2004 to struggling to finish fourth in May 2006.

They will forever wonder what might have been had they made it 50 games unbeaten that afternoon. They might have gone 60 or 70 games unbeaten, they might have been involved in one of the great title races with José Mourinho's Chelsea, they might have won the Champions League.

Arsenal should have been tougher, of course, and their reaction reinforced the perception of many of that United side – articulated in Gary Neville's autobiography – that the Invincibles had a "soft centre" and the team of 1997-99 was Arsenal's best. Even so, it's so rare to find a sporting injustice so great in both scope and significance – and against your hated rivals – that you can understand why they lost the plot as well as their unbeaten run. Let it go? No chance. Most of those involved will take their frustration to the grave.

# Contributors

***The Blizzard*, Issue Fifteen**

**Luke Alfred** is most recently the author of *When the Lions came to Town*, the story of Willie John McBride's all-conquering Lions rugby tour of South Africa in 1974, available in the UK from December. He writes for a variety of local publications, including the *Sunday Times* and the *Mail* and *Guardian*. He lives in Johannesburg.

**Philippe Auclair** is the author of *The Enchanted Kingdom of Tony Blair* (in French) and *Cantona: the Rebel Who Would Be King*, which was named *NSC Football Book of the Year.* His biography of *Thierry Henry* has just been published. He writes for *France Football* and *Offside* and provides analysis and commentary for *RMC Sport.* Twitter: **@PhilippeAuclair**

**Robin Bairner** is a French football writer primarily found working for *Goal.* He also holds a keen interest in the Scottish game. Twitter: **@RBairner**

**Nicholas Blincoe** is a novelist and screenwriter. He was born in Rochdale and now lives in London. His interest in football developed late in life, during the few years he lived in Bethlehem, Palestine, when he often felt homesick. Twitter: **@NicholasBlincoe**

**Dominic Bliss** is the author of *Erbstein: The Triumph and Tragedy of Football's Forgotten Pioneer.* He is founder and editor of *TheInsideLeft.com.* Twitter: **@theinsidelefty**

**George Caulkin** has been writing about football in the North-East of England for 20 years and for the *Times* since 1998. He ghost-wrote *Sir Bobby Robson's* final book, *Newcastle, My Kind of Toon,* and is a *Patron of the Sir Bobby Robson Foundation.* Twitter: **@CaulkinTheTimes**

**Jim Davies** is a writer and creative director. After 10 years photo-editing at *The Sunday Times Magazine* he moved to Colombia where he established Bogotá's first international photo agency and the social art project *YoCreo!* to benefit disadvantaged children. He now lives in Cali and works with various magazines including *Monocle* and *SoHo.*

**Amy Lawrence** writes about football mostly for the *Guardian* and the *Observer.* She is the author of *Invincible: Inside Arsenal's Unbeaten 2003-2004 Season.* Twitter: **@amylawrence71**

**Iain Macintosh** is the author of *Football Fables* and the *Everything You Ever Wanted To Know* series of sports guidebooks and a co-author of *Football Manager Ruined My Life*. He writes for the *New Paper* in Singapore, *ESPN* and anyone else who'll pay him. Twitter: **@iainmacintosh**

**Ewan MacKenna** is a former *Irish Sports Writer of the Year* and has also been shortlisted for the *Irish Sports Book of the Year*. Originally from County Kildare, he left for the World Cup over a year ago, failed to return and is now based in Brazil. Twitter: **@EwanMacKenna**

**Thierry Marchand** is an international football editor for *France Football* and a contributor for *L'Equipe 21* TV channel. He writes a blog called *You'll never blog alone*, about English football. Twitter: **@ThierryMarchan**

**Alessandro Mastroluca** is an Italian freelance sports journalist. He's the author of *Ilsuccesso è un viaggio*, the first complete biography dedicated to *Arthur Ashe* in Italian. He has just published *Denis Bergamini: unastoriasbagliata*, an enquiry detailing all the unresolved controversies surrounding *Bergamini's* mysterious death. Twitter: **@mastrale**

**Scott Murray** writes for the *Guardian*. He is co-author of *And Gazza Misses The Final*, a history of the World Cup through the medium of minute-by-minute match reports. He also co-wrote *The Anatomy of Liverpool*, and *Phantom of the Open: Maurice Flitcroft, the World's Worst Golfer*.

**Marti Perarnau** is a former Spanish Olympic high-jumper turned journalist and author. In 2013-14, he was given unlimited access to Bayern Munich by Pep Guardiola and wrote *Pep Confidential*, published in October 2014. Twitter: **@martiperarnau**

**Harry Pearson** is the author of *The Far Corner*. His blog about North-East Football, *The First Thirty Years Are The Worst*, is unaccountably popular in Switzerland. Twitter: **@camsell59**

**Juan Felipe Rubio** is one of Colombia's most respected documentary photographers. He is known for his imaginative style of storytelling and portraits and is often published in Colombia's biggest selling magazines and other international titles. He is a bike fanatic and works regularly with the national Colombian cycling team.

**Jonny Singer** is a freelance sports journalist for *Mail Online, ESPN* and the *Sunday Times.* Not that long ago, he wrote his undergraduate dissertation about the history of football tactics. Twitter: **@Jonny_Singer**

**Rob Smyth** is co-author of *Danish Dynamite: The Story of Football's Greatest Cult Team* and *And Gazza Misses The Final,* a collection of minute-by-minute reports on classic World Cup matches.

**Will Unwin** is a sportswriter for *ITV Sport* and *ITV News online.* A former resident of the Basque Country, he enjoys the region's food and football in equal measure. Twitter: **@will_unwin**

**Michael Walker** is originally from Belfast but has lived in North-East England for the bulk of the last 30 years. For the last 20 he has reported on the area's football for several national newspapers. He currently writes a Saturday column for the *Irish Times.*

**Paul Watson** is the author of *Up Pohnpei,* the story of his attempts to coach the world's lowest-ranked football team to glory. He co-writes the satirical football blog *Back of the Net* for *Four Four Two* and will appear in the documentary *The Soccermen,* due for release in Spring 2015.

**Jonathan Wilson** is the author of *Inverting the Pyramid.* He writes for the *Guardian*, the *National*, *World Soccer* and *Sports Illustrated.* He is writing a book on the history of *Argentinian football.* Twitter: **@jonawils**

# ***Blizzard* Subscriptions**

*Subscribe to the print version of* The Blizzard, *be the first to receive new issues, get exclusive Blizzard offers and access digital versions of all back-issues FREE*

## Subscription Options

### Set Price for Four Issues

Get a four-issue subscription to *The Blizzard* — for you or as a gift — for a flat fee including postage and packing (P&P):

| | |
|---|---|
| UK: | £35 |
| Europe: | £45 |
| Non-Euorpe: | £55 |

### Recurring Pay-What-You-Like

Set up a quartely recurring payment for each edition of *The Blizzard*. The recommended retail price (RRP) is £12, but pay what you like, subject to a minimum fee of £6 plus P&P

*See www.theblizzard.co.uk for more*

### Digital Subscriptions

If the cost of postage is prohibitive, or you just want an excuse to use your new iPad or Kindle, you can set up a subscription to digital versions of The Blizzard for just £3 per issue.

See www.theblizzard.co.uk for more

## Information for Existing Subscribers

*The Blizzard* is a quarterly publication from a cooperative of top class football journalists and authors from across the globe, enjoying the space and freedom to write about the football stories that matter to them.

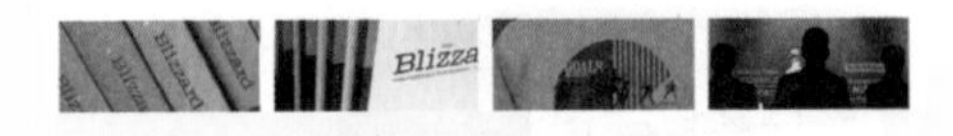

### Free Digital Downloads for *Blizzard* Subscribers

Whether you have taken advantage of our set price or pay-what-you-like offer, for the duration of your subscription to *The Blizzard* you are entitled to download every issue FREE.

*See www.theblizzard.co.uk for more*

We very much value the commitment of our print subscribers and have a policy to make available new issues, special offers and other limited access events and benefits to print subscribers first.

# About *The Blizzard*

*Distribution & Back Issues*
*Contact Information*
*About Issue Fifteen*

## Buy *The Blizzard*

We want as many readers as possible for *The Blizzard.* We therefore operate as far as we are able on a pay-what-you-like basis for digital and print versions.

### Digital Version (Current & Back Issues)

All issues of *The Blizzard* are available to download for Kindle, Android, iOS and PC/Mac at: *www.theblizzard.co.uk.*

- *RRP: £3*
- *Pay-what-you-like minimum: £0.01*

### Printed Version (Current & Back Issues)

Purchase a physical copy of *The Blizzard* in all its luxurious, tactile, sensual glory at: *www.theblizzard.co.uk.* If you haven't felt our rough textured cover-varnish and smelled the inner genius, you haven't properly experienced its awesome true form. Read it, or leave it on your coffee table to wow visitors.

- *RRP: £12* (+P&P)
- *Pay-what-you-like min: £6* (+P&P)

## Contact *The Blizzard*

**All advertising, sales, press and business communication should be addressed to the Central Publishing Office:**

*The Blizzard*
Ashmore Villa,
1, Ashmore Terrace,
Stockton Road,
Sunderland,
SR2 7DE

Email: info@theblizzard.co.uk
Telephone: +44 (0) 191 543 8785
Website: www.theblizzard.co.uk
Facebook: www.facebook.com/blzzrd
Twitter: @blzzrd

## About Issue Fifteen

**Editor** Jonathan Wilson
**Publisher** The Blizzard Media Ltd
www.theblizzard.co.uk
**Design** Daykin & Storey
www.daykinandstorey.co.uk

### Copyright

 Thanks to Jeanette G Sturis at the Kingsley Motel, Manjimup, for kind use of Warren Walker's original sketches of Dog.